The Short Fiction
of Kurt Vonnegut

The Short Fiction of Kurt Vonnegut

ca *Peter J. Reed* ca

Contributions to the Study of American Literature,
Number 1

GREENWOOD PRESS
Westport, Connecticut • London

Library of Congress Cataloging-in-Publication Data

Reed, Peter J.
 The short fiction of Kurt Vonnegut / Peter J. Reed.
  p. cm.—(Contributions to the study of American literature,
ISSN 1092–6356 ; no. 1)
 Includes bibliographical references and index.
 ISBN 0–313–30235–9 (alk. paper)
  1. Vonnegut, Kurt—Criticism and interpretation. 2. Science
fiction, American—History and criticism. 3. Short story.
I. Title. II. Series.
PS3572.05Z82 1997
813'.54—DC21   97–2236

British Library Cataloguing in Publication Data is available.

Library of Congress Catalog Card Number: 97–2236
ISBN: 0–313–30235–9
ISSN: 1092–6356

First published in 1997

Greenwood Press, 88 Post Road West, Westport, CT 06881
An imprint of Greenwood Publishing Group, Inc.

Printed in the United States of America

The paper used in this book complies with the
Permanent Paper Standard issued by the National
Information Standards Organization (Z39.48–1984).

10 9 8 7 6 5 4 3 2

Copyright Acknowledgment

The author and publisher are grateful for permission to use the following material:

Excerpts from interviews collected in *Conversations with Kurt
Vonnegut*, edited by William Rodney Allen (Jackson: University
Press of Mississippi, 1988), are used with permission of Kurt
Vonnegut.

For Maggie

Contents

Preface		ix
Acknowledgments		xi
Chronology		xiii
1.	Placing the Short Fiction	1
2.	Apprenticeship: High School and College Journalism	9
3.	The Early Stories: *Collier's*, 1950–1953	27
4.	The Prolific Years: 1953–1958	41
5.	The Later Stories: 1960–1963	75
6.	The Collections: *Canary in a Cat House* and *Welcome to the Monkey House*	93
7.	The Novels: Stories, Mosaics, and Jokes	111
8.	Other Voices: Kilgore Trout	125
9.	The Short Fiction and the Canon	137
Appendix:	Contributions to the *Shortridge Daily Echo* and the *Cornell Sun,* by M. Andre Z. Eckenrode	157
Bibliography		167
Index		171

Preface

Kurt Vonnegut's career as a novelist encompasses virtually the whole second half of the twentieth century. He stands as one of America's longest-publishing and most widely read novelists. Film, television, and theatrical productions have been made from his books. Yet Vonnegut enjoyed another career in fiction that these days goes almost unnoted, that of a short story writer. One of the ironies of the present obscurity of this phase of his career is that at the time it made him highly visible to a very large audience. His stories, illustrated by some of the best artists in that business, were featured prominently in such wide-circulation magazines as *Collier's*, *Saturday Evening Post*, *Ladies Home Journal*, *Cosmopolitan*, and *Argosy*.

Commentary on Kurt Vonnegut has tended to perpetuate this separation between two careers. Most critics have felt free to talk about Vonnegut the novelist while setting aside the short stories, as I did myself in the first book-length study of this writer. But I have come to think increasingly that to do so means to impose an artificial compartmentalization upon the body of his work. The short fiction merits consideration in part because there is where he learned and practiced many of the skills and techniques also employed in the novels. At the same time, however, it is not accurate to see the short stories simply as preceding the novels; there is an extensive period of overlap. More than that, it is possible to see the techniques and the impulses of the short story writer continuing on even into the most recent novels. To examine successive manuscripts of one longer work is to see the short fiction content—that is, the vignetttes, the parables, the comic episodes—survive from one version to the next within substantially changed contexts.

So one cannot simply regard Kurt Vonnegut as having had one incarnation as a short story writer and another as a novelist, as has been the tendency. And if "he child is father to the man," one should look back also to those apprentice years as a high school and college journalist where Vonnegut learned writing and made it a part of his daily life. This book does that, attempting by paying attention to these all-too-often overlooked parts of Vonnegut's work to contribute to seeing his canon completely and with better understanding.

Acknowledgments

A group of scholars who for years have studied Vonnegut's writing with intelligence and admiration, and who also have been loyal friends and generous helpers, again proved supportive in this endeavor. Among these are Marc Leeds, Loree Rackstraw, Asa Pieratt, and Jerry Klinkowitz.   A newer acquaintance whose painstaking research into the high school and college writing has overtaken my own and aided me greatly is Andre Eckenrode. Paul Baepler assisted tirelessly in research for this project. Most helpful of all has been Kurt Vonnegut himself, graciously patient and generous with my questions over many years, an unfailingly kind and decent man.

It will be obvious to any reader that three books have been of particular assistance to me. The *Vonnegut Encyclopedia* by Marc Leeds must now be indispensable to any serious student of Vonnegut. A practical compendium of a hoard of knowledge, it can save hours of searching. *Kurt Vonnegut: A Comprehensive Bibliography,* by Asa Pieratt, Julie Huffman-klinkowitz and Jerome Klinkowitz, likewise remains an essential book. *Conversations with Kurt Vonnegut*, edited by William Rodney Allen, brings together a collection of previously published interviews. Because of the convenience of having these interviews in one place, both for me and for any reader wishing to make further use of them, I have drawn all of my references to interviews from this one source.

Over the years my research in the work of Kurt Vonnegut, and specifically for this project, has been assisted by support from the Department of English, the College of Liberal Arts, and the Graduate School of the University of Minnesota. The Indiana Historical Society and the *Cornell Sun* assisted generously in my research into Kurt Vonnegut's high school and college writing. Scott Swartz, with his knowledge of computers and his flair for design, assisted in the preparation of the manuscript. And the ever-patient and gracious staff at Greenwood, particularly production editor Gillian Beebe, could not have been more helpful.

Having met me in graduate school, my wife Maggie has had to suffer through the emotional vacillations associated with everything I have written since. Her advice, suggestions and support with respect to this book were as invaluable as they have always been in the past.

Chronology

1848	Clemens Vonnegut, Sr. (1824–1906), the author's great-grandfather, arrives in the U.S.A.
1913	November 22, Kurt Vonnegut and Edith Lieber, the author's parents, marry in Indianapolis.
1922	November 11, Kurt Vonnegut, Jr., born Indianapolis. Siblings Bernard, born 1914, and Alice, born 1917.
1928–36	Attends Orchard School, Indianapolis.
1936–40	Shortridge High School. Works on the *Shortridge Daily Echo*, daily student newspaper, as reporter, columnist and editor.
1940	Enters Cornell University, to major in biochemistry. Writes for the *Cornell Sun*.
1943	March, enlists in U.S. Army as a private. Enrolls in training courses at Carnegie Institute and University of Tennessee.
1944	May 14, mother commits suicide while Vonnegut home on leave.
1944	December, the Battle of the Bulge. Vonnegut captured on December 22, while serving with the 106th Infantry Division.
1945	February 13 and 14, Dresden bombed and at least 35,000 inhabitants killed. Vonnegut and fellow POWs shelter in underground meat locker, the basis for *Slaughterhouse-Five*.

1945	April, Soviet troops occupy Dresden, Vonnegut liberated and later returns to U.S. Awarded Purple Heart.
1945	September 1, marries Jane M. Cox, whom he has known since high school.
1945–47	December 1945, moves to Chicago. Enters M.A. program in anthropology at the University of Chicago, and works as reporter for Chicago City News Bureau. M.A. thesis rejected.
1947	Joins his brother Bernard at the General Electric Co. Research Laboratory in Schenectady, New York, as a public relations writer. Later begins writing short fiction.
1950	Vonnegut's first published fiction, the short story "Report on the Barnhouse Effect," appears in *Collier's* for February 11. Also short stories "Thanasphere" and "EPICAC."
1951	Leaves G.E. to pursue writing professionally. Moves to Provincetown and later West Barnstable, Mass. Short stories "Mnemonics," "The Euphio Question," "All the King's Horses," "The Foster Portfolio," and "More Stately Mansions."
1952	Vonnegut's first novel, *Player Piano*, published by Charles Scribner's Sons. Short stories "Any Reasonable Offer," "The Package," "The No-Talent Kid," "Poor Little Rich Town," and "Souvenir."
1953	Short stories "Tom Edison's Shaggy Dog," "Unready to Wear," "The Cruise of the Jolly Roger," and "D.P."
1954	*Player Piano* published in paperback by Bantam as *Utopia 14*. Various work to supplement his income, including teaching at Hopefield School, free lance advertising copy writing, and opening a Saab automobile dealership. Short stories "The Big Trip Up Yonder," "Custom-Made Bride," "Adam," "Ambitious Sophomore," "Bagombo Snuff Box," "The Powder Blue Dragon," and "A Present for Big Nick."
1955	Short stories "Unpaid Consultant," "Deer in the Works," "Next Door," and "The Kid Nobody Could Handle."
1956	Short stories "The Boy Who Hated Girls," "Miss Temptation," and "This Son of Mine...."

1957   Father dies October 1. Short stories "Hal Irwin's Magic
                Lamp," and "A Night for Love."

1958   His sister Alice dies of cancer and her husband John Adams is
                killed in a train crash the day before. Kurt and Jane adopt three
                of Alice's four children (Tiger, Jim and Steven Adams), adding
                to their own three children Mark, Edith and Nanette. Short
                story "The Manned Missiles."

1959   *The Sirens of Titan* published by Dell.

1960   Short story "Long Walk to Forever."

1961   Collection of short stories, *Canary in a Cat House*, published
                by Fawcett. Short stories "Find Me a Dream," "Runaways,"
                "Harrison Bergeron," and "My Name Is Everyone," which was
                later collected as "Who Am I This Time?"

1962   *Mother Night* published by Fawcett. Short stories "HOLE
                BEAUTIFUL Prospectus," "2BRO2B," "The Lie," and "Go
                Back to Your Precious Wife and Son."

1963   *Cat's Cradle* published by Holt, Rinehart & Winston. Short
                stories "Lovers Anonymous," and "The Hyannis Port Story."
                (Latter did not appear until 1971.)

1965   *God Bless You, Mr. Rosewater* published by Holt, Rinehart
                and Winston. Begins two year appointment at the Writers
                Workshop, University of Iowa.

1967   Guggenheim Fellowship. Visits Dresden to research
                Slaughterhouse-Five.

1968   *Welcome to the Monkey House* (short stories) published by
                Delacorte Press/Seymour Lawrence. Includes new short story,
                "Welcome to the Monkey House."

1969   *Slaughterhouse-Five* published by Delacorte Press/Seymour
                Lawrence.

1970   January, visits Biafra shortly before its collapse in war with
                Nigeria. Literature Award from National Institute of Arts and
                Letters.

1970–71   October 7, *Happy Birthday, Wanda June* (play) opens in New
                York, runs until March 14, 1971. Published by Delacorte
                Press/Seymour Lawrence in 1971.

1971   Anthropology Department, University of Chicago, accepts
            Cat's Cradle as an M.A. thesis and awards degree. Moves to
            New York. Separated from wife Jane. Short story "The Big
            Space Fuck."

1972   March 13, *Between Time and Timbuktu,* 90-minute television
            play based on characters and situations from K.V.'s fiction.
            Published by Delacorte Press/Seymour Lawrence with
            introduction by K.V. the same year. In a letter to Marc Leeds
            (November 15, 1989), Vonnegut clearly denies authorship. "It
            is what it is, and doesn't belong in the canon of my work
            anywhere since the idea of doing such a thing *did not in the
            least originate with me.* (Vonnegut's emphasis.)
            I was so lacking in passion about what people were doing with
            my ideas within the demands of their own art form that I didn't
            even protect the title of a short story of mine, "Between *Timid*
            and Timbuktu." In small dictionaries, the word between Timid
            and Timbuktu is Time."

1973   *Breakfast of Champions* published by Delacorte
            Press/Seymour Lawrence. Awarded honorary L.H.D. by
            Indiana University.

1974   *Wampeters, Foma & Granfalloons* (essays, interviews, etc.)
            published by Delacorte Press/Seymour Lawrence.

1975   Elected Vice President of the National Institute of Arts and
            Letters.

1975   *The Eden Express*, by son Mark, published by Praeger
            Publishers. Recounts Mark's breakdown in 1972.

1976   *Slapstick, or Lonesome No More!* published by Delacorte
            Press/Seymour Lawrence.

1979   October 11, musical adaptation of *God Bless You, Mr.
            Rosewater,* produced by his daughter Edith, opens at
            Entermedia Theatre, New York.

1979   November 24, marries Jill Krementz, photographer and
            author.

1979   *Jailbird* published by Delacorte Press/Seymour Lawrence.

1980   *Sun Moon Star*, by Vonnegut and Ivan Chermayeff,
            illustrator. In October, one-man exhibition
            of his drawings at Margo Fine Galleries, New York.

1981   *Palm Sunday : An Autobiographical Collage* published by
            Delacorte Press.

1982   *Deadeye Dick* published by Delacorte Press/Seymour
            Lawrence.

1982   December 15, adopted daughter Lily Vonnegut born.

1985   *Galapagos* published by Delacorte Press/Seymour Lawrence.

1987   *Bluebeard* published by Delacorte Press.

1990   *Hocus Pocus* published by Putnam.

1991   *Fates Worse Than Death: An Autobiographical Collage of the
            1980s* published by Putnam.

1996   Stage adaptation of *Slaughterhouse-Five* by Eric Simonson at
            Steppenwolf Theatre, Chicago. Opera version of it in Munich,
            musical in Moscow. Film of *Mother Night* released.

The Short Fiction
of Kurt Vonnegut

1

Placing the Short Fiction

In the Preface to *Welcome to the Monkey House,* Kurt Vonnegut wrote: "The contents of this book are samples of work I sold in order to finance the writing of the novels. Here one finds the fruits of Free Enterprise."[1] That disclaimer has been referred to quite frequently by people writing or talking about Vonnegut's work, and it appears to have become a generally accepted assessment. As a result, there has been relatively little critical interest in Vonnegut's short fiction, particularly as he has grown in stature as a novelist through a long and productive career. In two of the earlier books on Vonnegut's work, Jerome Klinkowitz and Stanley Schatt include chapters on the short fiction and maintain stoutly that, in Schatt's words, "some are certainly memorable."[2] On the whole, though, the tendency has been to follow Vonnegut's disclaimer and to regard the short stories as separate from and inferior to the novels.

Of course, one has to wonder a little about that disclaimer. It certainly stops short of Vonnegut's disowning these stories; and if he had truly regarded them as such inferior work, would he have wanted to publish the collection? That same preface goes on, rather defensively, to respond to critical assessments that cast him as a science fiction writer, and science fiction writers and public relations writers—another group in which he had membership—as "equally vile." And it notes that *The New Yorker* had called *God Bless You, Mr. Rosewater* "a series of narcissistic giggles" and allows that "This may be another" (xi). Vonnegut frequently used a stance of embattled self-deprecation in the autobiographical revelations in his earlier books. But in this preface, particularly in the seeming acquiescence in the denigration of one of his best novels, there is surely a note of defiance. Some of that must extend to the stories, too.

In interviews, many of which are cited in the pages that follow, Vonnegut speaks frequently of differences between short story writing and novel writing. He emphasizes that in his short stories he had to meet the demands of a market, its audience, its editors. That imposed conditions on what he wrote in terms of length, tone, and subject matter. In books he wanted to preserve the freedom to write "truth," to speak of the world as he saw it. He therefore draws a distinction and holds the novel as being of a higher order. But there are several points to be remembered about his distinction, and they are connected. First, his distinction is based not on the characteristics of the short story as a form but of the market-imposed formulae. Second, he speaks frequently of the craft of short story writing and the skills it requires with serious respect. Third, his novels, too, usually have been viewed as popular fiction. And fourth, many of the same techniques learned and practiced in the short fiction—and even readership considerations—carry over into the novels.

To isolate the short stories from the rest of Vonnegut's work, then, may be both to distort the perspective taken on the stories themselves and to misinterpret their position as an intrinsic part of the Vonnegut canon. The short stories prefigure techniques and content that sometimes emerge years later in the novels. Vonnegut's interest in the sociological impact of technology, his use of science fiction techniques and themes, his visions of regenerative utopias and crushing dystopias, and his registering of the psychological burdens of contemporary life on the individual, all emerge in the earliest writings. Two later books on Vonnegut's fiction, Lawrence Broer's *Sanity Plea: Schizophrenia in the Novels of Kurt Vonnegut* (1989) and Leonard Mustazza's *Forever Pursuing Genesis: The Myth of Eden in the Novels of Kurt Vonnegut* (1990), have titles reflecting themes evident in the earliest stories, helping to demonstrate their importance to an overall understanding of this author's work.

One of the earliest circumstances that seems to have contributed to Kurt Vonnegut's subsequent career in fiction writing was his being the baby of the family, almost eight years younger than his bother Bernard and five years the junior of his sister Alice. He found that the most successful way to compete for attention was to be funny, and early family movies show him clowning. His sister shared his sense of humor, including the kind of slapstick humor that sees a pedestrian's stepping off the sidewalk into a puddle only to disappear down a hidden manhole as hilarious. He grew up listening to radio comedians like Fred Allen, Jack Benny and Henry Morgan. So it is not surprising that some of his school and college writing consists simply of telling jokes, his own and other people's. The steps from jokes to comical vignettes to humorous stories come progressively.

There were other more literary influences in Vonnegut's early life. His parents, and indeed the German-American community in Indianapolis, had a cultured background. His father was an architect who loved music and poetry, and in his later years turned to painting and pottery. His mother actually tried short story writing. "She was a good writer, it turned out," says Vonnegut, "but she had no talent for the vulgarity the slick magazines required."[3] The house was full of books, and Vonnegut read widely, though indiscriminately.

Shortridge High School in Indianapolis, located in one of those fine, well-fenestrated buildings that typified large schools of the time, offered Vonnegut splendid opportunities to develop as a writer. Shortridge was one of the first two high schools in the country to have a daily newspaper. During his four years there, 1936–1940, Vonnegut wrote for the *Echo* almost continuously, beginning with the publication of a paper he had written for his English class. He went on to become a regular weekly columnist and to be the managing editor. When he went to Cornell University in 1940 he quickly became involved with the *Cornell*

Sun, again going on to have his own column and to become managing editor. Vonnegut was socially very active both in high school and college, and it is easy to suspect that some of his writing served as an adjunct to those activities, rather as his cutting up at the dinner table had as a tot. Much of what he wrote in high school relates to student social life, just as at Cornell he wrote about the fraternity scene and the like. Of course, those are natural subjects for school journalism. What increasingly distinguishes Vonnegut, however, is his facility in making comedy out of this material. But other important growth went on, too; Vonnegut developed the habit of daily writing and meeting deadlines, he tested out narrative voices, and he learned social observation, beginning to nurture the insight of the satirist. Equally important, he began to learn about the timing of making a joke snap shut, later to be vital to his short story writing, and he developed the spare, clipped prose style that has remained a lifelong characteristic.

Vonnegut went into the army in 1943. In 1944 he had to confront the suicide of his mother, capture by the Germans, the loss of over forty pounds while in captivity, and a second narrow escape from death in the firebombing of Dresden—traumas that would later fuel his fiction and impact the nature of his humor. He returned to marry and go to graduate school, quickly resuming journalism by writing for the Chicago City News Bureau. From there he moved to Schenectady, New York, as a public relations writer for the General Electric Company, but found little reward in the work. He also needed more income, so, doubly motivated, he began writing short stories in evenings and on weekends. When he sent his first story, "Report on the Barnhouse Effect," off to *Collier's* it was spotted by Knox Burger, who at Yale had known of Vonnegut when they were managing editors of their respective school papers. Burger directed Vonnegut to the helpful advice of Kenneth Littauer and Max Wilkinson, agents whose past experience in magazine editing proved invaluable, and before long he was selling enough stories to leave G.E. and move to Cape Cod, writing full-time.

While Vonnegut has several times said that one of the requirements for writing for the popular, "glossy" magazines was that the stories be happy, Vonnegut's subjects are often serious. Indeed, one of the functions of his comedic stories is that of most good comedy, to face a generally recognized fear and diminish it with laughter. Not all of his endings are happy, or at least not happy in the sense that the main characters are smilingly bidding farewell to all of their troubles. Quite often the happiness is the reader's, in that good old American common sense and basic values have been vindicated. The characters will have come to their senses, but at a cost. Vonnegut thinks, he says, that in real life people probably do not change after age thirty-five, whereas in the short story they change all the time. In some of his stories, characters who realize their life's dream quite late in life are just as prone to discover its falsity as those with the foolish ambitions of youth.

Dreams, literal and in the sense of wished-for objectives, play a role in a number of the stories. Sometimes their influence is benign or even positive, offering motivation or a goal by which the character finds a sense of purpose and identity. Sometimes the dream has the opposite effect. Dreams of material acquisition usually corrupt and dehumanize. The values that the stories approve are usually traditional middle-class virtues of honesty, industry, modesty and decency. Show-offs, exploiters, cheats and those obsessed with material gain usually end up exposed to others for what they are and dissatisfied with themselves. Children are often the focus of sound values and are exposers of frauds. These tests of values, then, quite naturally intersect with another major theme, the quest for identity.

In Vonnegut's novels, the quest for identity becomes a consistent and prominent theme. Already in the two earliest novels there are excellent examples of this. In *Player Piano*, Paul Proteus, shifting between multiple roles as his name suggests, striving to sort out his ambitions, his attitudes toward his wife, father and best friend, and whether he finds the technological age to which he has contributed an improvement or not, essentially is trying to determine who he is. In *The Sirens of Titan*, Malachi Constant, the millionaire playboy who becomes "the Space Wanderer," is above all trying to find himself. In the stories, Vonnegut approaches aspects of the identity quest that return for more extensive development in his novels. There are the characters who live dual lives, pretending to be one thing and secretly being another. There are those whose identity is dependent upon a role or a job—and those who, having none, make one up, sometimes living by a fantasy. The impact of domestic or family relationships on identity makes a common subject. In the earlier years of these stories, at least, women's identities were often perceived as being tied to their husbands' roles, and influenced—or even dictated—by the expectations authenticated in women's magazines. For the males in the stories, the father-son relationship repeatedly tests the self-identity of those in both generations.

Such themes generally require domestic settings, and many of the stories have just such a familiar quality. The domestic drama makes a comfortable vehicle for upholding ordinary daily values, for vindicating "plain horse-sense," and frequently for introducing elements of suspense that can be quickly resolved and humor that does not ultimately hurt anyone. Some of Vonnegut's topics cannot be so easily accommodated. Writing in the era of the cold war, the dawn of the technological age, the coming of space travel, and at a time when the global population began to explode, he shows a compulsion to deal with these issues, as might be natural in a writer who has seen first hand the consequences of economic depression, warfare, and science unleashed without conscience. Hence there are stories that deal with war and its consequences to veterans, children and refugees. There are stories that warningly portray dreams of technological panaceas turned to nightmare. And there are stories where the pursuit of longevity has made Earth itself a sterile hell.

To treat these latter topics, Vonnegut needs to show the long-term consequences of the dangerous trends he sees implicit in them. To do that, he frequently makes use of a fictional future. In that way he can project a world where the extension of life and the preservation of youth create a society jammed with robust and handsome centenarians living on dried seaweed. Sometimes perspective demands distance in space rather than time. These removals in time and space, together with the sometimes technological subject matter, result in stories that qualify as science fiction or contain elements that do. Hence, as Vonnegut himself was to protest, he became more generally classified as a science fiction writer than was justified. Certainly in most instances, Vonnegut's motivation in the use of the science fictional is sociological. It comes not from a fascination with speculations about technology but from a desire to show the moral and practical consequences of patterns of behavior.

But also to have fun. However serious the purpose or profound the moral message, Vonnegut consistently lightens his stories—and usually heightens their didactic impact—by comic invention and an almost adolescent sense of fun. That holds for most modes he employs, but it is particularly distinctive in his science fiction. Sometimes the humor in his stories rests simply in events or dialogue. Sometimes it is in the very nature of the story, such as the traditional American tall tale, as seen in "Tom Edison's Shaggy Dog." And sometimes it is structural, as in the use of a narrator or an internal observer, or in the timing of a snap-shut ending. Narrators serve his humor well, often permitting a kind of relaxed, colloquial voice that can put a personalized comic stamp on the retelling of a story. Or the narrator can become the focus of humor out of the disparity between his (as it usually is) version of events and that conveyed by events themselves. Sometimes there is no persona created for this kind of narrative voice, but the narration has the same kind of easy, amused flavor. The internal observers often come in figures like the wise old guy behind the drugstore counter who can punctuate the words and actions of the lead character with undercutting good sense.

Vonnegut has said that one of the differences between writing short stories and writing novels is that with the former the writer has to know exactly how it will end from the start.[4] Many of his stories hinge on a turn in the plot very close to the end. The conclusion of the story—it may be as short as a paragraph or sentence—will snap the story to its close almost like the punchline of a joke. There may be steps in the story that follow a similar pattern, though not to so pronounced a degree. It is easy to see a connection between this technique and that applied to the longer fiction, where short chapters may work in much the same way, or even themselves be made up of a series of joke-like segments. Timing and compression are essential to sustain such a narrative technique, and it is in the stories that Vonnegut learns and refines the method that underlies the construction of the novels.

Looking back at the high school and college writing, one of the things that becomes evident is an occasional awkwardness in the assumption of a narrative voice. Vonnegut the reporter has learned to keep himself out of his columns, but Vonnegut the humorist and featured columnist longs to speak directly. The result is the sometimes clumsy use of "we" in a clearly singular situation, for example. In the short stories there are experiments with narrative voices: omniscient third-person narrators, almost disembodied first-person voices who write reports, first-persons who have roles as characters, too, and such narrators where there exists the sense of an authorial view as well. Vonnegut continues to employ such devices in the novels. After two omniscient third-person narrated novels, he comes to *Mother Night* with a first-person memoir, but outside of that an editor, "K.V.," or Vonnegut as persona, and *then,* with the 1966 edition, Vonnegut the author speaking personally as a third narrative presence. Another example is *Slaughterhouse-Five,* where Vonnegut frames the story in his own voice and interjects "That was me. I was there" in the course of a third-person narration. In that novel he wants the immediacy of that first-person voice, but he also needs the distanced, objective third-person voice to address the Dresden events as a public, historical issue. The narrative stance continues to be an interesting technical problem in his novels, and the experience of the short stories doubtless proved useful in finding solutions.

The topics or themes dealt with in the short stories recur in the novels, not surprisingly, so it is predictable that some of the images associated with them— EPICAC, Ethical Suicide Parlors, equalizing handicaps, for example—should recur, too. Actually, since the short stories and the novels are not simply successive, there can be a degree of cross-fertilization, as it were, between them. It is less important that a novel succeeds a short story in the development of a topic than that it affords a different context in which to do so. Obviously the novel's greater length affords the opportunity for more complexity, for the consideration of more aspects, and consequently for more profundity. The novel is also less subject to the requirement to keep the reader happy. Differences in the treatments of repeated themes or topics are therefore likely to be due as much to the requirements of the genre as to one's being earlier than the other.

One can say at the outset, then, that Vonnegut's short fiction enjoyed much success in its intended role. As popular fiction written for wide-circulation magazines, it commanded a ready market, appeared in the best of those magazines, and continued to be in demand as long as those publications thrived. It was ingenious, varied, and well written. Anthologized, or as collected in *Welcome to the Monkey House*, it has continued to find a readership. By those criteria, the short fiction must be judged successful. Whether being popular fiction excludes it from more serious consideration is another issue, and one, incidentally, from which the rest of Vonnegut's fiction has not always been removed. That, and the question of to what degree the short fiction can be separated from the novels, are questions the pages that follow will consider. Kurt Vonnegut is prolific and various in his artistic expression, for besides the novels and short stories he has produced poems, plays, assorted nonfiction prose, screen scripts, a requiem, drawings and paintings—and on-stage performances. These are the products of one mind, and there are inevitable connections between them. The short stories have their place in this spectrum of achievement, and just how intrinsic that place is to the written canon must be another issue to be evaluated.

NOTES

1. Kurt Vonnegut, *Welcome to the Monkey House* (New York: Seymour Lawrence/Delacorte Press, 1968), x.

2. Jerome Klinkowitz and Donald Lawler, eds., *Vonnegut in America* (New York: Delta Books, 1977), 53–60; and Stanley Schatt, *Kurt Vonnegut, Jr.* (Boston: Twayne Publishers, 1976), 119–135.

3. *Paris Review* Interview, in William Rodney Allen, ed. *Conversations with Kurt Vonnegut* (Jackson: The University Press of Mississippi, 1988), 177.

4. Telephone conversation with Kurt Vonnegut, May 17, 1996, wherein he said that with the short story there is no time to experiment, "you must know

the end before you begin, you must know where you are going." He observed that such writing taught the lesson of doing things with precision and economy. It was in this conversation that he suggested, as noted above, that in reality people seldom change much after age thirty-five, whereas in these stories they often do.

2

Apprenticeship: High School and College Journalism

Kurt Vonnegut's earliest publications appeared in his high school and college newspapers. In themselves they do not appear exceptional in the quality of either their prose style or their ideas. That is natural enough, since they are intended primarily to entertain student readers by being catchy and topical. Anyone who has written regularly for a student newspaper will know that trying to remain entertaining, not to mention actually funny, while drawing on the limited material an educational institution affords and meeting a deadline week after week is not nearly as easy as it appeared to be when eagerly undertaken. Indeed, Vonnegut actually resorts to using the difficulty in coming up with material as subject matter itself.

These early writings *are* interesting, however, for what they reveal of their author in his younger years, and for what they show of stylistic mannerisms and interests in subject matter that can be traced on into his much later writing. One important contribution of this experience with working journalism to Vonnegut's later writing career appears to be its accustoming him to the discipline of regular, daily production and the meeting of deadlines. Obviously, this approach to writing was to be furthered when he became a public relations writer for the General Electric Company in the late 1940s, but it has characterized his approach to his whole literary career. Vonnegut has always written steadily, even in bad patches where much of what was written ended up in crumpled paper balls on the floor. He has written to various audiences and markets, he has taken an active interest in the publishing and contractual side of writing, and he has undertaken the usual round of lectures and public appearances. All of this has contributed to his remaining a productive and popular author over an exceptionally long career.

Stylistically, too, the influence of journalism on his fiction writing made an impact that remains visible much later. The pun on his name in that his style is "curt" has often been remarked. The propensity to adhere to the newspaperman's short, direct sentences and paragraphs is evident in all of the novels, even becoming a predominating feature of *Cat's Cradle* (1963) with its 127 mini-chapters. Frequently the episodes that punctuate his novels seem drawn from everyday life, like so many human interest stories. Often, too, the foundations of the story line in a Vonnegut novel are drawn from historical fact or from invented situations based on historical circumstances, related as reportage. *Jailbird* (1979) is a prime example of this, drawing on the Sacco and Vanzetti case of the 1920s and later events such as the McCarthy hearings and Watergate, while also creating a history of the McCone family and the strike at Cuyahoga Bridge and Iron. This novel features unusually extensive mingling of the historical and the fictional, in the best postmodern fashion, but the reporting of "real" events in a journalistic manner occurs frequently in other novels. Sometimes, as with the recounting of the Sacco and Vanzetti case in *Jailbird*, the reportage has an educational function, especially where it seems intended to instruct younger readers on events now all too often forgotten. In this the didactic element sometimes detectable in the early journalism, primarily at the *Cornell Sun*, finds continuation in the moral and ethical judgments of the novels' social commentaries.

Such serious matters have little place in Vonnegut's contributions to the *Shortridge Daily Echo*, the newspaper of Shortridge High School in Indianapolis where his earliest writing is found.[1] But an interesting narrational characteristic does emerge. Vonnegut in later years spoke of the fact that he kept himself out of his novels because he had been taught in journalism that his writing should be impersonal. He says he broke free of this during his tenure as a visiting writer at the Iowa Writers' Workshop, when others there told him it was acceptable for him to declare himself in the first person.[2] Indeed, tracing Vonnegut's search for the appropriate narrative voice in his successive fictions makes an interesting exercise. What emerges in the high school writing, and to a lesser degree in his subsequent *Cornell Sun* pieces, is an apparent struggle with the impulse to be directly and intensely personal, both in the use of the first person singular voice and in using his daily experiences and feelings as the subject matter. A distinction should be kept in mind here, however; the prohibition against the injection of self in voice and opinion that Vonnegut had been taught applied chiefly to reportage. The writing in these student newspapers that can be identified as Vonnegut's occurs primarily in editorial or gossip columns, which are a different matter. It is intriguing, though, that in the *Echo*'s "Bull Session" columns, where he uses a *nom de plume*, he—as it were—peeks around the persona to reveal himself.

The earliest reference to Vonnegut in the *Echo* occurs in its social columns on January 13, 1937, his freshman year. Others occur in that year and the next.[3] By Kurt's junior year he was becoming a veritable "Big Man On Campus," on the Student Council, president of the Junior Social Committee, in the "B" band, the Press Club, the Drama League, the ROTC, and the Junior Pin and Ring Committee (*1940 Shortridge Annual, 75th Anniversary Edition*). The September 15, 1938, "In the Swim" column includes this: "Tip to Kurt Vonnegut. Please look at the person to whom you are going to speak. It is rather disturbing to have you look the other way and then say 'hello.'   Shortridge girls." It is not the only indication the girls were noticing him. In the Christmas 1938 issue, "Dear Diary" reports his passing notes, with two guesses as to whom. Another gossip column, "Flames and Soot" (September 22, 1938), seems to credit him with a little more social grace: "Plug for Kurt Vonnegut, who is planning on running for Junior Vaudeville chairman. Don't you think he would be a keen one, though? For if he applies a touch of that subtle Vonnegut wit to the Vaudeville, it should be really whizz-bang!" He got the job.

Vonnegut continues to be mentioned in the paper's social columns into his senior year, where "Popular Poison" nominates him "an intriguing personality" (September 21, 1939) and notes that he "is giving Baba Kiger a whirl" (September 28), while "Flames and Soot" gives more credit to his charms: "That President of the Social Committee, who is worshipped by freshmen femmes; thought of as 'wonderful' by Sally Evans, and 'intriguing' by Baba Kiger—Kurt Vonnegut remains oblivious to all. Universal opinion Kurt—we need more people like you." What it is to have friends in the press!

By this time, however, there is much evidence of Vonnegut's own writing. In the September 19, 1939' issue, for instance, there are gossip items that, while unsigned, might well be his, punctuated with expressions like "anyhoo," "oodles," "ho hum" and "Whoo! Whoo!" "Excelsior!" which occurs in two pieces, foreshadows his later title, "Excelsior! We're Going to the Moon! Excelsior!" in the *New York Times Magazine* of July 13, 1969. No doubt such words, like other Vonnegut favorites such as "keen" and "peachy," were common parlance among his peers and therefore not necessarily reliable clues to his authorship, but the conspicuous usage of some of them in later Vonnegut work, particularly in such novels as *Breakfast of Champions* (1973) and *Slapstick* (1976), is suggestive. At about this time, which of course coincides with the outbreak of the Second World War, there is also an editorial that takes a strong anti-war stance (September 29). There is nothing to confirm Vonnegut's authorship, though the contents accord with what he was to write in the *Cornell Sun* and with his later anti-war attitudes. It may simply indicate prevalent sentiments in this middle-American city at this time.

During this period, Vonnegut did some sports reporting, mostly of track and field, under his own by-line. The style is rather more dramatic that in most sports reporting, with a touch of the cheerleader, but clearly aims to bring appropriate credit to Shortridge contestants for their efforts. Vonnegut also commented on track and field while at Cornell, including references to a fellow Hoosier, the contemporary middle-distance running star Don Lash.

It is in the aptly name "Bull Session" column from September 1939 through January 1940 that Vonnegut's style and spirit show best. Throughout these weekly columns Vonnegut uses some variant of the name "Ferdinand" as a *nom de plume*. The name derives from that marvelous children's book *The Story of Ferdinand*, which Vonnegut acknowledges was a childhood favorite. It tells the story of a Spanish bull, raised for bullfighting, who disdains the pawing and snorting of his feisty brethren and prefers to sit under his shady cork tree and smell the flowers. It seems natural that this story would strike a chord with the boy who would go on to oppose wars, militarism and violence, and to reveal a sharp interest in animals. His novels often introduce animal behavior and biology, and he several times uses cruelty to animals as a measure of barbarity. One thinks of Ferdinand's literary relative, the cow in *Galapagos* (1985), brutally hoisted onboard ship by a noose around its horns. The oft-repeated point that Vonnegut remains too much of an anthropologist to have any real villains in his books comes closest to being contradicted in the obvious revulsion to such cruelty as Paul Lazarro's vicious murder of the dog in *Slaughterhouse-Five* (1969).[4]

In the *Echo* columns there are no such serious overtones, however, and the name seems to serve mainly as an apt play on *"Bull* Session." In the earliest of these columns, he signs himself simply "Ferdy." The column needles his chums Bud Gillespie and Dick Lieber and shows his efforts to give these columns a casual informality and a personal stamp with some of his favorite diction, like "keen" and "snooze." The October 3 column, signed "Ferdinand," contains added betrayal of authorship in its advertising for the Social Committee, of which he was then president.

About this date it appears that while Vonnegut finds himself popular and busy with the social whirl—within a month he becomes publicity chairman for the Senior Drama League, joins the radio and music committees for the Gym Jam Jump, and enters his candidacy for class treasurer—he has trouble finding time to create material for the column. In the October 10 "Bull Session" he writes: "There comes a time in every inquisitive reporter's career when timely questions are nowhere to be found and he is forced either to resort to pure nonsense or find some subject not so timely." He signs this one "Ferlfendelfinalfund," which is described as "Alfalfa Language." In the October 17 issue "Ferdy" says little, and on the 24th he laments once more, "Sometime you're going to find an awfully big hole on this page, and then you'll know I've had a nervous breakdown. If I'm to retain my buoyant health and general well-being, I'll be forced to compose this thing some other time other than Saturday midnight!" The following week "Foidinando" still dwells on the same theme: "It has been suggested that this column attack more major and timely issues and cease being so slap happy."

Was it nudging from someone else—readers, an editor, a colleague—that led to this harping on his lack of serious and "timely" content, or something within himself? The problem of coming up with subject matter week after week, especially when distracted by so many other activities, might well be enough in itself. But something in the nature of this issue seems peculiarly Vonnegutian. The boy clearly enjoys the role of entertainer, chatting breezily about friends and school social life, being a bit smart, making verbal plays—what he calls "resort[ing] to pure nonsense." On the other hand, there is the person who wants to be thought of as having ideas, even of being intellectual. He wants to be the entertainer but the challenger, too. That duality becomes even more apparent in the *Cornell Sun* columns, and it is one that continues to demand some care in the balancing even in his mature fiction. Even in the novel many regard as his masterpiece, *Slaughterhouse-Five*, the competing strains remain. To my thinking they cohere (or perhaps collide) in a way that gives that novel its richness, but there have been those, like Roger Sale and John Gardner, who have seen the serious issues raised by that novel trivialized or dismissed by the repeated "so it goes" and various comic gestures.[5] Certainly such objections were made about *Breakfast of Champions*, where the irreverent diction and childlike drawings blinded some to the thoughtfulness with which a number of serious social issues are addressed. That dilemma faces many comic writers, of course, as they range between farce, where serious purpose loses out to humor, and the darker hues of satire, where didacticism may overwhelm the comic.

Meanwhile, although he has created a persona in the *nom de plume*'s variant Ferdinands, he still feels the need to reveal himself directly. That evinces itself in the progression from the October 10, 1939, passage where he speaks of "the inquisitive reporter" in the third person, to the October 24th lament that is all first person and personal. Again, the search for an appropriate voice continues in his school and college writing, and even in the mature fiction. At times he seems to welcome the authority, as well as the anonymity, that the third person gives, while elsewhere he clearly wants to be heard and felt personally.

For all this, there is no discernible movement toward more of the "major and timely issues" in the remaining "Bull Session" columns. The November 21, 1939, column mentions the Second World War briefly at the start, but quickly reverts to the usual chit-chat about school personalities. There are more of the verbal plays like those that have reappeared in his fiction, such as the close of the November 7 column with "Ooooooooodles of X's Ferdy" and the interjection of "hm-m-m" into the narrative voice. There are some other notes of interest. Alan Nolan, subsequently to become an Indianapolis attorney, and friend Bud Gillespie continue to get ribbings. Incidentally, Bud failed to be elected class president at the same time that Kurt failed in his effort to be treasurer. The signature continues to go through permutations, to "FERDy" (November 11) to "Sturdy Ferdy" (November 28) to "Pferdy" (January 6, 1940) in an issue where everyone talks like a "Popeye" comic strip and initial p's are liberally distributed.

The November 21, 1939, "Bull Session" clearly labels his persona, concluding, "I like it better here where I can sit just quietly and smell the flowers . . . Ferdinand." But Ferdinand's days are numbered. In January he and an often-mentioned friend, Ben Hitz, are named co-editors of the Tuesday *Echoes* for the spring semester. The "Bull Session" on the 23rd, his last, has the usual social content then ends:

Here's a fellow you've never heard interviewed in this column. It's me by golly! I'm gonna tell you what I think! I think that the school is foolish to buy any 'good' entertainment when the students don't want to be entertained. Give the money to the Student Aid Fund. This is the last of these and so the last of your old pal. FERDINAND

"Bull Sessions" now passes to "Filbert," who is identified as Phil Huston.

The demise of "Ferdinand" does not the end Vonnegut's presence in the *Echo*. The 1939 Christmas Special Edition of the *Echo* was in magazine format, complete with advertisements from various Indianapolis businesses. Inside the back cover an advertisement for Block's department store features a photograph of Kurt Vonnegut, posed with two young women. One of these is identified as Betty Jane Mitchell, the other as Marilyn Clark, who wrote the regular weekly fashion column sponsored by Block's called "Block's Snooper." Vonnegut is included "for sponsoring the sartorial cause of the male." Later (February 15, 1940) there is an advertising column called Spring Song for Block's signed "Koort II," another on March 14 signed "Koort Snarfield Vonnegut II," and a final one on May 23 which he signs "KOORT MCVIII." During 1939 and 1940 as many as twenty-two Block's advertisements have participation by Vonnegut.[6] These must be Vonnegut's first ventures into writing advertising copy, significantly since his first full-time job after the war was as a public relations writer for the General Electric Company in Schenectady, New York. Even after his first short story successes and his retirement from G.E. in 1950, he still periodically freelanced writing public relations copy.

Apart from the Block's columns, convincing evidence of his editorial writing in his last semester at Shortridge is not easy to come by. An April 30, 1940, editorial on "Mental Apathy and Propaganda," pointing out how mental apathy makes people vulnerable to propaganda, suggesting that this has happened in the Axis countries, and asking if Americans are alert enough to be safe, sounds remarkably like Vonnegut. There are some editorials on books and music that could conceivably be his, but there is no persuasive internal evidence. An interesting note appears in the gossipy "Flames and Soot" column for April 25: "Kurt Vonnegut may even be plus his woman by now unless he hits another 'woe is he' mood." Context does not explain this, but it may suggest that the popular young socialite was nevertheless prone to some of the depressive mood swings that were to plague him periodically later in life.

Shortridge High School had a fiction club that appears to have produced much good writing. There were literary publications and literary pages in the *Echo*. Vonnegut apparently had no part in these activities, with one possible exception. The *Echo* occasionally published student writing from people not on the staff, sometimes classwork. There is a piece, written when Vonnegut was a sophomore, called "This Business of Whistle Purchasing" (February 18, 1938). It recounts an embarrassing experience on a first date, and appears to be something written for his English class, being signed "Kurt Vonnegut, English IVx." Perhaps Vonnegut's generally nonliterary approach confirms the impression that he saw working with the *Echo* largely as a social activity and his writing as a form of entertaining. He has spoken of himself as being the baby of his family and having to play the comic cut-up to get attention, and family movies which include him as a child tend to confirm this role (*Self-Portrait*). "Ferdinand" appears to be an extension of that role, as may have been his involvement in the Vaudeville (he had the winning act in his junior year), the Entertainment Committee and the Drama League. Such interests were to continue. Short stories use the setting of community or summer stock theater, for instance, and he went on to write plays. In later years his public appearances under the title "How to Get A Job Like Mine" were largely stand-up comedy routines.

So some significant patterns were set in this early writing: The use of personae but the need to speak personally. The routine of daily work and the requirement of meeting deadlines—even if done late Saturday night! The fascination with verbal play, interjections, and lengthened vowel sounds. Clipped sentences. Allusions to friends. Moments of denigrating his own writing—as he will later several times, notably in *Slaughterhouse-Five*, referring to the book as "a failure" (19). And some slight indications of the later deep concerns with jingoism, war and propaganda.

In the fall of 1940, Kurt went off to Cornell University, in Ithaca, New York. His major has been variously spoken of as chemistry or biochemistry, although it is likely that in the two and a half years he was there he was occupied largely with general education courses. Vonnegut must have involved himself in the *Cornell Sun* soon after arrival, since he was publishing under his own by-line by the spring semester of his freshman year. The content of his columns shows that he also involved himself in an vigorous social life, as he had at Shortridge, and much of what he writes centers around the fraternities and extracurricular activities. There are more serious columns, however, and some evidence of a concern with those "major and timely events" he felt he neglected in the *Echo*.

Vonnegut's identifiable contributions to the *Cornell Sun* include eleven "Innocents Abroad" columns, nine "Speaking of Sports" entries, twenty-one columns under the "Well All Right" heading, and two under "Berry Patch." The latter are the most interesting in being the most original and the most revealing of their author's evolving style and thought. His work under each of these titles began in the spring of 1941, although most of the sports columns appeared in spring 1942. "Well All Right" runs from April of 1941 through to May of 1942.

"Innocents Abroad" was a humor column that initially consisted of material clipped from other student newspapers. Vonnegut recognizes this in his first (March 25, 1941) column:

With the hilarious nature of this golden age we live in, with Adolph Hitler, labor riots, and the Cornell Widow, one cannot help but see the screamingly funny side to everything—or such is the hope of one dope who spends his time clipping witticisms from exchange papers and having the gall to demand a by-line for it.

He quickly makes his point:

> **Quip Clipped By Dip**
> Little ear of corn: "Where did I come from?"
> Big ear of corn: "The stalk brought you." —Northeastern News

There are many more like this in the columns that follow. The second one (April 9, 1941) concludes apologetically,

One of these days we're going to publish an original joke and see how long it takes to get around the college circuit. Anybody know an original joke?

The columns of April 15 and April 21, 1941, are in the same vein. By the fifth "Innocents Abroad" (April 23, 1941) there are items that are not simply clipped from other papers, though one might question the strength of their originality. A mini-story about three visiting Yale drunks concludes with one of them shouting back at a bus driver, "I'm no pedestrian, I'm a Methodist." In the next, April 30, Vonnegut produces more of his own humor, characteristically in short narrative episodes that may be the precursors of the short stories. One concerns a visit to the infirmary, one getting lost driving, one a "peachy" variant of stud poker, and one a gin cooler. Like the earlier *Echo* pieces, they rely on sensationalizing daily student life. But by May 2 he writes in mock-defense, "The Dean has suggested our leaving school so there's no point in your writing us about it too." He caps this column with an "old chestnut": "Cream is more expensive than milk because it's tougher for the cows to squat on the little bottles."[7]

As Vonnegut emerges from total reliance on clipped material he begins to reveal more of himself, although he insists on retaining the sheltering first person plural rather than the more declarative "I." One autobiographical revelation occurs in his May 3 column, where he invokes "the Shortridge High School Daily Echo (the first high school daily in the country) . . . located in the garden spot of America, Indianapolis, Indiana (home of Allison Engines, and the world's largest inland city)." (Later in life Vonnegut was to modify the claim for Indianapolis to "the largest city not on a navigable waterway," no doubt in deference to metropolises such as Chicago, Delhi, Berlin and Moscow!) The column then consists of seven two-liners (example: "Nomination for the meanest man in the world: The guy who was deaf and never told his barber"), every one of them followed by the acknowledgment:

Shortridge Daily Echo
(first high school daily in America)

On May 9 he is more autobiographical, with humor at the expense of the Cornell Military Department that one gathers he kept up in person. He talks about the army's need for zoologists such as himself to do bigger things than blowing up targets with Lieutenant Wilcox, such as identifying butterflies. He claims he is "not just being a sorehead because we didn't get a blue and gold medal like the rest of the fellows" and notes how his name gets mixed up as "Vontegal."

In April Vonnegut had written his first "Well All Right" column and was to produce three more in May, so possibly he found the effort to produce two columns simultaneously too demanding. As at Shortridge, however, he continued to adopt the stance that denigration of his efforts forced him to give up. The May 14 "Innocents Abroad" takes an ironic reverse tack:

Thousands of fans from all over America have asked how it is humanly possible to keep up such a consistent flow of top-flight humor. We can only say that we are not, as many people seem to believe, perfect, and that we, like anyone else may slip—such a thing is plenty remote, however.

The editorial in that issue is all about the flight of Rudolph Hess to Scotland. Vonnegut's "True Story" in his column, which appears right next to the editorial, recounts how four students went to the infirmary to see if a perfectly healthy student would be kept in if he reported. It turns out that the volunteer had German measles and was kept in, while the other three were quarantined. He remarks that to have German measles is "treason in these times," a nod toward topical events and the only revelation in "Innocents Abroad" of ambivalent feelings that have more direct expression in "Well All Right." The last "Innocents" by Vonnegut appeared on May 26, 1941; it jokingly alludes to the brief tenures of writers of this humor column, and, suggesting that he can take a hint, implies that he will be stepping down.

Taken together, the "Innocents Abroad" columns hardly prefigure the emergence of one of America's foremost comic writers of the century. On the other hand, they do show that the writer has a sense of humor, and if that humor sometimes seems rather sophomoric it should be remembered it was written by a freshman., It shows a sense for the ridiculous and a predilection toward the clipped, two-line joke (even if they usually are not yet his own) that stay with Vonnegut in his later fiction. Writing a humor column that appears on average twice a week and that contains three or more jokes a time amounts to having to produce a joke a day, a tough assignment for a student writer. Coming up with nine such columns in two months, along with other writing, demonstrates again the young Vonnegut's commitment to being a working journalist, meeting deadlines and producing copy.

Kurt Vonnegut wrote the "Well All Right" columns from April 7, 1941, near to the time he was to leave "Innocents Abroad," until May 4, 1942, by which time his career at Cornell was faltering. There are twenty-one in all. They are typically about 350–400 words long, they once again use the first person plural when speaking of the writer, and they range in subject matter from trivial campus social chat to the long-delayed ventures into "major and timely" topics. As a consequence they reveal more of the young Vonnegut than does any of the previous writing.

Of the 1941 spring semester pieces, the first column continues the previously-seen drawing on items from other college papers and the social focus. It alludes to pacifism in the mention of a student's parent who considers that "war is not the way to settle international misunderstandings." He refers to "our kid sister," which would be either fictional or an address that Alice, the sister five years his senior, would not appreciate (April 7, 1941). The second contains chat about campus building construction and train travel (April 11, 1941). The third recounts a sojourn in the infirmary with German measles, and the predictable high-jinks that enlivened it (April 18, 1941). A more serious column with the long title of "Bayonet Drill at the Rate of Seven in 20 Seconds, or, Oh For A Couple of Nazis," is one of several that address war-related issues (April 22, 1941). As narrative it may point toward the short fiction, though it is noticeable that here he reports his characters' speech whereas later in this series he would use dialogue. The situation describes meeting a young soldier on a bus back to Ithaca and listening to him revel in bayonet drill, lamenting only that he had no live Nazis to practice on. "He hates Germans—all of 'em." Vonnegut shows not just his distaste for such brutal militarism, but also his resentment as a German-American; "We were going to ask him what he had against Beethoven but we decided that we probably wouldn't get a very good answer."[8] This is a characteristic piece at an early age.

In the column "In Which We Dare to Enter a Stronghold of Evil" (May 10, 1941), he had probably decided he needed something in a lighter mood. It recounts a visit to the "XYZ Club," a gambling hall, and is told in rather exaggerated and somewhat clichéd images. A narrative, it involves description and the creation of an atmosphere, so constitutes another step toward fiction. Another light column, "Harvard Men Turn Tables on Sally Rand" (May 12, 1941), purports to review an account in "The Oil City Blizzard" of fan dancer Sally Rand's invitation to the Harvard College freshman smoker. Rand was purportedly kidnapped by MIT students, talked then into taking her to Harvard, and them persuaded the assembled students to strip while she escaped fully dressed, causing a riot. Once again he appears to appreciate that "Joe College" behavior and Ivy League social life find a receptive audience. "Gloomy

Wednesday–or Why We Wish We Were an an [sic] Independent" (May 21, 1941) discusses the impact of defense taxation and the prospect of the draft upon fraternities. Its argument seems rather curious, in that it is hard to see how the lot of independents would be any better than that of the fraternities in these circumstances. Vonnegut has another column the very next day, "Finding the News in the News." This one is more serious and is reminiscent of the column he wrote for the *Echo* called "Mental Apathy and Propaganda" (April 30, 1940). It discusses possible bias in news reports of the British defense of Crete and how the way news is presented visually can influence a reader's response to it. He also suggests that British colonial behavior remains under-reported. He concludes:

If the British are having the trouble in Malaya that they seem to have had in many of their colonies and protectorates, we should know it. We must know the shortcomings of the British—and of ourselves—as well as of the Germans if we would create any kind of lasting remedy, when the dangers of the moment are averted.

This column might seem to show again a German-American's concern for fairness, and to reflect some of the isolationist and frankly anti-British sentiment that was still quite widespread in the country at this time. It also demonstrates two more enduring characteristics, however—a concern about censorship and fair reporting, and an ability to see two sides of an issue. The final column of the semester, "We Impress Life Magazine with Our Efficient Role in National Defense" (May 23, 1941), makes his third column in three days. The awkwardness of the narrational "we" becomes apparent here, where it refers both to the Cornell ROTC and to Vonnegut personally. It is a light column about the visit by *Life* Magazine, which was evidently running a series, in the patriotic spirit of the times, on college military corps. Vonnegut shows some of his usual disdain for military discipline and authority, again including some humor at the expense of Lieutenant Wilcox (see "Innocents," May 9, 1941).

When Vonnegut returned for his second year at Cornell, he initially struck a personal and flippant tone. The first column, "Doomed to Look Like a Freshman All Our Lives" (September 22, 1941) and lamenting just that, actually tries to assert his "savior [sic] faire" with its casual talk of smoking, drinking and rushing. "In Which We Get Trimmed and Find the Barber—in The Same Boat" (September 26, 1941) is again personal and light, about his experience getting a haircut. It has some interest, however, in the movement toward short fiction, in that this little story includes an extended passage of dialogue, with dialect. The moral of this story appears to be that if there had been union barbers in Ithaca, the cost of the haircut would have been twice as much— implying a conspicuously different attitude toward unions than the mature Vonnegut would show. The next, "Ramblings of One Who Is Weak in the Exchequer, and in the Mind" (October 8, 1941), contains more fraternity-man chat about being broke and about rushing. Its only interest comes in its final paragraph: "We wrote a letter to Jane, too. You haven't met Jane yet, but she'll be up here for Fall House Party. We're getting married in '45, you know." This refers to Jane Marie Cox, to whom he did indeed become engaged in July 1945 and was married on September 1 of that year. But that was after she had graduated from Swarthmore and he had been repatriated from a prisoner of war camp in Germany.

In contrast to the careless spirit of these first three columns of his sophomore year, the fourth, "We Chase a Lone Eagle and End Up on the Wrong Side of the Fence" (October 13, 1941) holds considerable interest. Vonnegut launches into a staunch defense of Charles Lindbergh, defending him against those who had questioned his patriotism for opposing America's entry into the war. Vonnegut himself presumably held similar views to Lindbergh's; his earlier columns suggest that, and his German ancestry, the influence of his family's part in a rich German-American culture in Indianapolis, and his general distaste for war and patriotic jingoism, all suggest that. The column is often sarcastic and consistently angry.

The great work is spreading. Give the stout, red-blooded American—the average mental age is fourteen, we're told—a person to hate, tell him to do so often, and he and his cousin Moe will do a damned fine job of it, providing there are plenty of others doing the same.

Sarcasm and disgust at the misuse of patriotism seethe through this piece:

The mud slingers are good. They'd have to be good to get people hating a loyal and sincere patriot. On second thought, Lindbergh is no patriot—to hell with the word, it lost it's [sic] meaning after the Revolutionary War.

His politics at this point appear a little different from what they would be later in life:

Why . . . would anyone lay himself open for such defamation if he wasn't entirely convinced that he must give the message to his country at any cost? To offer an obstacle to the premeditated Roosevelt foreign policy is certainly to ask for a kick in the face.

Having compared Lindbergh's stand to that of Chief Justice Charles Evans Hughes in 1917, he goes on to assert the cost of war and the lack of an economic justification for America's entry:

Crusades . . . cost about five million men these days. It's America's purpose to defend it's [sic] way of life, to bankrupt itself rather than let Hitler take our South American trade—a farce which ends in red ink every time—and to send the best crop of young technicians the country has known, who could make this fabulously wealthy nation self-sufficient within itself, into battle.

There is irony, of course, in his use of the "young technicians" argument, because by the time Vonnegut had been through war and the General Electric Company, and came to writing short stories like "Deer In the Works" (1955) and a novel like *Player Piano* (1952), he took a very different view of the self-sufficiency they would bring. His conclusion to the column exudes sarcasm and defiance:

Lindy, you're a rat. We read that somewhere, so it must be so. They say you should be deported. In that event, leave room in the boat for us, our room-mate, Jane, mother, that barber with the moustache in Willard Straight, and those two guys down the hall—you make sense to us.

While this column may be a little peevish at times, it sounds more like the mature Vonnegut, especially when venting anger verbally from the stage, than most of the college writing. The willingness to take a public stand, particularly against anything militaristic, and the seeming relish in defending the underdog, are characteristic, too. The editor, it should be noted, saw fit to add that the opinions in the column were the author's and did not necessarily reflect those of the *Sun.*

That the stout defense of Lindbergh is the work of a young man is underlined by the fact that the next column, "A Challenge to Superman," appeared on the writer's nineteenth birthday, November 11, 1941. Vonnegut has again shifted to a light, spoofing tone, to create a parody of the comic strip Superman. "PEACHY-FELLOW" (using that word of which he was so fond) is the hero inverted—narrow shouldered, smoking, drinking, burping, and bludgeoning cops. His story ends thus:

The next step was simple. He took the keys from the bleeding corpse and opened the jail doors. Happy as little children, murderers, swindlers, burglars and other nifty people poured into the streets, no longer to be cruelly cooped up and treated like animals.

PEACHY-FELLOW would have none of their thanks; rather, he modestly passed out in an unobtrusive opium den, once more simply Kent Trent.

While "Kent Trent" is obviously a play on Superman's Clark Kent, it also suggests (at least in initials) the name of the anti-heroic short story writer of Vonnegut's later fiction, Kilgore Trout. This column points toward the very kind of short and often satirical stories Trout tells, and to the playfulness and hyperbole characteristic of much of Vonnegut's later writing. The Lindbergh and PEACHY-FELLOW columns, so different in tone and content, seem more accomplished and confident than those that have preceded them. It may be important that in each Vonnegut has hit upon a subject that he can invest himself in, that offers a generic form that he can work in, rather than seeming to try to make something of campus society topics.

In the first of the "Well All Right" columns of his final semester, Vonnegut reverts to rather insubstantial pieces with a personal focus. "A Worrysome Thing to Leave You to Sing the Blues—in the Night" (February 11, 1942) recounts a morning after; "All This and English 2" (February 19, 1942) has some suggestions for Cornell's freshman English course; and "Unaccustomed As We Are to Public Speaking . . ." (February 25, 1942) endorses a suggestion for cooperative dorms and laments the rationing of Coca-Cola. "In Defense of the Golden West" (March 4, 1942) answers the previous day's column by defending "the far West; Indiana, Illinois, and Ohio."   That line signals the comic intent behind his hyperbole, but Midwestern perceptions of Eastern xenophobia are implicit in this column, and sometimes reveal themselves much later in Vonnegut's writing. "Albino for a Day, or in the Pink" (March 24, 1942) recounts a visit to the dreaded infirmary to be diagnosed with pink eye. Again there is narrative form, and again "we" is used doggedly despite its being clear that only "I" is involved. Another characteristic feature is that the tale involves reversal—the "little Bastille" turns out to be hospitable, the staff pleasant, and the food good. Other than that, the humor depends on hyperbole and youthful rebelliousness, and there is little that points toward what was to come.

As in the previous semester, the last two columns prove the most significant. "The Drunken Mr.'s Pro and Con" (April 24, 1942) is another narrative built around a dramatic situation, and it also involves a reversal of a taken position. Vonnegut describes sitting in a Boston bar and meeting a seaman who, recognizing him as a college student, rails at him about the unfairness of reserve officer commissions that put immature young men in command positions while experienced enlisted men are overlooked for promotions. His seaman friend, he says, has been in the Navy eight years, while some " 'young jerk from Left Armpit, Ohio, who's never seen salt water, steps in for an ensignship. Does that make sense to you?' It didn't." Two other enlisted men in the bar tell the student the same thing. Then an older serviceman approaches Vonnegut saying, " 'Don't let 'em kid you, sonny. If you've got the chance, get a commission in the reserves.' "   He says he heard the same complaint from enlisted men in the First World War, and he concludes, " 'the reserves are a plenty good bunch of officers. It's a swell thing that they're taking their officers from colleges. What the hell, it makes sense, and what's more, it works.' " After that Vonnegut can only say, "We feel like apologizing to captain Schaefer and trying to get into advanced drill." The defense of the reserve commission sounds as if it came straight off of a recruitment poster, and Vonnegut here sounds more like the embryo public relations man than the short story writer. There were good reasons for that, as became apparent in the next column, but the argument in this one still leaves an impression because it contrasts so starkly with the views of the veteran Vonnegut who in later years would say, "All officers are shits."[9]

In the last "Well All Right," nothing at all in Vonnegut's life seems right. "The Lost Battalion Undergoes a Severe Shelling" (May 4, 1942) recounts his interview with the dean where it becomes apparent that because of his grades he won't be continuing at Cornell. That means "the Army of the United States." Because of his past performance and expressed attitudes toward the corps, he has been refused entry into advanced drill. He has no specialized training.

He [the dean] reached a grim conclusion—we knew it was coming—that we would soon be a private in the Army of the United States. It was like stepping into a cold shower: we couldn't conceive of good old us being nothing but a private. "Why not be a private?" our counsellor asked. We didn't have an answer, and still don't. "As Professor Marcham says," he went on, "there is a whole lost battalion in Cornell, composed of worried young men like yourself."

Vainly the student urges that he get credit for his extracurricular activities but is told, "Why not get a job and forget college entirely?" And so the end of Cornell:

Our little dream world had tumbled about our ears. Highly intelligent us was slated for two pretty bourgeoisie [sic] things: being a private in the army or working for a living. A sheepskin is not for us—we are a member of Professor Marcham's "lost battalion."[10]

Despite his academic problems, Vonnegut lingered on at Cornell into the autumn term of 1942. He continued as Assistant Managing Editor of the *Sun* and wrote two signed "Berry Patch" columns. The first, "Mr. Anthony, What I Want to Know," poses as an "advice-to-the-lovelorn" type of column, presenting the disappointments in love of one "Stinky" and inviting readers' advice (October 24, 1942), while the other, "Adventures with Dynamite in the Land of the 20-20 Duck," recounts Buster Keatonesque slapstick with dynamite (November 2, 1942). The humor and substance of both columns seems thin, and they are scarcely up to the standard of his better earlier efforts.

As in high school, Vonnegut did some sports writing while at Cornell. It had little direct bearing upon his later writing of short fiction, except that it again demonstrated his working journalism and it doubtless contributed to his education as a writer. There are nine signed sports reports in all. The first two, "Cornell's Rugby Club Tries to Forget Harvard and 38–0" (April 16, 1941), and "Mood Indigo on Upper Alumni, or, It Ain't Cricket" (May 1, 1941), are rather boosterish pieces about rugby, urging more students to turn out for this sport. The other seven all concern the Cornell track team. "Everything's Okely Dokely with Moakly" (December 4, 1941) talks about Coach Moakly's track team and urges more recruits to join it. "16 Thousand Witnesses—The Milrose Story" (February 13, 1942) recounts the performance of Cornell's two-mile relay team in the Ivy League contest of the Melrose Games. The next four columns, written March 2, 5, 6, and 7, all talk about the forthcoming IC4A Championships at Madison Square Garden. While supportive of Cornell's athletes, these three are less boosterish, and are generally well-written and informative previews of the event. The final sports column, dated March 11, 1942, reports on the IC4A meet, focusing on the issue of a disqualification that could jeopardize Penn State's winning of the championship.

It should be noted while on the subject of Vonnegut's journalistic writing, that after the war while he was a graduate student in anthropology at the University of Chicago, he worked "as a police reporter for the famous Chicago City News Bureau for twenty-eight dollars a week."[11] His experience on the *Echo* and the *Sun* obviously helped him to secure this employment and his subsequent position with General Electric.

This varied writing for student newspapers, then, was Vonnegut's apprenticeship. Its quality seems uneven, though perhaps it proves too tempting to review it with the later novelist in mind rather than the teenager who wrote it. In the range of subjects he can approach, the confidence evident in the writing, and particularly in the ability to use dialogue, he exhibits growth. He writes at his best when a topic presents itself for lampooning, satirizing, or even blistering, rather than when he evidently scratches for something to meet a deadline.[12] That would remain true. In later years he would justify his move from Cape Cod to New York by saying that his long seashore walks would leave him tranquil but uninspired, whereas a walk in the city usually left him with something to be mad about (*Self-Portrait*). In the short stories there is little anger—he wrote Stanley Schatt that editors wanted happy stories—but in other work indignation has inspired some of his strongest prose, just as it does in the Lindbergh piece. [13] Social issues, particularly to do with war and the military, prompted a number of these columns just as they would later fiction, and it was to be with the anti-war novel *Slaughterhouse-Five* that he achieved the peak of his fame. Interestingly, the distrust of scientists and technology, evident in the short stories and novels, did not emerge in this youthful writing, where on the contrary there are signs of optimism for what they could achieve.

What does carry over from this early writing into the short stories? Most obvious is the humor. "Innocents Abroad" was assembled from clipped jokes, and a format similar to that was built into some of the other humor columns. Years later, in his *Playboy* interview, Vonnegut was to speak of his novels as being like mosaics where each tile was a joke (*Conversations,* 91). The humor often depends upon exaggerated situations rendered in hyperbolic terms; in the short stories the situations are often heightened for effect but without the "whizz-bang" language. Vonnegut's love of slapstick films shows in the emphasis on the visual in some comic settings, and that becomes more pronounced in the short stories. Comic uses of dialect or fancifully distorted diction are occasionally evident in both high school and college columns. That device appears less evident in the short stories than it becomes in the novels, most conspicuously in *Cat's Cradle.* Pace is naturally important to comedy, and Vonnegut's general use of brisk, short sentences, or of a somewhat longer, slower preamble to a short, sharp clincher, becomes even more pronounced in the mature work. Finally, his ability to see two sides of an issue often allows him to see both funny sides, as it were. In more serious work, as in discussing reserve commissions to college students, he can lead from one point of view then switch to a conclusion based on the opposite stance. That serves him well in a satirical story like "Harrison Bergeron" (1961), where he can target both social inequality and the consequences of trying to eliminate it. It also forms the basis of comedy derived from a character's having perceptions of life utterly at odds with reality. Sometimes, too, it serves as the vehicle for the kind of "shaggy dog story" ending that characterizes a number of stories.

The search for a comfortable narrative voice also begins to emerge in these columns. For the most part Vonnegut appears to resolve this by adopting a first person plural "we" form of address. There are times, particularly when he creates a dramatic situation in which he becomes a participant, where "we" proves clumsy and awkward, and even, as we have seen, ambiguous. Sometimes, in these narrative episodes, the "we" participant appears at least as much fictionalized as autobiographical, and hence a kind of persona. Vonnegut would find this device increasingly useful, especially once he could bring himself to use the first person singular. In the short stories there are repeated personae—some sort of salesman or representative as story teller becomes a frequently used formula. He reveals an impulse to involve himself, to be not just a narrative voice, like James Joyce's godlike artist, "invisible, refined out of existence, indifferent, paring his fingernails," [14] but a presence in the writing.

That impulse continues—and continues to present difficulties in arriving at the most appropriate narrative stance or voice. It reveals itself in the number of columns where he makes himself the subject. In the short stories it appears mostly in some of the settings (Cape Cod, plants like G.E.) and characters (returned vets, writers, salespeople) that have biographical associations. Those trends continue in the novels and become complex where Vonnegut wishes to retain the personal immediacy of the situation while also addressing a broader social relevance. That dual purpose explains his 1966 addition of a highly personal Introduction to the original 1961 edition of *Mother Night*. It also emerges when the story of Dresden in *Slaughterhouse-Five* is punctuated by his intrusion, saying, "That was me. I was there."

NOTES

1. On his writing for the *Shortridge Daily Echo*, Vonnegut had this to say in an interview: "The high school I went to had a daily paper, and has since about 1900. They had a printing course for people who weren't going on to college, and they realized, 'My goodness, we've got the linotypes—we could easily get out a paper.' So they started getting out a paper every day, called the *Shortridge Daily Echo*. It was so old my parents had worked on it. And so, rather than writing for a teacher, writing for an audience of one—for Miss Green or Mr. Watson—I started out writing for a large audience. And if I did a lousy job, I caught a lot of shit in twenty-four hours. It just turned out I could write better than a lot of other people." William Rodney Allen, ed., *Conversations with Kurt Vonnegut* (Jackson: University Press of Mississippi, 1988), 92. (Hereafter cited as *Conversations*.)

Another revelation about Vonnegut's early interest in journalism comes in a 1973 interview with Frank McLaughlin: "One writer I admired a lot was H. L. Mencken. When I was young I knew something about his life—that he had had a very exciting time as a newspaper reporter—and I guess later as a city editor. I read a couple of his autobiographical works, and as a result of this I wanted to be a newspaper man and did a certain amount of newspapering" (*Conversations*, 67).

Dan Wakefield, who worked on the *Echo* some ten years after Vonnegut, records how Vonnegut was known to the aspiring high school writers of his generation as someone who had gone on to achieve success, as did a number of other writers in various fields. See Jerome Klinkowitz and John Somer, eds., *The Vonnegut Statement* (New York: Delacorte Press/Seymour Lawrence, 1973), 56.

2. *Kurt Vonnegut: A Self-Portrait*, filmed interview produced and directed by Harold Mantell (Princeton, N.J.: Films for the Humanities, 1976). (Hereafter cited as *Self-Portrait*.)

3. I am grateful to M. Andre Eckenrode for his assistance with Vonnegut's high school and college writing. His painstaking research enabled him to add significantly to the number and accuracy of my own discoveries. His index of this early writing is the most complete I have seen.

4. In the summer of 1937, Vonnegut was one of fifteen boys and five staff who went on the annual "Prairie Trek Expedition for Boys" to Base Camp Cotton-Wood Gulch, Thoreau, New Mexico. The trip went through dust bowl areas and destroyed farms in Colorado and included the Grand Canyon. There is

one photograph (by "Howie") of Vonnegut with the whole group, kneeling in the front row, and another of him, head down, with a row of dead rodents. He is listed under "Staff" as "Archaeologist-Mammalogist. Indianapolis, Indiana. First Year Man. Famous clarinet player. Stock company comedian. Tarzan yell man," in the *Twelfth Annual Report of the Prairie Trek Expedition for Boys*, Summer 1937. This document is typed, with no printer or publisher credited, but possibly produced by the participants themselves at Shortridge, and now in the care of the Indiana Historical Society. It shows Vonnegut's early interest in biology and anthropology—as well as comedy and the clarinet!

5. John Gardner, *On Moral Fiction* (New York: Basic Books, 1978), 87; Roger Sale, Review of *Slapstick, New York Times Book Review* (October 3, 1976), 3, 20–21.

6. Andre Eckenrode points out that in Vonnegut's dedication of his 1973 novel *Breakfast of Champions* to Phoebe Hurty, and in its preface, Vonnegut says that it was Hurty who hired him to write Block's advertisements for the *Echo*. She was then working for the Indianapolis *Times* and writing Block's department store advertisements for that paper. Vonnegut describes Hurty as a "liberating" influence on his life and writing. "She taught us to be impolite in conversation not only about sexual matters, but about American history and famous heroes, about the distribution of wealth, about school, about everything" (*Breakfast of Champions* [New York: Delacorte Press/Seymour Lawrence, 1973], 2).

7. As late as 1977, Vonnegut would own that this was one of the two that he and his sister agreed were "world champion" jokes (*Paris Review* Interview, *Conversations,* 192).

8. Robert Scholes, in "Chasing the Lone Eagle: Vonnegut's College Writing," in Klinkowitz and Somer, (*The Vonnegut Statement*, 49), observes: "At this time, of course, Vonnegut was having an experience rare for white Protestant Americans. He was a member of a minority group which was feeling the active antagonism of others. Before and during World War II anti-German feeling in the United States was not as virulent as it had been at the time of World War I, but it was there, and the German-American Vonnegut was very sensitive to it."

9. *Playboy* interview, *Conversations,* 96.

10. In a 1987 interview, Hank Nuwer asked Vonnegut about his parents' reaction to his "flunking out" of Cornell. Vonnegut said: "I think their feeling about it—as I was very close to being thrown out and would have been thrown out for academic reasons because I had no gift for science really, and that's what I was in—was they would have said, 'That's it.' But I myself wanted to be a journalist and wondered if I wanted to go to college at all. I thought maybe I'd go to work for the *Indianapolis News* or the *Star* or *Times*" (Hank Nuwer Interview, *Conversations,* 246).

11. Kurt Vonnegut, *Slaughterhouse-Five* (New York: Delacorte Press/Seymour Lawrence), 7–8. There is a brief account of these activities, including the first story he was assigned to cover.

12. Vonnegut recounted to Robert Scholes in 1973: "And I became managing editor of the *Sun* and I wrote about, oh, three columns a week, and they were impudent editorializing, as college-humor sort of stuff. . . . And I

continued to editorialize. That was congenial, and so I've always had to have an ax to grind in order to write" (Robert Scholes Interview, *Conversations*, 114).

13. Stanley Schatt, *Kurt Vonnegut, Jr.* (Boston: Twayne Publishers, 1976), 119.

14. James Joyce, *A Portrait of the Artist as a Young Man* (New York: Viking Press, 1965), 215.

3

The Early Stories: *Collier's*, 1950–1953

In 1947, Kurt Vonnegut left Chicago after the Department of Anthropology at the University of Chicago failed to accept his Master of Arts thesis, which was titled "Fluctuations between Good and Evil in Simple Tales." (In 1971, a different departmental administration recognized the merits of his novel *Cat's Cradle* [1963] as a contribution to the field of anthropology and he was awarded the M.A. degree.)[1]   He and Jane moved to Schenectady, New York, where he joined the General Electric Company for whom his brother Bernard was already employed as a scientist.   Vonnegut was hired as a public relations writer and notes that "because of all this background in science that I had had, they made me a flak, a publicity man for the research laboratory there, which is an excellent industrial research laboratory."[2]   He did not like the work, in part because it sometimes involved evading the whole truth—in later fiction the dilemma of writers faced with compromising their ethics for survival or success becomes a repeated theme.   Ollie Lyon, with whom Vonnegut formed an enduring friendship, was a colleague in this work.   The two of them recount how in those days when one landed a job there would be a celebratory party, and about three hours into it someone might ask, "By the way, what's the job?"[3]   Despite gratitude for secure employment, Vonnegut's heart was not in the job, and he sought escape in other writing.   Ollie Lyon recounts that while a number of their colleagues were aspiring writers, it was Vonnegut who dedicated hours at night and on weekends to writing, and they were glad to celebrate with him when Kurt's first story was accepted.

Vonnegut has accounted for his turning to writing short fiction in a number of ways.   He has alluded a number of times to having come back from the war feeling that he must have witnessed a major event in Dresden, only to find that few people knew about it, and to therefore having the urge to write about it.   By the time his Dresden novel (*Slaughterhouse-Five*) appeared in 1969, he spoke to interviewer Richard Todd of having been trying to write it for twenty years, which would put its origins back in his G.E. era (*Conversations,* 34).   He also makes mention of the fact that in the 1930s, when the Great Depression caused his architect father's fortunes to dwindle, his mother aspired to writing short stories to supplement their income. "She was a good writer," he says, "but she had no talent for the vulgarity the slick magazines required." With characteristic self-deprecating humor he adds:

Fortunately I was loaded with vulgarity, so, when I grew up, I was able to make her dream come true. Writing for *Collier's* and *The Saturday Evening Post* and *Cosmopolitan* and *Ladies' Home Journal* and so on was as easy as falling off a log for me. I only wish she'd lived to see it. (*Paris Review, Conversations,* 178)

Vonnegut sums it up breezily by telling Laurie Clancy in an interview, "I disliked my job at General Electric so much and in order to quit and hang on to my family I wrote short stories on weekends and at nights" (*Conversations,* 51). He goes on to explain that in those days there were a number of magazines publishing five or more stories a week, so there was great demand, and money came easily.

While Vonnegut obviously achieved considerable success in the short story market quickly, it was not quite instantaneous, and it was achieved with some important help, as he recounts:

When I was working for General Electric, I wrote a story, "Report on the Barnhouse Effect," the first story I ever wrote. I mailed it off to *Collier's*. Knox Burger was fiction editor there. Knox told me what was wrong and how to fix it. . . . And Knox got me a couple of agents who were as shrewd about story telling as he was—Kenneth Littauer, who had been his predecessor at *Collier's*, and Max Wilkinson, who had been a story editor at MGM. (*Paris Review, Conversations,* 190–191)

Burger remained a friend, later becoming son Mark Vonnegut's literary agent. Littauer, to whom Vonnegut would later dedicate *Cat's Cradle*, he was to acknowledge as "my mentor."

There was a time when I was a very earnest student writer and had a teacher, Kenneth Littauer, an old-time magazine editor, agent, and splendid old gentleman. And we would talk about things like that, that is, after dark passages you have a light one . . . and use short sentences when people are running, and long sentences and long words when people are sleeping. (Bellamy & Casey, *Conversations,* 158)

Much of Littauer's advice, with its emphasis on short sentences and paragraphs and a light hand with adjectives and adverbs would have accorded with Vonnegut's own journalistic experience.

"Report on the Barnhouse Effect" earned Vonnegut seven hundred and fifty dollars when it appeared in the February 11, 1950, edition of *Collier's*. His second and third stories ("Thanasphere" and "Epicac," both also in *Collier's*) earned seven hundred and fifty and nine hundred dollars, respectively. At the time, Vonnegut was earning ninety-two dollars a week at General Electric, which he points out was a respectable wage at the time, but prospective advancement in the company was slow. Since he now found he could earn more than six weeks' salary for one story, he resigned from the company and moved to Provincetown to devote himself to a career as a writer (Charles Reilly,

Conversations, 197–198). Later the family would move to West Barnstable, a location used in several of his stories.

The relationship with *Collier's* was to be a fruitful one, in that all of the first ten short stories Vonnegut published appeared in that magazine, and within the space of two years. They were illustrated by some of the preeminent glossy-magazine illustrators of the time, typically with one large representation of a scene from the story across the opening two pages, above or below the title, with a short teaser to elicit interest in the story. For "Report on the Barnhouse Effect," for example, the illustration by Glen Fleischmann fills the entire page facing the title page of the story. It depicts a man with his hand raised thoughtfully to his mouth and a frown of concentration, surrounded in both the foreground and the background by images of aircraft plunging in flames and blazing warships. Beneath the title and author's name is the teaser: "Nobody knows where he is. But he controls the destiny of the world. . . . And I know his secret."[4]

"Report on the Barnhouse Effect" is in the form of a report on the experiments of Professor Arthur Barnhouse written in the first-person by his assistant. In summary, Barnhouse has discovered what he calls "'*dynamopsychism,*' or *force of the mind.*" He has found that by following a "thought train that aligned the professor's brain cells," Barnhouse has the power to move physical objects. At first he learned to roll dice to whatever numbers he wanted; eventually he becomes "about fifty-five times more powerful that a Nagasaki-type atomic bomb" and can destroy objects thousands of miles away. Naturally, the armed services become interested in this potential weapon. The professor, who has wanted to use this power for peaceful purposes such as "moving cloud masses into drought areas," becomes increasingly recalcitrant about sharing the secret of his powers, but does agree to a demonstration. Before service chiefs he destroys squadrons of decoy aircraft and flotillas of warships, but in the midst of their celebrating his awesome power he slips away into hiding. Thereafter he sets about destroying weapons in all nations in an effort to bring about world peace. The professor is "of short-lived stock," and his death would mean the end of his singlehanded imposition of peace, but at the close of the report the writer reveals that he has decoded the last message Barnhouse left him and is now increasingly able to exercise "dynamopsychism" himself. With the clear implication he will take up Barnhouse's role, he ends the report with a simple "Good-by."

This first story remains one of Vonnegut's best. It was collected in *Canary in a Cat House* and *Welcome to the Monkey House* without changes. The central premise may seem farfetched, especially when taken to such extremes, but it retains just enough plausibility to sustain the plot. After all, the notion of persons' having some degree of psychokinetic power is a persistent one, occurs in other story and film plots, and has even fueled rumors of the Russians experimenting with it for military purposes. That it imparts an element of the "tall tale" puts this story squarely in an American tradition with works such as Thorpe's "The Big Bear of Arkansas" or Twain's "The Celebrated Jumping Frog of Calaveras County." Vonnegut continues to use exaggeration for humorous or dramatic effects, just as he did in his student writing. The first person narration in the form of a report works comfortably for him, though characteristically the reporter slips into the role of agent at the end. There is an element of suspense that engages the reader, heightened by the revelation of Barnhouse's coming from "short-lived stock." The solution—the younger narrator's carrying on the professor's work—is a surprise turn in the plot at the end that is not really a surprise. There have been clues, like the professor's puzzling last message and the assistant's being a disillusioned war veteran, and it is not an outcome that was difficult to predict. Such an ending becomes a characteristic trick in Vonnegut's short stories: there is often a sudden turn in events at the end, what has the appearance of a surprise ending, but the reader will in effect have been let in on it before it happens. The effect is for the reader to have the double satisfaction of the relief that the last-minute reversal typically gives, plus the somewhat smug pleasure of having suspected what was to come.

Several topics touched on in "Report of the Barnhouse Effect" become thematic in Vonnegut's fiction. Two of the most obvious (and persistent) ones express his anti-war sentiments and raise questions about the ethical responsibility of scientists for the uses of their discoveries. The narrator's futile sympathy with the laboratory rats—doing "an experiment that had been done to everyone's satisfaction in the nineteen thirties"—hints again at his feelings for animals. There are some details of this story that have personal, biographical associations to them. Barnhouse's suggestion for moving clouds to drought-stricken areas echoes Vonnegut's brother Bernard's pioneer work in cloud seeding.[5] The narrator is a veteran of overseas service and works in a laboratory. And the prediction of Barnhouse's mortality because he comes of short-lived stock sounds reminiscent of Vonnegut's own tendency to make life predictions for himself and others based on parental lifespans.

While the imaginative plot and relevance of theme make this story worthwhile, the narrative richness determines its quality. The narrative voice remains consistent, with a personal perspective that makes possible hyperbole and colorful vernacular that would not be available to an omniscient third person narration. An economy of syntax moves the plot purposefully, but there are also some lively images. An effective pausing for details that contributes a touch of familiar realism to the sci-fi plot can also add suspense on the brink of dramatic action. For example, right before the great military test of Barnhouse's powers, action stops for this description: "Inside, a log fire crackled in the fireplace, and the flames were reflected in the polished metal cabinets that lined the living room. All that remained of the room's lovely old furniture was a Victorian love seat, set squarely in the center of the floor" (64). Vonnegut continues to use this device for varying the pace and throwing the futuristic into relief against objects from the past, perhaps most conspicuously in *Player Piano* (1952).

If "Report on the Barnhouse Effect" borders on science fiction, or science fiction with parapsychological overtones, the next story, "Thanasphere," goes further. It appeared in *Collier's* for September 2, 1950, illustrated by Tran Mawicke. The plot relates the secret launching of Major Allen Rice into orbit 2,000 miles above the earth. Soon the Major's transmissions to the team below become distracted, and he complains of hearing voices, often more clearly than those from earth. He provides identities to some of the voices, which the ground personnel check out and find to be those of people who are deceased. The team on earth goes through much anguish, fearing that Rice may be having a breakdown or that security of communications has been breached. It emerges that Rice has entered a sphere populated by the spirits of the dead who then bombard him with requests to be communicated to the living on earth. Finally he can see beautiful shimmering phantoms, among them his dead wife Margaret. Seeking to keep the mission secret, the earth team can do nothing but jam the transmissions and bring Rice down. But they recognize that the orbiting Rice may now not wish to return safely but prefer to join his wife, and indeed he does crash the satellite, assuring the continued secrecy of the mission and of the existence of this "dead space," the "Thanasphere."

Having been written more than a decade before the first manned space flight, "Thanasphere" contains some details that later readers might find rather quaint. An audience that has viewed mission control at Houston, for instance, will find it odd that communications from earth are handled by three people in a small laboratory on a university campus. The rather basic nuts and bolts of the operation, however, help to preserve a measure of plausibility in a story with such an imaginative premise—just like those household furnishings in "Barnhouse." The story fits into a genre popular in a time when supersonic flight was new and rocketry was still in its infancy, tales that told of certain speeds and directions and altitudes leading to regressions in age or entry into other dimensions, and so forth. One feature that is distinctive with Vonnegut, and continues to be, is his introduction of humor into the science fiction elements. The whole concept of a "dead zone" where spirits compete to be heard by an astronaut is comic in itself. The particulars, like the late Hollywood actor's trying to rectify his nephew's tampering with his will, and the amateur radio operators' trying to make sense of this when they intercept a transmission, add delightful touches of the absurd. This would not be the last time Vonnegut would entertain with comic visions of an afterworld or of communications with it. There are sustained renditions in the play *Happy Birthday, Wanda June* (1971) and in the novel *Slapstick* (1976).

Like a number of the other stories of this era, "Thanasphere" is an artifact of the cold war. In fact, at one point General Dane says that if it is discovered that America has an observer in space "that's the start of World War III. . . . That's when the cold war gets hot, my boy" (60). Once again the scientist responsible for the space flight is negligent of moral responsibility; the threat of war has made possible the funding of what remains for him "*the experiment*," regardless of its application. A conspiratorial atmosphere pervades the world of this story, as scientists, military men and politicians collude in secret. It is a jaded world, dispossessed of its sense of wonder: "Science had given humanity forces enough to destroy the earth; and politics had given humanity a fair assurance that the forces would be used. There could be no cause for awe to top *that* one" (62). Variants of that statement continue like a refrain in Vonnegut's writing.

"Thanasphere," then, combines suspense (will the secret launch be discovered, what will be the outcome of hearing the spirits, will Rice survive?), humor, meaningful reference to the cold war world of its audience, and ethical reflection. Its premise, like those of so many of Vonnegut's fictions, involves a "What if?" This imaginative capacity to envision the unpredictable or to question the generally assumed, to stimulate the sense of wonder or, to use his word here, "awe," remain characteristic of Vonnegut's work and of its appeal. "Thanasphere" is a well made story, and its failure to be included in the later collections is no doubt due mainly to the fact that actual space flight overtook it.

The third story to appear in 1950 (in the November 25 *Collier's*) was the frequently anthologized "EPICAC."[6] This story also deals with technology and might be called borderline science fiction. As Vonnegut said to the *Playboy* interviewer about this, "There was no avoiding it, since the General Electric Company *was* science fiction" (*Conversations,* 93). EPICAC, the subject of the story, is a vast computer that cost $776,434,927.54 and occupies "about an acre" of the fourth floor of the physics building at (as in "Thanasphere") Wyandotte College. Once again a scientist has financed the implementation of his genius through the military, and EPICAC is designed to "plot the course of a rocket from anywhere on earth to the second button from the bottom of Joe Stalin's overcoat, if necessary" (36). For all its great (and dated!) size, EPICAC does not fulfill its promise, faltering and seeming unhappy in its work. Until, that is, its operator tells it of his love for Pat Callaghan, a woman colleague. The machine then pours forth romantic poetry that the narrator signs off on and uses to woo Pat. But EPICAC is in love, and realizing that it/he cannot win Pat, commits suicide.

One might argue that Vonnegut again shows technological foresight, and that a situation like this might yet arise in the interaction between humans and artificial intelligence, but obviously the plot is again farfetched. Yet once more it is an intriguing "what if" that invites suspension of disbelief, again given a touch of brass-tacks plausibility in that the mathematically-accomplished operator and the supercomputer can come up with no more sophisticated means of communication than "a childish numbers-for-letters code: 1 for A . . ." and so forth.

The story is wholly dependent on the effectiveness of its narrative persona. A factual, third-person omniscient reportage of the events would fall flat. So Vonnegut acts boldly to establish a characterization behind the narrative voice from the first sentence: "Hell, it's about time somebody told about my friend EPICAC." The careless informality of a young man's telling a tale establishes a different level of acceptance from the measure of veracity that might be applied to an objectively stated story. It also sets the giving of EPICAC gender, personality and relationship in place from the outset. Above all, the narrator is what saves the story from succumbing to its sentimentality. The emotions are *his*: the reader may share in them but is not asked to be the primary receptor of them, as would be the case without his presence. Vonnegut's stories quite often show a level of sentimentality that must make some readers hesitate. Frequently, though, the sentiment is undercut by the humor and something rather offhand or rough-hewn in the narration, and that is true here. EPICAC's falling in love, its being told it cannot be loved because it is a machine and that it is inferior because it isn't protoplasm is poignant—but also absurd.

Computers named EPICAC reappear in the novel *Player Piano*. More importantly, computers (or robots) who are more "human" than humans—or humans who are machine-like and chemically controlled—become themes throughout Vonnegut's writing. The robot Salo in *The Sirens of Titan* (1959) is another machine with "human" feelings that attempts suicide. These machines become a useful means of highlighting aspects of human behavior—the programmed steadfastness of the machine contrasting with human inconstancy, for example.

The anti-war note evident in "EPICAC" owes less to Vonnegut's wartime experience than to the cold war environment in which it existed, and the same is true for the next story, "All the King's Horse's" (*Collier's*, February 10, 1961, and included in *Canary in a Cat House* and *Welcome to the Monkey House* unaltered). This is the story of the survivors of the crash of an American military transport in a communist Asian country. Their leader, Colonel Bryan Kelly, has his wife and two sons with him, so when his captor, Pi Ying, suggests a game of chess for their lives the stakes are high. They stand on a floor marked out as a huge chess board, and while Pi Ying controls human-sized chessmen from his seat in the balcony, Kelly must use his survivors as live pieces. Those who are taken by Pi Ying's pieces are led out to be shot.

Naturally this story generates a good deal of suspense. Beside Pi Ying there are a Russian advisor and a young courtesan. Will one or the other intervene? Will one of the crewmen who are given personalities, like the brave, loyal sergeant, be taken? Will Kelly be able to save at least his wife and sons? Will open-faced American bravery and Yankee resourcefulness triumph against the insidious evil of the inscrutable East? And so on. The story ends with the seeming promise that the Russian and the American, worthy antagonists, may square off again in some future contest, larger and far more deadly than this has been.

"All the King's Horses" is an omniscient third-person narration, though its chief focus is on Kelly. The narration is as if over Kelly's shoulder, and the voice reflects his tense, tight-lipped control. The characterizations are swift and somewhat stereotypical, as they must be in a story of four magazine pages, but effectively vivid. The story grips; one expects an American victory, but at what cost? Chess players (like Vonnegut himself) must weigh the moves: *Collier's* illustrations include a chessboard with the numbered moves. At a time when the two superpowers made matching moves of global strategy, with communist subversions at the borders of the Soviet Union being countered by the airbases and missile sites of American "containment," the intimate scale of this story serves as a reminder of the personal, human consequences of this game that was not a game.

The other four stories published in 1951, all in *Collier's*, and the three *Collier's* stories of 1952, mark a shift in emphasis away from technological and cold war contexts to more domestic settings. They look at social behavior— the things people do to try to make themselves happy, often by finding an identity. Man-woman relationships begin to become more important as Vonnegut dares slightly larger roles for women. The kind of narrative persona that was used in "EPICAC" begins to appear more frequently, and will continue to in subsequent stories. Often this narrator is some kind of salesman or representative, a person who logically has moments of entry into other people's lives. Such narrators can add plausibility and a touch of folksy charm to a tall tale, humor through the observation of *their* reactions within the story, and color through a vernacular language less suitable to an objective narration.

"Mnemonics" (April 28, 1951) is the shortest of the stories. Alfred goes to a memory clinic where he learns to remember items by making mental images of pleasant things that create associations. Most of Alfred's involve screen goddesses, and there is humor in the stretches he makes to include all that must be remembered: "In Alfred's mind, Ava Gardner executed a smart manual of arms with a rifle. Emblazoned on her sweater was a large 16A" (38). The suspense comes when his list of things to be remembered gets so long and his mnemonics so involved that the reader expects complete failure and consequent disaster at work. But he survives and comes out of his fantasies to face his secretary, whom he has admired for two years but has felt afraid to approach. Still in his reverie he clutches her and says, " 'Now, Baby, what's on your mind?' " He catches himself: " 'Oh, gosh! I'm sorry. I forgot myself.' 'Well, praise be, you finally remembered *me*' " (38). So the story achieves a slick ending, with a verbal play on remembering and romantic fulfillment. There is a touch of the shaggy-dog story about "Mnemonics," in that it appears to be building up to a climactic crash of Alfred's seemingly over-imaginative formula for remembering, but that never happens. The closing event is something more mundane, the answering of Alfred's two-year wish to "break the ice" with Ellen.

In being narrated in the form of a report, "The Euphio Question" (May 12, 1951, and included in both collections with some very minor changes) harks back to "Report on the Barnhouse Effect." But this is an oral report, more chatty and informal in style, and the situation itself is lighter and farcical. The story also looks back in being the only one in this group that leans on a comic presentation of technological invention for its plot. Despite that "science" element, however, it has the flavor of the other stories in this group in its context of daily, American middle-class life.

In the story, the narrator, a sociology professor, reports to the Federal Communications Commission about the discovery he and two friends, a radio announcer and a physicist, have made. The physicist has been trying to pick up radio signals from space. When he gives a public radio demonstration the hiss that emanates from his equipment induces a state of supine euphoria in the listening audience. Their heads filled with visions of making themselves fortunes with schemes to market guaranteed happiness, the three friends come up with a "euphoriaphone" and run a home test. The scene that results becomes a mix of Laurel and Hardy and the Three Stooges, as more and more people arrive and in careless abandon trash the house. They would all continue in their hypnotic state indefinitely, it appears, but for a tree's falling on the power lines to cut the machine off. The twist to the end of the story is that the unscrupulous radio announcer plans to push ahead with the euphoriaphone, and mounts a demonstration model in the hearing room, and . . .

"The Euphio Question" touches on a theme soon to become prevalent in some of Vonnegut's work (notably in the soon-to-be-published *Player Piano*) in showing the downside of the pleasure principle, or the Utopian becoming nightmare. While there are serious issues implicit in that theme, Vonnegut clearly enjoys handling it with comic exaggeration in slapstick scenes. The comic ending resolves the moral issues the situation raises, and in that sense this piece also has some of the tone of a shaggy dog story.

The other five *Collier's* stories in this group, "The Foster Portfolio" (September 8, 1951), "More Stately Mansions" (December 22, 1951), "Any Reasonable Offer," (January 19, 1952), "The Package" (July 26, 1952) and "Poor Little Rich Town" (October 25, 1952) have plots relating to middle-class life, with its domestic situations and its concerns with estate and status.[7] In "The Foster Portfolio" a contact man for an investment counseling firm tells of a client, Henry Foster, who leads a frugal existence while secretly possessing a huge portfolio. The narrator puzzles over the secrecy and Foster's persistence in his meager life. Then he discovers that Foster works on a second job on three nights a week playing jazz piano in a bar. By day he lives by the dictates of his puritanical mother and "shrewish" wife; three nights a week he can be free to "play piano in a dive, and breathe smoke and drink gin, to be Firehouse Harris, his father's son" (72). The salesman narrator works well; his puzzlement becomes the reader's, and the story is driven in part by his "want," his irrepressible desire to shape and build the stock portfolio, his frustration that he cannot make Foster take an interest in something for which he has a real enthusiasm. Foster's "want" remains a puzzle and a frustration until the final revelation. A reader may get caught up in the narrator's desire to build that portfolio—Vonnegut's salesmen usually have an enthusiasm for their products—and be drawn into the story by frustration with Foster.

"The Foster Portfolio" introduces a theme that becomes a major one for Vonnegut, namely the question of identity. He explores the need for identity and people's efforts to achieve or retain it in various ways. Frequently identity is tied to purpose, to job. Sometimes it resides in an invented role or persona. Sometimes pretense becomes reality and the mask becomes the soul. As *Mother Night's* 1966 Introduction would warn, "We are what we pretend to be, so we must be careful about what we pretend to be" (v). The relationship between fathers and sons also becomes recurrent, with an autobigraphical basis that Vonnegut, in the dual roles of father and son, has acknowledged in several of his books. His interest in jazz also emerges quite frequently.

"More Stately Mansions," which is collected in both *Canary in a Cat House* and *Welcome to the Monkey House* with only minor stylistic changes, explores identity in a different way. For the male characters, identity frequently seems synonymous with career, but in the era in which Vonnegut was writing, this was far less likely to be true for middle-class American women, especially if they were married. Vonnegut's exploration of this problem is unlikely to earn the approval of feminists of later decades, but it is not unsympathetic. He appears to suggest that, just as the women of the eighteenth century British bourgeoisie found their social models in the novel, so their transatlantic descendants were guided by the numerous women's glossy magazines. Anita Proteus, the main female character in the 1952 novel *Player Piano*, illustrates the pattern. Anita does not come off well in that novel, yet Vonnegut takes pains to make clear that she comes from a background that does not prepare her for the elite managerial society into which she moves, and that she has neither great intellect nor education. In the circumstances, her efforts to glean from magazines the dimensions of her role as "company wife" and how best to fulfill them can hardly be ridiculed. If Vonnegut *does* have subjects for satire here they are some of the contents in the magazines themselves and the society that presses women into such a role. Some of the same observations can be made of "More Stately Mansions."

In this story (which in manuscript was originally called "Build the More Stately Mansions"), the narrator and his wife Anne have moved into a new house and are greeted by neighbors Grace and George McClellan. Grace immediately starts making suggestions for how the house can be redecorated and refurnished. She continues frequent visits to Anne over two years, bringing more and more magazines, clippings and suggestions. The newcomers grow increasingly curious about the McClellans' own house and how much they must spend on it. Then one day Grace asks the narrator, who deals in office furniture, for a derelict filing cabinet. When he delivers it, he and Anne are astonished to find a ramshackle, unkempt house with broken-down furniture. This is explained partly by the fact that for five years George has been making very little money. Then two things happen; Grace is hospitalized, and George comes into an inheritance. While Grace is away, the other three, making use of her files, spend George's inheritance refurbishing and refurnishing the house into her dream home. Perhaps inevitably, in true *Collier's* story fashion, Grace's reaction is a surprise. She reacts as if the house has always looked like that, remarking only that George has kept it dustfree, and she totally dismisses her magazines, saying, "Read one and you've read them all." The McClellans' earlier repetition of "someday" perhaps serves as another reminder that dreams are sometimes more sustaining than their fulfillment.

The comic exaggeration is extreme. While such rapid short stories often depend on farcical eccentricity, Grace's painstakingly walking around imaginary furniture or rocking to nonexistent music is demented. In fact, the serious point one has to overlook in this obviously light comedy—another shaggy dog story even—is Grace's being crazy as a bedbug both before and after hospitalization, and that this does not seem to worry anyone. The description of Grace's house resembles a *New Yorker* cartoon by Booth:

The couch springs had burst through the bottom and were resting nakedly on the floor. The chief illumination came from a single light bulb in a cobwebbed chandelier with sockets for six. An electric extension cord, patched with friction tape, hung from another of the sockets and led to an iron on an ironing board in the middle of the room. (62)

Obviously representationalism is not the goal of such detail. This is an early example of Vonnegut the fabulist at work, creating fables of modern existence out of the cartoons, helpful hints and advice columns of television's predecessor, the glossy magazine. He shows Grace creating an identity out of the printed page, making a fiction of her own life. He will elaborate on this pattern of behavior several times in later novels.

Real estate figures prominently in the plots of the other three stories. In "Any Reasonable Offer," a real estate man recounts having taken a couple to view an extremely expensive property. They quickly take command of the situation, maneuvering themselves into drinks, dinner, and even several days residence as pampered guests all to see if they feel comfortable in the place. Finding the estate unsuitable, they express interest in another even more expensive one, but, at the crucial moment, the "Colonel" announces he has been called as a government consultant to go to Bangkok. Later, on the telephone, what the estate agent overhears confirms that the Colonel has a lowly position in an office and that he and his wife manage an luxurious vacation every year as confidence tricksters. Next year, the Colonel says, he will try Newport, where there are some lovely homes. The narrator declares, understandably, that he needs a vacation, and the light dawns for the reader who remembers that the story opens with the narrator's telling that he is on vacation in Newport. So this story, like its predecessor, comes around to a sly, shaggy-dog style conclusion. The reader has foreseen the Colonel's scam; Vonnegut's real surprise is the second one. Once again the narrator shows a lively interest in his job, enthusing about houses, vintages, commissions and his ability to gauge clients. The dialogue remains lively, the pace brisk, the tall-tale scenes comical. Part of this story's charm resembles that found in Twain and Faulkner when their roguish confidence tricksters pull off their scams with flamboyance.

"The Package" reverts to a third-person narration and a more serious tone. The "package" of the title is a push-button dream home into which Earl and Maude Fenton move, having achieved affluence from modest beginnings. The third major character in the story, an old college friend named Charley, arrives the day they move in. Charley remains an object of resentment to Earl for having been born rich. Earl repeatedly tells Maude how Charley and others in their college fraternity had constantly made him aware of his less favored circumstances. As the story progresses, it appears that more of this denigration was imagined than real, and the initial sympathy a reader might feel for a couple who have struggled to success dissipates as the Fentons emerge as prejudiced and mean spirited, and quite as snobbish in their own way as they describe Charley as being. Eventually they invent a story to get rid of Charley, only to discover afterward that he had sunk all of his own money into a charity hospital in China and been imprisoned for years by the communists. The story ends with Earl turning to the contractor: " 'Maude and I'd like to start today all over again,' said Earl, smiling dryly. 'Show us which button to push' " (53).

Retrospectively it is difficult to read this story without being aware that it foreshadows situations to be developed subsequently in the novels. Much of the reflection on affluence resembles that in *God Bless You, Mr. Rosewater* (1965), with Charley Freeman in some respects prefiguring Eliot Rosewater. On the other hand, Charley's Albert Schweitzer-like running of a charity hospital looks even more like the behavior of Julian Castle of *Cat's Cradle* (1963), and Earl Fenton's racist dismissal of shiftless Asians sounds like the bigotry of Pop Crosby in that novel. Again there are heightened effects throughout; the futuristic house, the excesses of Earl and Maude, Charley's inevitable saintliness, the abrupt reversals, are all larger than life. But they are also recognizable, and they characterize familiar behavior. Once again there comes the surprise that is not a surprise, the reversal that the reader knows will arrive while in suspense waiting to see how. When Charley is revealed as saint, not ex-con, the Fentons are set down but the reader is rewarded.

"Poor Little Rich Town" also has reminders of the novels, in particular the contemporary *Player Piano* (1952). Most obviously, both use the same setting—or setting *name*—Ilium. More generally, "Poor Little Rich Town" has a similar nostalgia for traditional small town ways, contempt for big business impersonality and efficiency, revulsion from the arrogance of wealth and power, and delight in folksy dialogue and humor.

The large Federal Apparatus Corporation decides to move its corporate headquarters to Ilium, New York, which is jubilant, having languished since its textile mills moved to the South. Newell Cady, Federal's brilliant efficiency expert, rents a mansion in the nearby village of Spruce Falls, with option to purchase. The villagers are also jubilant, foreseeing other executives following Cady's lead and driving property values sky high. As Cady begins to enter village life, the locals' awe gradually turns to dismay. First he shows the revered old postmistress how to make sorting more efficient, then he decries the Volunteer Fire Brigade's order for a new fire engine. At the annual Hobby Show he derides the tradition of giving every entry a ribbon and belittles the entrants' efforts. When he suggests that the post office and the picking up of mail there are redundant and that there could just be delivery from Ilium, he has finally gone too far. The villagers rebel, deciding their way of life is more important than potential profits from property, and they all refuse to talk to the real estate agents about selling. They invoke a residency requirement to revoke Cady's membership in the Volunteer Fire Brigade, *but* they do agree to see how he adapts himself, because "he's got a good heart . . . and we're all rooting for him" (95).

Vonnegut himself was a volunteer fireman while living on Cape Cod, and volunteer brigades appear elsewhere in his fiction, notably in *God Bless You, Mr. Rosewater*. They are extolled as people who will risk their own lives, without pay, to save anyone else, without question. Hence they are models of what citizenship and community should be. There are also comic dimensions to the firemen in this story. Like the ordinary citizens in *Player Piano*, they are unable to resist gadgetry and the chromium glitz of a new fire truck even though it will take them twenty years to pay for it and the old one is perfectly serviceable.

Vonnegut's last contribution to *Collier's* came just four months later. "Tom Edison's Shaggy Dog" appeared on March 14, 1953.[8] It is a story about two retired men sharing a bench in Florida park. Harold K. Bullard is an inveterate raconteur of his past business successes. "But he faced the problem that complicates the lives of cannibals—which is that a single victim cannot be used over and over" (46). The other, a stranger, merely wants to sit and read, but Bullard's dog is a plastics addict and keeps after his suspenders, and Bullard himself continues to press his repetitious monologue. The stranger moves to another bench but soon feels the dog's wet muzzle at his ankle. Before Bullard can resume his story, the stranger launches into one of his own. When he was a boy, he says, he lived next door to Thomas Edison's laboratory. He became great pals with Edison's dog, Sparky, and one day that led him into the laboratory. Edison showed him a black box he was working with which proved to be an intelligence analyzer. To test it they attach it to Sparky's head, and it at once reads off the scale. It turns out that dogs have been smarter than humans all along, just letting humans have the worry and stress of providing while they lived in comfort. To repay Edison for keeping this secret, Sparky tells Edison to use carbonized cotton thread as a filament for the light bulb, and gives the stranger a stock tip that has made him wealthy for the rest of his life. Sparky, however, is ripped to pieces by a pack of dogs who have overheard him revealing the secrets of man's best friend.

Vonnegut has moved toward the shaggy dog story before, but this one is a self-proclaimed example. Part of its delight is seeing the tables turned on the boring Bullard (and his intrusive dog), and watching his mounting incredulity as the stranger's story escalates. The culmination of the stranger's tall tale is slipped in craftily. Edison protests that he has been working for the last year, " 'Slaving to work out a light bulb so dogs can play at night.' 'Look, Mr. Edison,' said Sparky, 'why not—' 'Hold on!' roared Bullard" (49). The purple-faced Bullard's finally being caught as the story takes its last step over the edge of credulity is a delightfully contrived moment. It bears out what Vonnegut has said about the need for the short story writer to know exactly how the story will end (as opposed to the novelist, who may explore in the course of writing) so that the close can be sprung deftly.[9] Much of the success of this brightly comic little story is in its dramatization—Bullard's dog's intrusions, the cross-purposes dialogue (" 'You know what Horace Greely would say today?' 'His nose is wet . . . ' "), Bullard's credulity, and the avenger's evident delight. The use of a story teller within the narrative, particularly one who mixes scientific history and the farfetched, makes this a short story that points directly toward the use of Kilgore Trout and his vignettes later in the novels.

By 1952 Vonnegut has begun to place stories in periodicals other than *Collier's*: first *Saturday Evening Post*, then *Argosy*. The *Collier's* stories constitute his earliest corpus of published fiction, and as such they embody some shared characteristics for all that they cover a range of plot situations and narrative techniques. Vonnegut notes that the *Writer's Digest* of the time, and other advisers, suggested that a first step in getting a story accepted was to find copies of the magazine and see what it had previously published. Editors had a sense of their readership and what their market enjoyed. That necessarily imposed some restrictions on the writer, but it also gave the neophyte some very clear guidelines within which to work while honing skills in many of the basic elements of good fiction. That certainly appears true for Vonnegut's *Collier's* stories, many of which read well decades later despite sometimes dated plot situations. Several of these stories continued to thrive in the durable collection *Welcome to the Monkey House* and in anthologies.

NOTES

1. Asa B. Pieratt, Jr., Julie Huffman-klinkowitz, and Jerome Klinkowitz, *Kurt Vonnegut: A Comprehensive Bibliography* (Hamden, CT: The Shoestring Press/Archon Books, 1987), xviii–xix.

2. Robert Scholes, "A Talk with Kurt Vonnegut, Jr.," in William Rodney Allen, *Conversations with Kurt Vonnegut* (Jackson: University Press of Mississippi, 1988), 112. (Hereafter cited as *Conversations*.)

3. Conversation between the author, Ollie Lyon and Kurt Vonnegut, in the home of Mr. Lyon, Lexington, Kentucky, October 31, 1993.

4. Kurt Vonnegut, "Report of the Barnhouse Effect," *Collier's*, February 11, 1950, 18.

5. Marc Leeds, *The Vonnegut Encyclopedia* (Westport, CT: Greenwood Press, 1995), 615.

6. "EPICAC" is reprinted in *Welcome to the Monkey House* with changes. The last sentence is changed from "Say nothing but good of those who have never been born" to "Say nothing but good of the dead," and the name Pat Callaghan is changed to Pat Kilgallen, which it had been in an earlier manuscript. Before that, in manuscript, it had been Annie Kilgallen.

7. Of the five stories in this group, two, "The Foster Portfolio" and "More Stately Mansions," are collected in both *Canary in a Cat House* and *Welcome to the Monkey House,* with only minor changes.

8. This story appears in both collections, having only minor stylistic changes in *Canary in a Cat House. Welcome to the Monkey House* omits the last sentence: "His step was brisk and spry as though the Florida sunshine were already working its magic."

9. Conversation between the author and Kurt Vonnegut, New York, May 24, 1996.

4

The Prolific Years: 1953–1958

In 1952, besides the three stories in *Collier's*, Vonnegut had published the novel *Player Piano* and two stories in important new sources, *Saturday Evening Post* and *Argosy*. The novel, published by Charles Scribner's Sons, had a printing run of 7,600 copies in its first edition, though Richard Todd, on the basis of interviews, claims that it sold only 3,500 copies.[1] The next year a Doubleday Book Club Edition ran to 20,000 copies, and then in 1954 came the interesting development of the novel's being retitled *Utopia 14* (a title with no foundation in its contents!) and reissued by Bantam with a suitably fanciful cover. Since then it has reappeared many times, but in those early years it failed to provide the kind of income Vonnegut could derive from the short stories, and it was to be seven years before he would again turn to the longer form (in *The Sirens of Titan*).

SATURDAY EVENING POST

The 1952 *Saturday Evening Post* story, "The No Talent Kid" (October 25) was the first of four stories written for that magazine centered on the character of George M. Helmholtz, head of the music department and director of the band at Lincoln High School. The other three are "The Ambitious Sophomore" (May 1, 1954), "The Kid Nobody Could Handle" (September 24, 1955, and the only one collected in *Welcome to the Monkey House*), and "The Boy Who Hated Girls" (March 31, 1956). Vonnegut clearly draws on his own experiences as a clarinet player and band member at Indianapolis's Shortridge High School in these tales.

There is a formula to all of these stories. Helmholtz is good hearted and dedicated. His bands have won state championships with regularity, and he has nurtured generations of students, often leading misfits to find themselves through music. Usually a baffling problem with a troublesome student causes Helmholtz to fret and threatens the performance of the band in the next championship contest. These situations are well captured in Amos Sewell's Norman Rockwell-like illustrations for "The No Talent Kid" and "Ambitious

Sophomore." Both depict the fussy, pudgy Helmholtz, brow wrinkled in consternation, confronted by a willful-looking boy.

"The No-Talent Kid" tells of Helmholtz's struggles with Walter Plummer, a member of the C Band. Normally students graduated to the B Band in time or realized their lack of ability, but Plummer was a third-year clarinetist. He spent his summers swimming to improve his breathing (Vonnegut was a swimmer, too), the only consequence of which was that he could hold a note longer than anyone else. Despite Helmholtz's patient entreaties, Plummer persists, mainly because he wants to wear the proud uniform of the school's Ten Square Band. The solution comes from the conjunction of Helmholtz's and Plummer's wants. Helmholtz wants to have a giant drum to compete with or surpass the rival Johnstown band, and Plummer wants to be in the A Band. When the Knights of Kandahar sell their giant drum, Plummer beats Helmholtz to it. He won't give up the drum, and Helmholtz knows he'll never be able to play it. But he can pull it, in uniform, and that is the compromise they reach.

In an interview Vonnegut said, "When I used to teach creative writing, I would tell the students to make their characters want something right away—even if it's only a glass of water. . . . When you exclude plot, when you exclude anyone's wanting anything, you exclude the reader."[2] "The No-Talent Kid" plays two "wants," which give it suspense: Helmholtz's wish for something to give his band an edge against Johnstown, and Plummer's to get in that uniform. Helmholtz has always overspent his budget; he gets no miraculously discovered funds. Plummer has no talent; he does not by some surprise turn of events prove to have hidden ones. And yet there is a resolution, a surprise by understatement, another form of the familiar shaggy-dog ending. That humorous touch is complemented by the characterization of the two main participants: Helmholtz sweet but scheming, Plummer surprisingly adult in dialogue and cunning.

In "Ambitious Sophomore," Helmholtz's problem is roughly the reverse. Leroy Duggan is a talented piccolo player, but he is "bell-shaped" and self conscious, so the problem is to get him to play confidently in the A Band. Helmholtz experiences his usual trouble with Stewart Haley, the assistant principal assigned to keep an eye on band finances. The band director has already lavished funds he does not have on a hundred elaborate uniforms— " 'Every time I see one of those uniforms,' said Haley, 'all I can think of is a road company of The Chocolate Soldier' " (88)—but now needs another special one for Leroy, to give him the stature and confidence he needs. Helmholtz's strategy for winning this year's State Band Festival Trophy involves a production where Leroy's piccolo solo in "The Stars and Stripes Forever" will be accompanied by fireworks that will release parachutes bearing American flags. A uniform padded like a football player's jersey gives Leroy the confidence he needs and contributes to his banishing his usual timidity in responding to a female band colleague. Helmholtz sells his unused spare tire to Crane, the English teacher, to pay for the uniform. On the crucial day, a rival band member flirts with Leroy's new friend. Confronted, he rips up Leroy's padding, but Leroy triumphantly fights back. With Leroy forced to wear a spare uniform for the big event, Helmholtz imagines his key musician reduced to bell-shaped jelly again, but love overcomes all, Leroy rises to the occasion, the rockets spew parachutes, and Helmholtz staggers off with another trophy. His car has a flat and he has sold his spare, but Helmholtz rides home happily on the streetcar.

One part of this story is rather like the Charles Atlas advertisements that appear beside some of these stories, where the ninety-six-pound weakling gets his revenge on the muscular bully who kicks sand in his face. Except that Leroy does not take the Atlas course—love lends him boldness. It is a sentimental notion, just as Helmholtz's mothering of his band, scheming to raise funds, selling his spare tire for Leroy's uniform, and riding home misty-eyed with his trophy are sentimental. But there is also enough humor, enough wry undercutting in this story, much of it supplied by Haley, to keep it from going soft. Helmholtz, for all of his sweet gentleness, is enough of a confidence man—shades of Professor Harold Hill of "The Music Man"—to spice his characterization. As the story says, "Helmholtz often gave the impression of a man lost in dreams, but there was a side to him that was as tough as a rhinoceros" (31). There is also a side that shows the limits to his perceptions. While he is kindly and concerned with his students, and has used performance to help many to grow, he does not always understand them. He fails to see that infatuation has transformed Leroy's behavior, and despite his best efforts he misreads "The Kid Nobody Could Handle."

The story begins with the contrast between the unworldly Helmholtz and a cynical contractor named Bert Quinn. Helmholtz is contented because "Each year he dreamed the same big dream. He dreamed of leading as fine a band as there was on the face of the earth. And each year the dream came true" (37). Quinn is "humorless," "suspicious and self-pitying," "arrogant and boastful," and obsessed with making money. The contrast is one Vonnegut often uses, and it sets the context for the arrival of Jim Donnini. Jim is a high school student from South Chicago, tough, destructive, nihilistic, seemingly caring for nothing but his well polished boots. Challenged, Helmholtz tries to find something Jim will respond to, that will give him satisfaction or attachment, but without response. When he intercepts Jim's nocturnal vandalizing of the school's chemistry lab, he tries to make a deal, to swap Jim's most prized possession, his boots, for his own, a trumpet once owned by John Philip Sousa. Neither Jim nor Quinn sees the point in this gesture, the value of the instrument, or the opportunity for creating something worthwhile that it offers. In frustration and futility Helmholtz cries " 'Life is no damn good' " and smashes the trumpet. That evokes a response, and the story concludes with Jim's sitting in the last seat of the C Band with the repaired horn. " 'Our aim is to make the world more beautiful than it was when we came into it. It can be done. You can do it.' " When Jim asks how, Helmholtz replies," 'Love yourself, . . . and make your instrument sing about it' " (129).

Contemporary audiences may be skeptical of such stories of bad kids touched by adults who offer "uncritical love," but it does happen, and Vonnegut shows a continuing interest in prodigal sons, just as he does in fathers.[3] Jim appears to be reached not by Helmholtz's generosity and forgiveness, but when he, too, shows hurt and despair. Those feelings are familiar to Jim, and make Helmholtz relevant in a way he had not been in his "friendly scoutmaster" approaches. Quinn, too, rejects "the poor little sick boy" approach Jim has always "heard from social workers and the juvenile court," but for his part calls him "a no good bum of a man" (126). Quinn's demolishing the hill he has bought from Helmholtz, while the band director is described as "the mountain that walked like a man," symbolizes the contrast in the two approaches When the mountain starts to fall apart, that vulnerability helps Jim to see the value of what Helmholtz offers.

In "The Boy Who Hated Girls" Helmholtz's well-intentioned judgment comes into question even more. One of the boys to whom Helmholtz has given special attention, Bert has now been passed on to another tutor for music instruction but keeps inventing other difficulties to regain Helmholtz's attention. The school nurse recognizes that this fatherless boy has become dependent upon the teacher's nurturing, and she tells Helmholtz, "Will you please open your eyes, and see what you've done to Bert's life?" (60). Bert, she says, will seek a surrogate father until he finds a woman companion. At the same time he learns from the tutor that Bert shows no serious musical talent, and had worked desperately just to have Helmholtz's tutelage. These revelations stun the band director, and "guilt rode on his back like a chimpanzee with very bad breath." He contrives a situation where, though it causes him pain to do it, he embarrasses Bert in front of the band—and of Charlotte, the girl who has shown interest in Bert without response. That brings Bert and Charlotte together like old friends, and leaves Helmholtz without a problem that threatens his band. And at a window above the practice area, a small freshman looks down at Helmholtz and his band with adoration.

This last Helmholtz story, with its curiously inaccurate title, has many characteristic features.[4] Nurse Peach paves the way for later competent women with a perception that the men lack. Fathers, surrogate fathers, and father-son relationships provide recurrent themes in Vonnegut's fiction. The problem that the most altruistic intentions can sometimes lead to harm that Helmholtz encounters here also recurs—one thinks of Boaz in *The Sirens of Titan* claiming that " ' I found me a palce where I can do good without doing any harm' " at the very time he is killing the harmoniums he is feeding (185). Even the use of names with the same initials for recurrent plots in these stories—Helmholtz and Haley—resembles the "H subplots"—dependent on the names Homestead, Haycox, Hagstrohm, Hacketts, Halyard—surrounding the central "P plot"—the player piano and Paul Proteus—in *Player Piano*.

Helmholtz himself proves an interesting character, as Stanley Schatt has observed.

His obsessive devotion to this dream [winning the annual contest] makes him a comical yet strangely moving character. Helmholtz has much in common with the traditional Jewish *Das Kleine Menschele* figure, the little man of Eastern European Jewish folklore who is physically helpless to control his own destiny and who constantly lives in fear of the outside world entering his *shtetl* community.[5]

Helmholtz also shows a quality akin to that Vonnegut has admired in those embattled movie comedians, Laurel and Hardy:

The fundamental joke with Laurel and Hardy, it seems to me, was that they did their best with every test. They never failed to bargain in good faith with their destinies, and were screamingly adorable and funny on that account. (*Slapstick*, 1)

Helmholtz has little of their slapstick but his resourcefulness, his ability to make donors "see" and "hear" imagined bands, and his resilient belief in the good in people all show the influence of those comedians Vonnegut had grown up enjoying. These stories are not without their darker side, however, as Helmholtz himself acknowledges several times. He clings to the notion that "I've got at least one tiny corner of the universe . . . the air around my band. I can fill it with music. Mr. Beeler, in zoology, has his butterflies. . . . Making sure everybody has a corner like that is about the biggest job we teachers have" ("The Kid Nobody Could Handle," 126). This sounds similar to something Vonnegut said in response to a student's question once. The student asked if, given Vonnegut's general pessimism about the future of the planet, it made him totally nihilistic. Vonnegut replied that he still believed in acting decently and in trying to do the best one could where one could, hoping to make a difference in people's lives despite the long-term outlook.[6] Helmholtz appeals because he is generally undaunted, resourcefully clinging to a dream, helping children in their aspirations, and always striving to create something new.

Three of the *Saturday Evening Post* stories of this period can be connected by their all having to do with beautiful women and men's perceptions of them. While it must be remembered that the terms for discussing these subjects would begin to change radically in the following decade, and while in their own ways these stories express more sympathy for their female characters than for the males, nevertheless they remain less comfortable than the stories located in male worlds.

In "Custom-Made Bride" (March 27, 1954) the familiar investment counselor narrator goes to the aid of Otto Krummbein, a genius designer with no money sense. (An early manuscript of this story carries the title "The Krummbein Portfolio," which would underline the similar setup to that in "The Foster Portfolio.") Much of Otto's overspending has been on his bride of one month, the elegant Falloleen. The brief month of marriage has been spent mostly in the company of their set of bright young people. The quotation under the Robert Meyers illustration for this story sets up the problem: " 'You've taken me out every night,' said Falloleen. 'People wonder if maybe we're afraid to be alone with each other' " (30). And so it proves. The reason is that Otto has created Falloleen out of his "dowdy" secretary Kitty Cahoun. The make-over has left her with no sense of who she is, only the knowledge of a role to perform, while Otto doesn't know how to respond to Falloleen. The intrusion of the narrator provides the situation that can bring all this to light, and the resolution seems to be that Mrs. Krummbein can go on looking like Falloleen but the soul of Kitty must remain intact and shine through.

A saving touch in this story is the way in which the small steps Otto takes to adjust the narrator's appearance make plausible Kitty's submission, progressively, to her make-over. The ultra-modern house, Otto's obsessive passion for design, and the accolades he has received for his products all contribute to a consistent, more plausible setting. Kitty's eventual rejection of

her " 'dull and shallow, scared and lost, unhappy and unloved' " life as
Falloleen—with the appropriate swing at her husband's face—is the redeeming
moment of the story. "You think I'm striated plywood and plastic?" she cries, in
denunciation of her objectification. One may be reminded of Ed Finnerty's
derision of the magazine-molded Anita in *Player Piano* as something he could
replace in sponge rubber and stainless steel (46).

While both Anita and Falloleen/Kitty are shaped by male expectations, the
bit-part actress Susanna creates her own image, the fixing of her identity by men
occurring in their heads. The title figure of "Miss Temptation" (April 21, 1956,
and *Welcome to the Monkey House*) is "forever as startling and desirable as a
piece of big-city fire apparatus." Like Falloleen she affects "barbaric" gold
hoop earrings, with the rest of her physical description put in terms clichéd in
the convention of soft-porn fiction: "Her hips were like a lyre, and her bosom
made men dream of peace and plenty for ever and ever" (30). And so on. This
type of description brings the narration close to the male state of mind that the
story depends upon. It also furthers a third-person narration that sounds almost
first-person. This self-conscious usgae emphasizes the story's point. It recalls
the similar description in the portrayal of Mona Aamons Monzano in *Cat's
Cradle*. She, too, "was peace and plenty forever" and "[h]er hips were a lyre."
But Vonnegut underlines his point there by noting, "Her breasts were like
pomegranates or what you will, but like nothing so much as a young woman's
breasts" (138).   Both fictions in effect deconstruct the language and the
psychology of male objectification of the female body.

The objectifier of Susanna is a recently demobilized veteran named Norman
Fuller. He interrupts Susanna's daily visit to Bearse Hinkley's drugstore by
turning on her bitterly in full view of everyone at the counter. "American
women" are provocative then heartless, he says, stirring feelings then dousing
them. The excuse offered for Fuller is that in Korea he saw endless
temptresses—in movies or magazines, as pinups—"beckoning the Fullers to
come nowhere for nothing."

The wraith of a Puritan ancestor, stiff-necked, dressed in black, took possession of
Fuller's tongue. Fuller spoke with a voice that came across centuries, the voice of a witch
hanger, a voice redolent with frustration, self-righteousness and doom.

"What did I speak out against?" he said. "Temp-ta-tion." (60)

The old pharmacist, Hinkley, debunks Fuller's self-righteousness. He leads
Fuller to see how much he has hurt Susanna and occasions his going to her to
apologize. Susanna argues that she has been treated with his kind of harshness
all her life because of false conclusions based on her looks. The story ends with
Fuller's walking Susanna down the street to "welcome [her] back to the human
race."

Looked at from decades on from the date of its writing, "Miss Temptation"
may present more difficulties for its audience than it did for contemporary ones.
Imagining a contemporary actress greeting either Fuller's initial outburst or his
subsequent attempt at reconciliation as submissively as Susanna does is not easy.
One might even wonder whether the woman who makes the speeches she does

to Fuller about the way people have always looked at and treated her would then parade in "barbaric hoops" and with "tinkling bells" at her ankles. The bodily descriptions, even when done for a "moral" purpose, are troublesome, and so is the outcome, with the two parading self-consciously downtown. On the other hand, the story has its strengths. It does not simply take on Fuller's chauvinism, it challenges a more general and entrenched Puritanism in the culture that persistently intrudes on individual freedom and expression. And it goes behind stereotypes, finding the individuality behind the type-casting of both main characters. And there are some nice touches in the dialogue, characteristically where it is between men. Fuller fumes, " 'The beautiful girls in high school—by glory, if they didn't think they were something extra special.' 'By glory, if I didn't think so, too,' said Hinkley" (60).

The third of these stories on gender relations is "A Night For Love" (November 23, 1957). Again a woman's beauty provides the nub of the situation. At the opening, Turley and Milly Whitman are waiting for their daughter Nancy to return from a date. Nancy is out with Charlie, son of Louis and Natalie Reinbeck, who are also waiting up. The beautiful moonlight night has less to do with what romantic notions the young couple might be led to than with the memories and insecurities it stirs in their parents. For once the young Louis Reinbeck, now tycoon of the Reinbeck Abrasives company, had kissed Milly—then Mildred O'Shea—on just such a night. So now as Milly, "very beautiful and mysterious," looks up at the moonlight from her bed, Turley, Reinbeck company cop at the parking lot, begins to wonder. When he discovers that Milly has found that by bending and looking at a certain angle one can see the Reinbeck mansion from their kitchen, he wonders even more if she has not been thinking she made a mistake years ago.

At the same time, Louis Reinbeck is sitting in the moonlight looking at the spot where he kissed Milly O'Shea, and feeling nostalgic. When Turley calls Reinbeck to ask about the children he alludes to the earlier relationship. Natalie overhears this, and attributes the cold relationship of their marriage to Reinbeck's wishing he had married Milly instead of someone of his own social stratum. So things become uncomfortable in both households, despite the fact that the earlier "romance" had in fact been one kiss in the moonlight that at once began and ended a relationship both knew could not last. As Reinbeck tries to deny its significance to Natalie, he knows she is right that his life has never brought "anything as nice as that time in the moonlight with Milly." It has given him the joyless gifts of wealth, power, responsibility and status, but deprived him of "feeling human" such as he had had with Milly. But he tells Natalie—and himself—that that night had been just "beautiful, moonlit hokum," and that she is the only one he has ever loved. "So everything was fine." And Milly tells Turley she knew when Reinbeck kissed her that he was not the one, but when Turley kissed her, he was, so would he kiss her again? "Turley did, so everything was all right there, too." And Charlie and Nancy impetuously decide to get married. "So now there was a new household. Whether everything was all right there, remained to be seen. The moon went down" (84).

Vonnegut obviously recognizes the potential for this story of magical moonlight, of unrequited but never-forgotten love between a pretty but poor young woman and a rich but constrained young man, to topple over the edge of acceptable sentiment. But in fact the pessimistic undercurrents to this story and the undercutting in its narration actually overbalance its romance. Milly appears to be as genuinely adoring of Turley as Kitty/Falloleen was of Otto, but it matters little while Turley harbors uncertainties. He does—and Milly may, too. And despite Reinbeck's best-foot-forward reassurances, he and Natalie remain equally uncertain at heart. Milly and Reinbeck's moonlit Cinderella romance that they felt could not survive daylight's realities remains to be tested in the next generation, but with even less assurance of the possibility of success. Those ironical, throwaway assurances that "everything was all right" falter completely in the third case. The moon goes down—and the story certainly ends in darkness: two couples in the all-too-frequent situation of assuring themselves that their life choices were the right ones, and the equally familiar occurrence of a young couple prematurely throwing themselves into a commitment they do not yet begin to comprehend. If the incremental refrain of "everything was fine" does not alone make the point, the allusion to "Cinderella and Prince Charming" serves to clinch it.

The final *Saturday Evening Post* story from this period focuses squarely on a theme frequently woven into Vonnegut's fiction, the relationship between fathers and sons. "This Son of Mine" (August 18, 1956) involves two pairs: Merle Waggoner and his son Franklin, and Rudy Lindberg and his son Karl. Merle is the founder and owner of Waggoner Pump, for which he has just been offered two million dollars by a large corporation based, predictably, in Ilium, New York. He would like nothing more than for the company to pass to his son, but Franklin has just announced that he wants to be an actor. Rudy Lindberg meanwhile works at his lathe in the factory. He was Merle's first employee and could have been a partner for two thousand dollars but thought it too risky. His son Karl has followed in his footsteps and works at another lathe nearby. The two are close. They have simple, mutually understood hand gestures that signal their bond, and they accompany each other on clarinet and flute. Thirty-one years before, Merle had received as a gift a plate with a square hole and a cube that fit perfectly through it that were the tests of Rudy's apprenticeship. At his latest birthday he has received an identical set from Karl—and the parts of the two sets are exactly interchangeable.

Franklin's decision to become an actor shatters his father's dreams. And there is much emphasis on dreams in this story. Merle laments that none of the old firms are continued by the sons. " 'What is it about the sons?' " he demands. For a moment even Franklin is forced to see them as "the killers of their fathers' dreams" (76). When Merle dramatically threatens to sell the company on the spot, Franklin pleads with him not to throw away his life's dream just because he is not sure of his. " 'I'm not Karl Lindberg,' he said. 'I can't help it. I'm sorry, but I'm not Karl Lindberg.' " That reaches Merle, who responds, " 'I'm glad you've got big dreams of your own' " (76). But the turning point of this story occurs when the four go hunting and the two boys are left alone. It is Karl who tells Franklin to pursue his own dreams for the theater and leave the factory. Franklin *can*, he says. Merle has had his own dream, and he has his success. " 'All my old man's got is me. . . . I'm what he'd rather have than the half of Waggoner Pump he could have had for two thousand dollars' " (78). And then Karl reveals what drives the relationship he has with his own father:

he is supposed to be the son that *Merle* wants. To further that end, Rudy has even made the second cube and plate set supposedly made by Karl as a gift to Merle. Karl even threatens to miss the target on his next shot as his rebellion against a dream-killing father. But at the end the two pairs are regarding each other with troubled affection.

> The music . . . was speaking of all fathers and sons. It was saying hauntingly what they had all been saying, sometimes with pain and sometimes with anger and sometimes with cruelty and sometimes with love—that fathers and sons were one. It was saying, too, that a time for a parting in spirit was near—no matter how close anyone held anyone, no matter what anyone tried. (78)

It can be inviting to see thinly-veiled autobiography in this story. Franklin goes to Cornell and becomes much involved with fraternity life, as did Vonnegut. Ilium, Vonnegut's fictional equivalent of Schenectady, reappears as the home of the impersonal corporate giant. Franklin deviates from the career of his father, just as Kurt turned away from the careers of his grandfather and father, both architects. Vonnegut's father, like Merle, bought expensive guns and hunted. One parallel is with Karl rather than Franklin; like him, Vonnegut plays the clarinet. Vonnegut alludes to his relationship with his own father quite frequently in his writing. It was a rather distant one, particularly as by the time Kurt, five years younger than his next sibling, was growing up, his father was withdrawing increasingly into a reclusiveness resulting from his failure to find clients during the Great Depression. Vonnegut was also the father of a son himself by the time this story was written. The existence of the long-standing Vonnegut Hardware store in Indianapolis, in which Kurt had sometimes worked, also might have provided some background insights for the story.

Like "A Night For Love," then, "This Son of Mine" has a qualified ending. Its affirmation—"that fathers and sons were one"—is undercut, not least by the final paragraph. The being "one" is, like marriage, for better or worse, and as in the depiction of marriage, the dream of one partner can threaten the world of the other. Both stories seem to suggest that the dream relationship—marriage as moonlight romance, father and son fitting as perfectly as Rudy's cube and plate—is not likely, but that something reasonably good and sustaining can exist anyway. Relationships are difficult, be they Helmholtz's with his students, the romances and marriages, or the fathers and sons, but they can at least be workable where there is effort to understand and to allow the other person room to sustain his or her own sense of identity.

The key elements that unite these essentially domestic *Saturday Evening Post* stories are dreams and identities, and the two are related. Consistently the attainment of material success, be it by Bert Quinn or Otto Krummbein or Louis Reinbeck or Merle Waggoner, brings only sterile rewards. Dreams may be sustaining, lend purpose to lives, or be a source of identity, but they can also be obsessive, blinding one to the feelings and freedoms of others. Dreams, and the occupations or life-styles they lead to, can also be a source of vulnerability when threats to their existence endanger the person's self-identity. When Helmholtz finds his treasures and accomplishments mean nothing to Quinn and Jim he is crushed; Franklin's disinterest in inheriting his father's role threatens to make

Merle's life meaningless. In the novel that has been published by this time, *Player Piano,* and in several later ones, Vonnegut shows people feeling invalidated and lost when displaced from their jobs by technology. So while these stories remain frequently humorous and on the whole up-beat, their conclusions seldom prove as rosy as they first appear. The undercurrent is of a world where relationships are not always happy, dreams collide or fail, and success by society's standards may come at personal cost. These are not escapist happy stories, but more the kind of stories that recognize the rough and the smooth in the readers' worlds, and offer the reassurance of compromised outcomes such as those readers may encounter in their own lives.

COSMOPOLITAN

The stories for *Cosmopolitan* for this period seem less domestic and slightly more exaggerated in their plots and settings than do their contemporaries in *Saturday Evening Post.* Like their illustrations, which tend to emphasize glamour and romance, the stories frequently focus on dreams as escapes from everyday reality more than do the *Post* stories. They do, however, continue to undercut the high-flown with strong doses of the mundane, once again seeming in the end to endorse traditional American middle-class ethics. In fact, they tend to advise their audiences to be content with those values, to see the virtues of the often-overlooked rewards in everyday life, and not to be pulled off-balance by too unrealistic aspirations. The first story in this group is a reminder of the wonder in the everyday miracle of birth, posed against the specter of genocide.

"Adam" (April, 1954, collected in *Welcome to the Monkey House*) may be seen as a variant of the fathers-and-sons motif, but it is much more a story that harks back to the Second World War and its consequences. Set in Chicago, it tells of a Holocaust survivor, Heinz Knechtmann, at the time that his wife Avchen is in the hospital having their baby. Heinz is filled with wonder and excitement. Their first child was born and died in the wartime camp. The family name has almost died. But no one shares his elation. To Sousa, the huge man waiting with him and expecting his seventh baby, still in pursuit of a son, it is a familiar scene. The doctor is exhausted from thirty-six hours on his feet. When Heinz croons at the baby through the glass a nurse hushes him. And in the bar where he hopes to share his celebration, Sousa and the bartender quickly launch into a discussion of the White Sox. A disconsolate Knechtmann tells himself nobody cares. "What could be duller? Who would be so stupid as to talk about it, to think there was anything important or interesting about it?" (38). In the morning he rides to the hospital seemingly as emotionless as those around him. Now he can see Avchen.

> "Sweetheart, are you all right?"
> "Yes, yes," she whispered. "I'm fine. How is the baby, Heinz?"
> "Perfect. Perfect, Avchen."
> "They couldn't kill us, could they, Heinz?"
> "No."
> "And here we are, alive as we can be."
> "Yes."

"The baby, Heinz—" She opened her dark eyes wide. "It's the most
wonderful thing that ever happened, isn't it?"

"Yes," said Heinz. There was no question about it. Absolutely none. (38)

If "Adam" seems sometimes sentimental in the manner of its telling, it
might also be remembered that babies are a subject people generally wax
sentimental about, even in ordinary circumstances, and that the special
circumstances of this story justify sentiment. In fact, this story may be
sentimental by design, to emphasize the indifferent taking for granted of this
regenerative miracle. The horror that has preceded these events in South
Chicago—the Holocaust, the loss of the first baby in the camp, the murder of the
rest of the family—accentuate the meaning in the commonplace. The story
emphasizes continuance—Knechtmann is not simply to be subsumed
into a bland Americanized "Netman" but proudly preserved as
"*Khhhhhhhhhhhhhhh*NECHT! *mannnnnnnnnnnn*." And the baby's names, Peter
Karl, invoke the memories of an uncle who was a famous surgeon, a father who
was a virtuoso cellist. That Heinz has no one to share his news with underlines
the history behind this birth. "He had died a little as each member of his family
had been led away and killed by the Nazis, until only in him, at the age of ten,
had life and the name of Knechtmann shared a soul" (35–36). The story poses
the wonder of birth against the horror of genocide—and exposes the danger that
absorption in the daily round makes people too prone to indifference to both.
The exchange between Heinz and Avchen at the end of the story remains rich in
ambiguity. " 'They couldn't kill us, could they, Heinz?' 'No.' 'And here we
are, alive as we can be.' " This affirmation applies not only to their personal and
racial survival of Nazi genocide but to their feelings not being suppressed by the
busy indifference all around, in their being alive as can be to the wonder of birth
and continuance, of regeneration through generations.

One of Alex Ross's illustrations for "Adam" shows Heinz and Avchen as a
young couple crouching behind the barbed wire of a camp, itself improbable,
since men and women were separated in the camps. More surprisingly, someone
could not resist his creating another to illustrate the sentence, "The Knechtmann
men were ugly, but somehow the women they chose were lovely as angels" (39).
The full-page illustration has the face of a glamorous woman with an angel, a
serene young woman in white with wings, in the lower left foreground, one wing
trailing up the side of the portrait. The sentence seems an odd choice to illustrate
this story. The made-up and bejeweled face connotes little of the grim existence
Avchen has led, and Ross's angel seems singularly inappropriate to this story of
Jewish survival. The illustration appears fairly typical, however, of the way
those in *Cosmopolitan* tend to glamorize the plots. It stands out as particularly
unfortunate in this case, where Vonnegut addresses a historical episode that may
be especially sensitive to one of his war experiences and his German-American
background.[7] Although the story's initial premise remains a conventional one—
the husky Sousa and his "pop-up toaster" wife have a seventh girl, while bent
Heinz and the malnourished Avchen have a boy—"Adam" makes serious
comments on its times.

"Bagombo Snuff Box" (October, 1954) recounts a story about the aftermath
of the Second World War, husbands, wives, and children, that contrasts starkly

with "Adam." The central character, a salesman, bears little resemblance to the conscientious, steady hands who have narrated some of the earlier stories. And he sharply contrasts to the small, bent Knechtmann, being tall, straight and handsome. Eddie Laird makes a sales visit to the town where he was based in the Air Force during the war. Those days, as he recalls them, had been prime years when he was an adventurous hero in the eyes of pretty young women. Now much is changed, but Eddie still has plenty of bravado, and he decides to call his ex-wife. He and Amy had been married for only six months before Amy had enough of his restlessness. But that was eleven years ago. Now she was married to an unimposing credit manager named Harry and has a nine-year-old and an infant. Eddie's call catches her by surprise, but he invites himself in a way she finds hard to refuse, and soon he has taken a taxi to her door. While he and Harry wait for her to emerge from tending the baby, Eddie hands over a gift—a snuff box he says he picked up in Bagombo, in Ceylon. When Amy emerges, obviously having taken great pains with her looks, Eddie resorts to a silver-tongued-devil style aimed to contrast with the mundanity of her domestic round. " 'I can see you now in a Mainbocher suit, your high heels clicking smartly along the Champs Elysees, with the soft winds of the Parisian spring ruffling your black hair, and with every eye drinking you in—and a gendarme salutes!' " (37). He spins tales of his high living, flying a sheik in Iraq, pearls in Ceylon, and so forth, engaged in adventures only a single man like him can undertake. Now he is about to set up his own outfit uranium prospecting in the Klondike. He even teaches both Amy and Harry some phrases in the native tongue of Bagombo.

The first turning point in this story comes when the son, Stevie, arrives home and bluntly asks why the Bagombo snuff box has "Made in Japan" stamped on it. While Eddie tries to bluff through that, Stevie presses on the question of where Ceylon is located—off India or off Africa. A thoroughly flustered Eddie opts for the wrong answer and beats a hasty retreat to his waiting taxi. The second turning point comes when we see Eddie back in his hotel room calling his wife, asking about his four children in turn, and boasting of his success selling potato chips in Dubuque. When his wife Selma asks if he called *her* while he was in town, he replies " 'Naaaah. We'd hardly know each other. People change, people change' " (39).

"Bagombo Snuff Box" is comedy, where the slick pretender who threatens to beguile the woman is exposed and stolid old virtue prevails, but not until everyone has been titillated, at least a little, by visions of a fancier life. An interesting interplay takes place in this story between how the circumstances of the two main characters have changed and how they, in at least some respects, have not. Eddie, though obviously now leading a humdrum life as a not-very-successful salesman with a wife and four children, is still the fast-talking flimflam artist he was when he married Amy. And Amy remains susceptible enough that one sees how she succumbed in the first place. Even Amy's regular-Joe husband, Harry, starts to fall for Eddie's line. Hence one irony of Eddie's telling his wife, " 'People change, people change.' " The other levels of irony, of course, are that he has not changed in being the same old liar, and that he proves capable of Protean change between the life he leads and that he pretends to live.

Eddie's being exposed by the nine-year-old Stevie is apt. The parents are too vulnerable to tall tales of exotic places and doings as escapes from their tiring routines to catch the implausibilities. The smart no-nonsense kid bringing down the confidence man is stock comedy—a favorite of W. C. Fields, for instance, a comedian Vonnegut admired as a boy. In much of Vonnegut's fiction he introduces a writer or artist figure, a surrogate author within the narrative. That is Eddie's role here. Like the writer, he tells stories and beguiles people into believing false worlds. The snuff box becomes the emblem of this, the embodiment of his giving to his audience a world that is exotic and wish fulfilling, but fake. It resembles other such metafictional reflections on the role of the artist as liar or deceiver that recur in Vonnegut's work.[8] Another characteristic device within the story, the madeup phrases Eddie teaches Amy and Harry, represent a foretaste of *Cat's Cradle* with its San Lorenzan dialect.

Not Vonnegut's doing, but the illustrations by Paul Burns are interesting— and amusing. Amy, we are told, "was still young, but very tired. She was prettily dressed, carefully made-up, and quite self-conscious" (37). In two of the illustrations this tired housewife appears confidently ravishing in a strapless, low-backed ball gown and elaborate jewelry, with finely tapered fingers and long painted nails! Harry, described as a "short, blocky man," appears lean, tan, and handsome. The artists obviously had an important role in setting the tone of these magazines and luring readers to their stories.

"The Powder Blue Dragon" is another story of pretense and flights of romantic fancy. Young Kiah Higgins works three jobs to save money for the car of his dreams, a powder blue Marittima-Frascati two-seater. The dealer tells him the engine must be run in gradually over five thousand miles, and on his first drive Kiah shows restraint. He does a little showing off for the benefit of a blonde young woman in a Cadillac and follows her into a hotel cocktail bar after she parks. There he tries to impress her despite the undercutting of the bartender and his painful inability to make conversation. Kiah's efforts are cut short by the arrival of the woman's fiancé, who boasts of his Hampton sportscar's superiority to Kiah's. On the road back to town, Kiah outruns the Hampton but arrives back with the Marittima-Frascati's engine seized solid. Kiah's dream has been shattered in one day. At the end he bursts into tears. " 'I'm glad it's dead,' he said brokenly. 'I'm glad I killed it' " (53).

What Kiah has killed, of course, is delusion. His dream is not an uncommon one among American young men, that a magnificent car will lend him its sophistication and take him from being acned and awkward to suave and debonair. The encounter in the cocktail lounge, where the bartender calls him "sonny," the young woman refers to him as "that boy," and the boyfriend taunts him, leaves him humiliated. On the drive back he can triumph over the Hampton, but he knows it is futile. He can outrun the Hampton, but he cannot keep up with the Marittima-Frascati himself. He cannot transform his life and himself with one gesture, one dramatic purchase, and he learns that. A boyish dream dies with the car. Stanley Schatt likens the demise of the car to that of "Puff the Magic Dragon" of song that "cannot survive in the adult world. The lesson he learns is a common Vonnegut bromide, for a kindly old druggist tells the boy that expensive cars are part of a 'phony world, a toy world, full of useless trinkets' " (Schatt, 131).

Another person who lives by a delusion is Harry Divine of "Unpaid Consultant" (March, 1955). As in the later "Go Back to your Precious Wife and Son," the situation involves a man married to a rich and famous wife. The singer Celeste Divine appears regularly on television, gets offered movie roles, and enjoys wealth to equal her beauty. Harry has been an auto mechanic but has left that job as his wife's fame blossoms. After a period at loose ends, straining the marriage, Harry has found his role as a consultant to the catchup industry. Or so he tells the narrator, once again an investments counselor and a former classmate of Celeste, who has called on him for financial advice. The comedy of Harry's obsession with catchup occupies much of the story. At every point he turns the conversation to catchup, speaking as if the fate of the entire industry rests in his hands. Later, when the narrator goes to advise a man whose family has in fact been in that industry for three generations, he introduces his client to Harry, and the bubble bursts. It turns out that, after Celeste had achieved her fame, Harry had walked the streets seeking some occupation, and resting in libraries had read up on catchup. The job was a fiction, a make-believe grand role, that gave Harry a sense of importance and purpose that counterbalanced his wife's fame. Shocked out of his fantasy by his encounter with the real catchup manufacturer, he returns to being a mechanic and is last seen finding satisfaction in the gratitude of a customer for his fixing a broken fuel pump.

The title of this story proves the tip-off, telling readers that Harry is unpaid and therefore signaling the probability that Harry's job remains imaginary. That does not detract, however, because once the job is understood as probably imaginary the humor of Harry's obsession becomes the funnier. When his exposure is foreseen it becomes not the moment for the comic overturning of the deceiver, as in "Bagombo Snuff Box," for Harry hurts no one and mainly deceives himself, but a moment of potential pathos. It comes as a relief, then, that Harry can return contentedly to his old job and to acceptance of reality, and that he can actually josh with the narrator about the role he had been playing.

There is some amusement in the dialogue of this story, largely because of Harry's obsession. When after interruption he asks what he was talking about, the narrator reminds him "catchup"—and one can almost hear his exasperation. When Harry explains that the industry is "trying to lick thixotropy" the humor lies in the ambiguity of the verb. By and large this remains a lighthearted story. Its "moral" again points to the virtue of solid, homespun values, without heavy didacticism. Once again much emphasis falls on the physical beauty of the woman, but it must be remembered that the impressionable narrator is a former suitor. The illustrator (J. Frederick Smith) certainly focuses on Celeste, however, although Harry does appear, sitting on the tiger-skin rug with his pitcher of martinis, looking rather like Fred Astair.

Vonnegut's stories frequently feature children, but rarely as centrally as in the rather curious one called "Next Door" (April, 1955, and included in *Welcome to the Monkey House*). Most of his stories snap shut with a brisk turn of events that brings closure, almost like the final couplet of a Shakespearean sonnet. The kind of ambiguity that hovers over the ending of "Next Door" remains rare.

Two families live next door in an old house divided by a thin wall "that passed on, with high fidelity, sounds on either side" (81). On one side the

Leonards live with their eight-year-old son Paul, and on the other the Hargers. The Leonards go off to a movie, leaving Paul playing with his microscope. Soon he hears arguing next door, and the radio, turned on to cover the raised voices. As the shouting increases, so does the volume of the radio. Increasingly frightened, Paul pounds on the wall and begs the Hargers to stop fighting. The radio program is a request show, with messages—the usual thing, "for so-and-so with love from." In a brain wave, Paul decides to call the disc jockey, who, hearing yelling in the background, thinks the boy's parents are fighting. Leaping on the chance to be a public Samaritan, he adds a homily of his own and announces the boy's request: "for Mrs. Lemeul K. Harger, from Mr. Harger—I love you!" In the course of this, all has grown quiet next door, the yelling replaced by "affectionate cooing," and Paul is impressed by the impact of the disc jockey's words. But the Harger message precipitates an explosion. The woman next door is clearly *not* Mrs. Harger.

Paul hears a woman call Harger a "philandering, two-timing, two-bit Lochinvar," and Harger yell, "Charlotte—put down that gun," and then three shots. He rushes into the hall where he and a disheveled woman startle each other equally. She tells him he has not heard a thing, shoves a wad of bills into his trouser pocket, and flees. Totally discombobulated, Paul hides in his bed until police arrive. Harger also appears in the hall, denying he has heard shots. He looks "sharply" at Paul: " 'Have you been playing with your father's guns again, young man?' 'Oh, no, sir!' said Paul, horrified." Moments later Harger adds: " 'I'm sorry I said that about the guns . . . I certainly would have heard any shots in this house. The walls are thin as paper, and I heard nothing.' Paul looked at him gratefully" (85).

At this moment a happily flustered Mrs. Harger bursts in, having heard the radio message. The Hargers retreat to blissful reunion, the police leave, and Paul retires to his bedroom. His returning parents awaken him, and in the course of undressing him discover the bundle in his pocket.

The ball bloomed like a frowsy chrysanthemum, with ones, fives, tens, and lipstick-stained Kleenex for petals. Rising from it, fuddling Paul's young mind, was the pungent scent of perfume.

Paul's father sniffed the air. "What's that smell?" he said.
Paul's mother rolled her eyes. "*Tabu*," she said. (81)

This suggests an atypically mysterious ending. The most logical explanation might be that "Charlotte" has indeed fired the three shots but has missed. Why would Harger be so anxious to cover up for her when the police arrive? To hide an affair? His wife has already left him—she arrives back after this with a large suitcase. To avoid the disclosure that there has been a gun, simply to avoid involvement? Quite possibly. Paul presumably feels frightened enough of Mr. Harger, especially after hearing the gun, to change his account when Harger asks if he has been playing with his father's guns again. Presumably he is young enough and frightened enough to feel threatened by the prospect of the police now turning to question him. It hardly seems rational; nothing suggests that his father has guns or that he has ever played with them, but an eight-year-old's fears in such a situation would hardly be rational. And what, when she flees, makes Charlotte so panicked and anxious to seal Paul's lips, if indeed her shots have missed? And the final question mark at the end of the story remains how the great wad of money in Paul's pocket will be explained.

Paul has had an experience of an adult world, a situation set up in the parents' deciding not to take him to the movies with them, ironically because the subject of the film was thought to be too grown up. As in the previous *Cosmopolitan* stories, there is verbal play, *double entendre*, at the end of the story when the mother says *"Tabu."* Paul has entered a tabu world. That receives emphasis in preceding paragraphs when the mother speaks of the short subject's being about bears, with "cunning little cubs." Paul has certainly been that in the course of the evening. Her blissful ignorance of that emerges with emphasis when she says, "Little boys' pockets! . . . Full of childhood mysteries. . . . A magic pocketful from a fairy princess?" (85).

The portrayal of Paul's reactions and fears in the course of this story works well. The building tension, his fear, his determinedly but distractedly adjusting his microscope in his attempt to escape the terrifying sounds next door, his sudden relief when the disc jockey seems to provide salvation, are all vividly conveyed. The inclusion of the microscope proves an effective device, too. The instrument is designed to explain, to make rational and ordered the minutia of life. The more chaos reigns next door, the more Paul tries to preserve order and rationality by peering more and more intensely into his microscope. But next door represents the outer, adult world, a world of chaos and ambiguity. It cannot always be controlled or put right by "the fantastic speed of modern communications" or the intervention of someone (like the disc jockey) who speaks "like the right hand of Providence itself." "Childhood's mysteries," as the mother calls them, are not all the fairy princesses and enchanted frogs that she imagines, but things of the adult world he is forced to try to comprehend during this evening. That is established early in the story when Paul accepts not going to the movie: "The why of their not wanting him to see certain movies, certain books, certain television shows, was a mystery he respected—even relished a little. He liked the notion of there being more to the world than he could sense" (81). The mysteries of the story's ending, then, are fully appropriate to its subject.

"Hal Irwin's Magic Lamp" (June 1957, collected in *Canary in a Cat House*) has much in common with some of the previous domestic stories. As in "The Foster Portfolio" there is a husband who has made much money in investments and not told his wife, and there are strong echoes of "The Package" in that husband's wanting to equal his erstwhile fraternity brothers and "reward" his wife with new house, car, servants and the rest.

The setting is Indianapolis (Vonnegut's home town) in 1929. Hal Irwin has made half a million in the stock market. He has also made a "magic lamp" by converting an old metal teapot with batteries and a buzzer. The idea is that one can seemingly rub it and push a button on the side so that the buzzer summons a servant. The Irwins don't yet have a servant, and they live modestly, but Mary does not mind this and the two-year-old marriage seems reasonably happy. Hal's dream is to surprise Mary with everything her heart could desire. He hires a cook—devastating to Mary who takes this as a rebuke to her excellent cooking. The cook then becomes his genie, to materialize from a closet at the sound of the buzzer when he takes Mary to the surprise new house. The day when he delivers "the package"—chateau, car, servant, and so on, is a disaster. To Mary it simply means that "Hal had thought he could make her happy with a big, greedy day. But she wasn't crying so much about greediness as she was about how her husband didn't even know her after living with her for two years" (95).

Hal feels his mistake, too.

Hal had diddled himself out of two years, too—and he knew it. Every time he'd wished, he'd felt a little of himself disappear. And he'd realized too late that he'd wished away the good man his wife thought she had. He'd wished his marriage all to smithereens. (95)

Mary has the last wish, that "the lamp would take back the house and the car and everything else" The now-depleted buzzer emits a *"Weep"* sound. Shortly thereafter, the great 1929 stock market crash assures the fulfillment of her wish. The story comes up to "the present" at this point, with the Irwins and their nineteen-year-old daughter Sue visiting the chateau, now for sale again, and eating the sole pear from the tree Mary had planted on that fateful day.

The domestic melodrama in this story resembles that in others, like "A Night for Love" or "Custom Made Bride," in the husband's insensitivity to his wife's feelings, especially in mixing up love and possession. And like "The Package" and "The Powder Blue Dragon," for example, it explodes the notion that the buying of a dream can suddenly create happiness and fulfillment. This story gains much greater significance, however, from the time of its setting. It effectively comments on the widely-held belief of the 1920s that dreams could be bought. The story, though different in tone, might be seen as revisiting the world of F. Scott Fitzgerald, where people rode the market to wealth, and possession became a decadent obsession. Mary's bitter rejection of making her "happy with a big greedy day" could stand as a commentary on the national obsession that led to the Crash and the Great Depression. That is the irony of the last sentence: "Personally, I never forgave her for the Depression" (95). Although Mary has indeed wished for all the trappings of wealth to go away, it is the greed of Hal, his two great fraternity friends, and the other dream buyers, who have sown the seeds of economic collapse. "Hal Irwin's Magic Lamp" looks forward to the later outspoken commentaries on economy-related issues in such novels as *God Bless You, Mr. Rosewater* (1965) and *Jailbird* (1979).

It is interesting to ponder why "Hal Irwin's Magic Lamp" should be the one story collected in *Canary in a Cat House* that was *not* also collected in *Welcome to the Monkey House.* Vonnegut himself, in May 1996, pleaded reasonably enough that "that was a long time ago" and he could not remember, although it was his recollection that the selection of stories for both collections was his. His suggestion was that at the time he probably thought there were the requisite number of stories that were better. One can imagine that some of the precepts of the story, like giving the wife an allowance and generally making decisions for her, though fictionally grounded in the 1920s, were less comfortable to a 1968 audience than they would have been to one in 1957. A lot had changed in that decade. The same might be argued about the caricaturing of Chinese-American English, and the extensive "black dialect" dialogue.

Another interesting feature of this story is its narration. Throughout it appears to be a third-person omniscient narration, although it is told with a conversational informality that is stylistically suggestive of one of the typical first- person stories. Only in the very last sentence is an "I" introduced to suggest the presence of a narrator. It comes as an ironic and humorous touch, and may be the nearest Vonnegut ever comes in his short stories to those moments in the novels, most famously in *Slaughterhouse-Five*, where he abruptly intrudes himself in the first person. A small point of biographical interest in this story is the mention of Irwin's buying a cabin on Lake Maxinkuckee. That is where the Vonnegut family had a summer home, as described in *Fates Worse than Death* (1991).

"The Manned Missiles" (July 1958, and in both collections) is another cold-war story and also, like "Thanasphere," deals with things going wrong with manned space flight. It is very much a "Sputnik era" story, overlaid with the national fears, competitiveness, suspicion and secrecy of those times. Like "Thanasphere" it precedes the actual placing of astronauts in orbit around the earth, reflecting a time when fears of what such an occurrence would mean in military terms were at their highest.

The story is told in epistolary form. That is, the first half of it consists of a letter dictated by Mikhail Ivankov, the father of a Russian spaceman, to Charles Ashland, the father of an American astronaut. The second half is Ashland's reply. Both sons have died on their respective missions. Just how they have been killed is veiled by secrecy and propaganda, but it appears that there has been some sort of collision, shattering their craft and dooming the two dead astronauts to orbit together indefinitely. The two fathers are men of an earlier generation, little understanding the missions of their sons, remembering them rather as the bright young boys whose promise made the fathers proud. While some suspicion of the role of the other son or of the other's national purpose lingers in each, the two fathers are drawn together by their mutual loss. They share an understanding of how this international, even cosmic event has special meaning for them individually. And each is lifted by the commitment of his son, and each strives to express to the other how his son was motivated by a youthful idealism that had nothing to do with politics or nationalism, but with the beauties of space and flight and a belief in ensuing benefits to all humankind.

The letters are effectively written. They may be longer perhaps than is plausible in reality, but they have a simple directness that captures their emotion with dignity. They convincingly portray the impression of two men reaching across a gulf, recognizing the political breach that separates them but striving to touch the common humanity they share. Their emotion shows the more depth for being controlled. They speak of work and family, and tell stories than humanize their sons. Each achieves a kind of simple eloquence.

"The Manned Missiles" obviously represents another rendition of the familiar fathers-and-sons motif in Vonnegut's fiction, and it works well at that level. It also might be seen as another variant of the anti-war story. It certainly reaches past national hostilities to show the shared humanity of people on both sides of the Iron Curtain. As do other of Vonnegut's fictions in various ways, it

uses the dimension of space to shrink the earth and put the political differences
that threaten it into perspective. It is even reminiscent of those college columns
where Vonnegut tries to remind his audience not to stereotype all Germans and
to remember their full human dimensions. Another familiar ingredient is of
political, military and even scientific leaders using technological advances to
destructive ends. The young spacemen have notions of what space exploration
can bring that transcend narrow national and political advantage. Those who
exploit them live in a dehumanizing world of secrecy and suspicion. But the
story is not all pessimistic. It offers the hope that resides in a shared human
condition, in the possibility that if people can talk across the divide they can find
community in the abiding, fundamental human emotions like love of family.

If the *Cosmopolitan* stories can be characterized, particularly as they may
compare with their contemporaries in the *Saturday Evening Post*, it might be
said that they are somewhat more reliant on heightened situations for their plots,
that they make more use of levels of meaning or ambiguity, both verbal and
situational, that their subject matter is more likely to involve some aspect of
conjugal relations, and that there is more likely to be a serious undercurrent,
even a note of pessimism, to what they have to say. That may add up to their
being more sophisticated, or at least aimed at a more sophisticated audience.
The differences are relative, and there is sufficient variety in both groups to
make compelling generalizations difficult. There is more worldliness implicit in
these stories than may be apparent from their plots. The escapist dreams of
contentment in wealth and status invariably prove delusional. Miraculous
ascents into worlds of unrelieved happiness invariably fail, whereas the genuine
marvels of a child's birth or of two fathers' reaching each other across the Iron
Curtain via the spaceflight of their sons offer promise. But didacticism does not
overwhelm these stories. While they invariably tell their message clearly, it is
embodied in a way that enhances rather than detracts from their function of
entertaining. Their moral or ethical messages usually espouse values familiar
and acceptable to their audiences, but ones it may be easy to overlook in the
appeal of the kinds of dreams that beguile Vonnegut's characters.

OTHER MAGAZINES

Between 1952 and 1955, Vonnegut placed a number of stories in magazines
other than the "Big Three" of *Collier's, Saturday Evening Post,* and
Cosmopolitan. Two were placed in *Argosy*, the first, "Souvenir," in the
December 1952 issue, and the second, "A Present for Big Nick," in December
1954. "Souvenir" combines elements of autobiography, cold war anxieties, and
characteristic Vonnegutian values. It tells a story within a story. The framing
story has a postwar, mid-American setting, while the story within is set in the
closing phases of the war in Europe. Joe Bane is a pawnbroker "obsessed by the
game" of acquiring things at the lowest possible cost then selling them for the
highest possible profit. Coming in from a rainstorm he has barely opened up his
shop when a shy, lean young farmer enters. The farmer, Eddie, wants to sell
Bane a jewel-encrusted gold watch for five hundred dollars. Bane quickly
discerns that the watch, with its jewels and chimes, is valuable and sets his heart

on buying it. But not for five hundred dollars. There is an inscription in the back of the watch. Eddie thinks it is German but does not know what it says. Bane makes an impression of it and gives a shoeshine boy a dime to run through the rain to a German shopkeeper and get a translation. Trying to convince Eddie that as war booty the watch could be considered contraband, Bane tries to beat the farmer down to taking a hundred dollars for it. At that point Eddie launches into the story of how he came by the watch.

Eddie and his older brother Buzzer were prisoners of war in a German camp when the war ended. Left untended, the two wonder off and eventually join a stream of refugees who are trying to stay ahead of advancing Russian tanks. They come upon two Germans in a stalled car who, though in civilian clothes, prove to be a general and his subaltern. The refugees' flight halts when they meet another column fleeing Russians from the opposite direction. At this point, while the four are hiding in a farm yard, the two Germans try to persuade the two Americans to take them prisoner and escort them through the Russian lines to Prague, where they can surrender to the Americans. When this fails, they offer to buy the two bothers' uniforms and dog tags. They offer a wad of money, which Buzzer dismisses as "Confederate money," an ornate automatic pistol, and finally the watch. Again the brothers refuse, but then, abruptly, the younger German shoots and kills Buzzer and wounds Eddie. Plunging into the darkened barn, Eddie finds a pitchfork and is able to jump and kill the younger German. He then finds the general dressing in Buzzer's uniform. When the general taunts him by waving the watch at him, Eddie shoots him, strips him, and redresses his dead brother. Later, with the help of four Australians, he "got Buzzer to Prague."

This story finished, Eddie tells Bane the watch has too much sentimental value and that he's changed his mind. Bane rapidly runs his offer up, all the way to the five hundred dollars Eddie had first asked for, but the farmer refuses it and leaves. The shoeshine boy returns and proves he can drive a hard bargain, too, forcing Bane to give him another fifteen cents to reveal what the inscription had said. It reads: " 'To General Heinz Guderian, Chief of the Army General Staff on this day'—and then there was an empty space for the date—'the glorious day on which the last enemy soldier was driven from the sacred soil of the Third German Reich.—ADOLPH HITLER.' " And the shoeshine boy's final taunt is, "Get your money's worth, Pop?" (79).

The autobiographical element here, of course, is in the fact that Vonnegut, too, had been a P.O.W. in a camp in an area liberated by the Russians, and that he too had wandered from the camp and witnessed the flight of refugees. There are descriptions of this situation in *Slaughterhouse-Five* and *Bluebeard*, and in interviews such as the *Playboy* interview reprinted in *Wampeters, Foma, and Granfalloons*. The influence of the contemporary cold war fears shows up most when the younger German says to the Americans of the Russians, "Now you will have to fight them" (77). The view that this was inevitable, and even that the Allies should have kept their advance going and overthrown Stalin's Soviets in a preemptive war was not uncommon at the time. The Russians are the bogeymen in this story, not to be trusted to respect even their allies, though in fact they prove to be too far engrossed in celebrating their victory to hinder the escaping P.O.W.s.

While the opening of "Souvenir" shows traces of Vonnegut's usual sympathy toward the diligent small businessman in his portrayal of Bane's enthusiasm and skill in his "game" of buying and selling, that is quickly overwhelmed by the equally characteristic distaste for those for those who put acquisition ahead of decency. When Bane is willing to beat the needy farmer down to a hundred dollars, even when he knows the asked-for five hundred dollars was already too little—and worse, when he continues to try to hold his bid down even after he has heard Eddie's story—Vonnegut's disapproval is obvious. As in other stories, it is the bright youngster who turns the tables on the pretentious older figure. The shoeshine boy's forcing Bane to ante up another fifteen cents is a small victory but a fitting one, beating the pawnbroker at his own game. His real triumph, though, is that he understands what the inscription means to the worth of the watch, and that revealing it will torture Bane all the more with the knowledge that his initial meanness has cost him something of great value. The boy's final taunt—"Get your money's worth, Pop?"—derides Bane for what his own greed has cost him. The same thing has happened within the war story, of course, where the two Germans try to take everything when the Americans are ready to trade for the watch. It is the general's flaunting of the watch that provokes Eddie into shooting him.

The moral message of this story is probably less heavily loaded than this summary may suggest, and the structuring of the tale, one plot supporting the other, each gaining far more significance than it would have standing on its own, is effective. It seems weaker in its dialogue, particularly that of the two brothers while bantering with each other and with the two Germans, than some other stories of this period. The abrupt and passively understated shootings— "And Buzzer fell dead, shot in the head by the blond"—leave the reader almost at the point of asking, "Wait a minute. What just happened?" There also remains a question about motivation. What is the emergency that prompts Eddie to sell a watch that means so much to him as a memento of his dead brother? If Eddie felt such an overwhelming need for five hundred dollars that he was willing to sell the watch in the first place, how has that need evaporated so easily at the end? Telling the story to Bane may remind Eddie again of his attachment to the watch, but could the balance of need and sentiment have shifted so dramatically? Finally, the brief mention that "we got Buzzer to Prague" does not resolve itself easily. How do Eddie and the Australians convey the corpse all the way to Prague?

"A Present for Big Nick" is a Christmas story, as emphasized in its earlier draft title, "Saint Big Nick." That is a situation that affords Vonnegut the opportunity to return to some themes about values and the use of children to bring down the pompous and bogus. Big Nick of the title is a Chicago gangster said to be the latest heir to the power of Al Capone. Bernie O'Hare, formerly the Shenandoah Blaster, was a middle weight controlled by Nick and now, since an eye injury, works as one of his bodyguards. With his wife Wanda and son Willy, Bernie shops for a Christmas present for Big Nick. In the store he runs into another couple who work for Nick with their son, Richard. Both couples are trying to find something tasteless, preferably something that glows in the dark, as a gift for their boss. Both boys, it turns out, are terrified of store Santa Clauses because of Nick's annual Christmas party. His habit is to dress as a

Santa, hand out presents, and use the occasion to pump the children for what their parents may have said about their boss at home. It is a ritual the wives and children dread equally, and which the employee husbands endure solely because it enables them to keep better jobs than they would otherwise have had.

At the party all goes as usual, and Willy remembers the proper responses to Nick's question about what his parents think of him. But then Willy asks for a rag to wipe off the boat Nick has just given him. When Nick demands to know why, he says it is because his and Richard's mothers have said everything Nick touches is bloody and dirty. The resulting confrontation leads to Bernie's punching Santa Claus Nick into the Christmas tree, and Nick's ordering everyone out with threats to have them killed, hurling their gifts after them. When the excited boys continue to taunt Nick for having no friends, he runs to fetch more presents to prove that he does. The second one he opens is from anonymous admirers in Italy, and when he pulls the ribbon it explodes, killing him.

The story is completely light-hearted in tone. Big Nick is no more than a cartoon figure, with his Edward G. Robinson gangster dialect, his outbursts of " 'You're all dead,' " and his fixture cigar. His valuation of gifts by how much they cost and whether they glow in the dark and his terrorizing of the children complete his portrait as a hyperbolic inversion of the Christmas spirit. The other characters are equally typecast, as befits this kind of comedy. The dialogue is humorous, too. When Santa Claus demands some gratitude from Richard, the boy always responds with Big Nick's own "T'anks," as if it were a special word to be used for the occasion. Nick boasts of the "hunnerd and twenny-four-fifty" train he will give Richard, but when it is mislaid he demands, " 'Now, where'd I put that stinkin' train.' " One little girl interrupts when things start to unravel to declare that her father " 'says kissing Santa Claus isn't any worse than kissing the dog. . . . I kiss the dog all the time and I never get sick,' " she concludes (72). Even Nick's death at the end is slapstick, a cartoon ending. It does not transform the tone of a story where the worms turn, the bully gets his comeuppance, and children expose the villain. Big Nick, as villain, may be Old Nick masquerading as Saint Nick, but he remains only the stuff of Christmas pantomimes.

Another play on names in this story is of interest. Bernie, or Bernard, O'Hare is the name of one of Vonnegut's old friends from the Second World War, later an attorney in Pennsylvania. As a joke Vonnegut uses that name several times in his fiction. Bernard B. O'Hare is the self-righteous super-patriot who hunts down Howard Campbell in *Mother Night* (1962); as Bernard V. O'Hare he appears as himself in *Slaughterhouse-Five* (1969); and the name recurs in *Slapstick* (1976) as that of the pilot of the Presidential helicopter.

In April of 1953, Vonnegut published two stories, one in the *Cape Cod Compass* and the other in *Galaxy Science Fiction* magazine. The former, "The Cruise of the Jolly Roger," has aspects of a local-color story for a regional magazine promoting Cape Cod; this, of course, was at a time when Vonnegut was living on the Cape. Another touch of biography to this story is in the central character's being a returning army veteran. The story begins with a simple declaration: "During the Great Depression, Nathan Durant was homeless until he found a home in the United States Army" (7). Seventeen years later, with the rank of major, he is invalided out after sustaining injuries in Korea. Another man in hospital sustains himself with dreams of the boat he will buy when he recovers. "For want of exciting peacetime dreams of his own, for want of a home or family or civilian friends, Durant borrowed his neighbor's dream" (7). He buys an old cabin cruiser, at the suggestion of children on the dock names it "The Jolly Roger," and sets off on a destinationless journey.

Out of the only role to have given his life purpose, Durant lacks a sense of who he is or how he relates to others. During a stop in Chatham he catches the eye of an attractive women, and recalls how "in the old days, about to leave on a dangerous mission, he and the woman might have strolled off together. Women had once treated him like a small boy with special permission to eat icing off cakes. But the woman looked away without interest. He was nobody and nothing" (7-8). Later a tourist wants to photograph him, asking if he is one of the resident artists. Still later, he joins more comfortably with three young men and a woman who *are* artists, and despite feeling excluded from their arty talk, enjoys being in a group again. And he likes the woman, who seems sensitive. When they ask him about his wounds he reluctantly begins to tell them. They listen respectfully at first, but he finds the subject hard to come to grips with, launches into a whole military history, and the conversation dies.

Durant next stops at a small fishing village where, he remembers, a buddy who had died beside him in the Second World War had lived. His inquiries finally lead him to Annie, a lawyer's secretary, who remembers the family of George Pefko. They were a poor family who had come to pick cranberries and stayed on in a summer cottage. Annie tells Durant all war dead in the village are commemorated in named squares—though the square may be no more than a traffic circle or a small plot. She duly leads them to George Pefko Memorial Square. Durant is dismissive of this gesture, but then the schoolchildrens' Memorial Day parade comes through, stopping to put flowers at each of the memorial plaques. Durant agrees that this is a lovely thing to do, but asks, "What does it mean?" A teacher prompts that they are "paying homage to one of the fallen valiant who selflessly gave his life," but the small boy placing the flowers has another answer. "He died fighting so we could be free and safe. And we're thanking him with flowers, because it was a nice thing to do. . . . Everybody knows that." Durant takes in "the beauty and the importance of a village at peace," and concludes, "This *is* what war is about, isn't it. This" (14). And the story closes with his taking Annie off to lunch.

The recurrent themes of dreams and identities have a central—and obvious—place in this story. Vonnegut had experienced the shock of battle and the trauma of having been a prisoner of war, had endured its privations (he lost forty-one pounds in captivity), and the difficulty of re-entering a civilian world. Like Durant he knew the difficulty of talking about his experience. In the firebombing of Dresden he thought he had seen a horror of historical proportions, only to find on his return that it had been hushed up and no one knew what he was talking about.[9] So he well understood the difficulty of men coming home from war, especially long-term or disabled soldiers, in rediscovering or recreating roles for themselves in a civilian world that understands little of the one they have just left. This was, after all, the era of the Korean War, a war with little of the glamour or moral clarity the public often perceived in the Second World War. Durant's psychological healing begins only after he completes his physical recovery. He borrows a comrade's dream. He takes a name from a children's story, suggested by children, for his boat. When the young artists derisively suggest that if he had a dog he would name it Spot, he replies with some embarrassment, "Seems like a perfectly good name for a dog." Even at the end, the definition he accepts for why his friend has died—and he himself has been nearly killed—is that of a child. These references to childhood emphasize his painful growth from a new beginning. The three encounters with women work similarly, each less associated with the stereotypical soldier's response, until the slow building of a friendship of equals with Annie promised at the end.

Readers familiar with Vonnegut may be surprised at the statements of "what war is all about" that come in the conclusion, and feel that they look surprisingly jingoistic in one who has been so often an outspoken opponent of war and militarism. In the context of finding a meaning in what George Pefko or any other soldier may have died for, the justification may not be hard to understand. But put in the terms Durant chooses—"This *is* what war is about"—it seems more problematical. The boy offers his explanation after the teacher's more conventional justification falls flat. "Tom looked at her blankly." The boy Tom's statement, stripped of patriotic flourishes, speaks modestly of the soldier's dying "so we could be safe and free," and thanks him "with flowers, because it was a nice thing to do." Nothing said here about flags or making the world safe for democracy. The reiterated "this" that war is about remains the simple, quiet life of a small village. If "The Cruise of the Jolly Roger" does represent a departure from other statements Vonnegut has made about war, it proves only a qualified one, and certainly not one couched in the jingoistic language of the super-patriot that would represent a real contradiction. And even in moments such as voicing his opposition to the Vietnam War, Vonnegut has never expressed anything but respect for the sacrifices of the men who fought and died or were captured beside him in war.

Once again this is a story with an interesting name: "Pefko" crops up again in later fiction. A Francine Pefko makes her appearance in *Cat's Cradle*, and assumes a larger role in *Breakfast of Champions*, where there is another Pefko, her husband Robert.

The other April 1953 story was the first of two Vonnegut was to publish in *Galaxy Science Fiction.* "Unready to Wear" is both inventive and a fine example of Vonnegut's comedic uses of science fiction, and it was subsequently reprinted in both *Canary in a Cat House* and *Welcome to the Monkey House.* It presents a world in which people have learned, thanks to a Professor Konigswasser, how to escape their bodies. Such people are called amphibians, in that they are like the first creatures that learned how to leave the water and live on land. Ironically, Professor Konigswasser (whose name means king's water) has discovered how to do this by walking *into* water. Ever absent-minded—in fact, his absent-mindedness is seen as the first step to his leaving his body—he has walked into a lake. Later he walks back out, sees a rescue team resuscitating a decrepit body and realizes it is his. To spare people inconvenience he gets back into the body and takes it home. But from then on he mostly leaves it in a closet, keeping it on low maintenance. He writes a book on how to do this and soon has millions of followers, among them the narrator of this story and his wife Madge. The amphibians have storehouses where bodies, usually just the best, are kept for people to check out whenever they want to exist in a body again. One such occasion is the annual Pioneer's Day Parade for which old Konigswasser always checks out the body of a tall, blond, and incredibly strong cowboy. Madge, when she first became amphibian, spent a lot of time trying out the body of a platinum blonde burlesque queen.

A considerable number of the human population has resisted becoming amphibian, however, and these the narrator refers to as the enemy. Actually, the amphibians are not much bothered by the enemy, but those corporeal folks feel threatened by the amphibians, their freedom and their invisibility. They have all kinds of detection devices, but they cannot detect amphibians who, unless they borrow bodies, are simply spirits. One day Madge and the narrator go over to observe the enemy, as they sometimes do, just to see the latest fashions and update the bodies in their storage centers. Lo and behold, the humans have built an elaborate storage center. Madge decides the enemy have seen the light and are preparing to become amphibians. The narrator remains more wary, but Madge spots a magnificent body—"six feet tall and built like a goddess. . . . The body had copper-colored skin, chartreuse hair and fingernails, and a gold lame evening gown" (107). Madge cannot resist, but it proves a trap, because the ankles are tied so that an amphibian cannot take the few steps that are necessary to leave a body. To try to save her the narrator enters the adjacent body of "a blond, male giant in a pale blue field marshall's uniform," but his ankles are also tied.

The human beings put the two trapped amphibians on public trial on the charge of desertion. The general who presides rails at them for abandoning responsibility and the cause of progress. The amphibians counter that humans allow fear, of pain or privation to their bodies, to rule their lives. When the narrator starts to describe the steps to become an amphibian and leave worry and fear behind, the authorities cut off television and halt the trial. They have long since banned Konigswasser's book. Convicted, the amphibians counter that this will mean war, that other amphibians surround the building, and that if the two of them are not released amphibians will enter the humans' bodies and march them off the edge of a cliff. This, incidentally, would be impossible, since only one person can inhabit a body at a time. The bluff works, and they escape the bodies and human capture, but not before Madge has left instructions for the copper-colored-chartreuse-haired body to be mailed to her local storage center. And so life for the amphibians returns to normal.

All comic spoof, "Unready to Wear" nevertheless finds ways to touch on some serious social issues. One of the concerns it incorporates, and to which Vonnegut returns repeatedly, is that of overpopulation, with visions of a future when the world is overcrowded and there simply are not the resources to meet the needs of all those human mammals. " 'Trouble with the world,' said Konigswasser, 'isn't too many people—it's too many bodies' " (101). "Amphibiousness" is not a serious solution, but it calls attention to the problem, which is one of the major issues facing humankind that it seems least disposed to confront. Similarly, Vonnegut draws attention to the frequency with which what people would like to do comes into conflict with the demands of the body—or is shaped by the body's appetites, or is made impossible by the body's limitations. In a comic way he draws attention to the implications of the old saying, "The spirit is willing but the flesh is weak." There is also another rendition of the identity theme, the question of "what are people for?" The narrator has been in the pay toilet business—one for which, obviously, there is no demand among amphibians. He speaks of how some people never get over the habit of worrying about their jobs, even after they have become amphibian, and have trouble defining themselves without such things.

In this respect, bodies are like jobs. They it is that often give identity, not the person within. Konigswasser is old and decrepit, the stereotype of the absent-minded professor, but he has a childlike curiosity that leads to invention. "As a matter of fact," says the narrator, "it's a respectful thing to say that somebody is childish in certain ways, because it's people like that who seem to get all the big ideas" (101). Vonnegut will pursue that line with characters like the creative genius Dr. Felix Hoenikker in *Cat's Cradle*. And even Konigswasser delights in assuming the body of the husky cowboy and crushing beercans with his fingers. Women, we are told, relate identity even more to the body, and delight in trying new bodies, and costuming them and making them up like oversized dolls. But bodies are the source of most human problems. "The moment you get in, chemistry takes over—glands making you excitable or ready to fight or hungry or mad or affectionate, or—well, you never know *what's* going to happen next" (101). This is the first instance of Vonnegut's speaking of people being controlled by chemicals, something that he returns to quite often in later fiction. It is a major component of the plot of *Breakfast of Champions* and *Slapstick*, where chemicals' control of human behavior is seen as sometimes reducing them almost to being robots. That also touches on the issue of free will, and how much of it humans actually enjoy, which is another perennial with Vonnegut.

"Unready to Wear" works well with its comfortable narration in the first person and its reveling in its own implausibility. Its creator rather resembles Konigswasser (who may even be seen as another German-named author-surrogate within a story) in his adolescent irreverence for the determined conditions of existence and the imagination to explore, if only in fun, what might happen if they were changed. This shows the same imagination that can conceive water that freezes at room temperature in *Cat's Cradle*, variable gravity in *Slapstick*, or *chronosynclastic infundibula* in *The Sirens of Titan*. One may even see a resemblance between Konigswasser's amphibian and the disembodied fictional character that an author creates. While its subjects are comically treated, this story may stand as another example of Eliot Rosewater's grounds for complimenting science fiction writers in *God Bless You, Mr. Rosewater*: "You're the only ones who'll talk about the *really* terrific changes going on" (13).

The other story in *Galaxy Science Fiction* (January 1954, included in *Canary in a Cat House* and *Welcome to the Monkey House* with the new title, "Tomorrow and Tomorrow and Tomorrow") similarly gives comic treatment to serious social issues, returning in its primary focus to the one of overpopulation. Set in 2185 A.D., "The Big Trip Up Yonder" depicts a world where the invention of anti-gerasone has enabled people to stop the aging process. That results in overpopulation and the rationing of food and space. Life becomes miserable for most people, yet they remain reluctant to leave it, to abandon their anti-gerasone and take "The Big Trip Up Yonder." Lou and Emerald Ford share their grandfather's apartment with twenty-three other relatives. The 172-year-old Gramps rules the household ruthlessly, using the tyranny of his will, which determines who will succeed to his bedroom and who meanwhile will sleep on the prized daybed. Others sleep crowded on mattresses on the floor. Rivalries for favor in Gamps's eyes or to end his rule lead to subterfuges like attempts to dilute his anti-gerasone, and eventually one of his own where he vanishes and appears to leave a suicide note dividing his belongings equally among all his descendants. This precipitates a riot among them that leads to their all being arrested. At the end Lou and Em are luxuriating in private eight-by-four prison cells with their own wash basins and hiring a good attorney to get them the longest sentence possible. And Gramps retains his apartment, which is private at last, and writes off for the new *Super*-anti-gerasone, which not only stops aging but enables the user to recover youth.

Incidental humor abounds in this story, in addition to the satirical treatment of overpopulation. It satirizes the advertising world's promotion of the desire among people to look young and alike: "Wouldn't you pay $5,000 to be indistinguishable from everybody else?" the *Super*-anti-gerasone commercial asks. Even soap operas are satirized; "The McGarvey Family" has been running for at least 102 years. The situation in Gramps's apartment and the childish shenanigans of the five generations trapped there are sheer slapstick. The jailer threatens the celebrating family inmates with eviction if they do not keep quiet, and with lifelong exclusion if they ever disclose how good conditions are in prison. The box number for *Super*-anti-gerasone is 500,000! The location of the manufacturer, inevitably, is Schenectady again, and Wyandotte College makes a reappearance. Only Gramps gets to eat *real* food; the rest get "buckwheat-type processed sawdust cakes" or "egg-type processed seaweed." And presumably because time has lost meaning, the Indianapolis 500 has become the 5000-mile Speedway Race.

The two *Galaxy Science Fiction* stories work well because they give Vonnegut's imagination free rein. The Cassandra in Vonnegut that always wants to warn, to alert his readership to what he sees as "real" issues confronting society, can speak out, but so can the comedian, the entertainer, who enjoys comic situations and childlike deconstructions of traditional assumptions about life. He finds a comfortable narrative voice in these pieces, and he can use science-fictional terms and futuristic settings with a comic hyperbole that banishes resistance to their implausibility. The plots are amusing and retain their own element of suspense that sustains interest. These are stories that prefigure some of the earlier novels like *The Sirens of Titan* and *Cat's Cradle*, where the same combination of science fiction tropes and comic hyperbole produces energetic novels that both entertain and educate.

Another magazine in which Vonnegut published during this period was *Ladies Home Journal*. "D.P." appeared in the August 1953 edition, and was subsequently reprinted in both of the collections. Set in Germany soon after the Second World War, ir depicts an orphanage for displaced children in a village overlooking the Rhine that houses a lone black child. He has been given the name Karl Heinz, but the villagers call him Joe after the legendary heavyweight champion, Joe Louis. His rumored origins are the predictable ones, that he had a German mother and an African-American soldier for a father, but no one knows with certainty. The villagers' calls to him are stereotypical though well intentioned, and they make him self-conscious about his difference. The nuns who run the school try to protect him as well as answering his questions by explaining that his father comes from far across the sea where there are many other brown people.

One day the villagers tell him his father has come, and looking up the hill where they have indicated he does indeed see a large black man. The nun refuses to let Joe go to him, but he sneaks back at night and encounters the American army sergeant whom he immediately claims as "Papa." These events occur before the integration of U.S. Army units, and Joe has stumbled into a Negro Company. The soldiers who gather around are astonished to find a black child who speaks only German in this setting. As the sergeant says, " 'this here's the most displaced little old person I *ever* saw.' " A German-speaking lieutenant translates, and eventually he and the sergeant drive Joe back to the orphanage, but not before the soldiers, with the legendary G.I. generosity, have given him a watch, a knife, a carton of (chocolate) D-bars, and an army hat. Joe has had to be pried loose from the sergeant, whom he still regards as his father. When next morning other skeptical children ask him how he knows the sergeant was not fooling him, he has his answer.

"Because he cried when he left me," said Joe simply. "And he promised to take me back home across the water as fast as he could." He smiled airily. "Not like the river, Peter— across more water than you've *ever* seen. He promised and then I let him go." (84)

The device of having the end of the story come in dialogue between the children the next morning, rather than in narrative description of how Joe, resolutely clinging to the sergeant, wrung the promise from a weeping soldier, provides a saving touch. This is an emotional story with a subject that invites lapses into excessive sentimentality. In that sense, and in aspects of its content, it appears akin to "Adam," which was published just six months later in *Cosmopolitan*. In both cases, the emotional intensity seems justified by the subject, and the handling of it to stay on the safe side of the boundary of bathos. This story comes nearest to sentimentality in the reactions of the soldiers to Joe. But does one really doubt the depth of emotional reaction there would be in African-American soldiers in finding a lone black child in these circumstances, especially one who so instantly and emphatically identifies with them? The affection and generosity of Second World War American soldiers toward children of any kind was of this order, as the present writer can attest. The use of the "Joe Louis" label might seem to be loading the emotional dice here, but can actually be seen to work in another, more important way. When the German villagers call him Joe Louis it accords with their efforts to make him "light up" and show his white teeth—well meaning, perhaps, but undeniably predicated upon a stereotypical perception of black Americans of his time. It apparently embarrasses the nun, and without his really understanding why, it causes Joe himself uneasiness. At the least it calls attention to his difference, and his feeling that he belongs somewhere else with other people. With the black American soldiers, the label, surprising to them in this child who speaks only German, turns around and becomes a badge of identification and pride.

Just as "Adam" comments powerfully upon the Holocaust without ever once saying specifically that its main characters are Jewish, "D.P." makes some powerful social comment by understatement and indirection. In the first place, the existence—and the plight—of the millions of Displaced Persons, as they were officially designated, adrift in Europe after the Second World War, is a circumstance easily forgotten or simply not known decades after the war. Vonnegut saw and felt it, both in the refugees flocking into Dresden from the East before the fateful air raid, and in the days following the collapse of his prison camp when he wandered among such human flotsam, as he recounts in interviews and in fiction such as the novel *Bluebeard.* For Vonnegut the D.P. represents an embodiment of the human condition—or at least the human condition as it exists all too frequently—of people not knowing where they belong, what they are here for, their purpose or their identity. The other social group on whom he makes comment is, of course, the Negro Company, the black soldiers in a segregated army. They remain as much alone and stereotyped in their larger community as does Joe in his. They, too, are still D.P.s within the army and in American society as a whole at this stage in history.

"D.P." brings together many of the characteristic features of Vonnegut's stories in the earlier nineteen-fifties: identity, children, the father-son relationship, the war and its human consequences, language and communication, and the sustaining dream, among others. Soldiers and veterans occur quite frequently in the stories of this section, another manifestation of Vonnegut's drawing on personal experience for material. In "Deer in the Works" (*Esquire*, April, 1955, and both collections) he draws on his civilian experience as journalist and as public relations writer.

The protagonist in "Deer in the Works," David Potter, runs a weekly newspaper in the small town of Dorset, which lies ten miles from Ilium. David has gone to the Ilium Works of the Federal Apparatus Corporation looking for a job; the company needs employees, having just won a large new defense contract. "Any kind of writing," he says. "You mean advertising and sales promotion," says his interviewer, in the second hint that this career change is a mistake. David presses ahead, pleased at the prospect of security and a steady one hundred and ten dollars a week. As he points out, his problem has been twins—two sets.

David calls Nan, his wife, from the plant. Stunned by his unexpected move, she points out that the paper has done well, and argues that the family will not be the happier for his salary if it entails work for which he has no enthusiasm. David's confidence in his decision undergoes further erosion when he reviews a graph of average salaries over a career, with an "x" to mark where he stands, and his future charted out for him. He feels resentment when told about the rating sheet, on which he will be rated, and will rate others, on everything such as "appearance, loyalty, promptness, initiative, cooperativeness." The impersonality of the giant corporation appalls him. When he finally reports to the department where he will work, his interview is interrupted by an event that demands coverage for the works paper. With the only staff writer off on another assignment, David is given directions and told he will be met at a location where a deer has somehow invaded the works grounds. David sets off, but the plant seems so vast, the streets and buildings so much alike, the numbers so baffling, and the directions so exasperating that he becomes increasingly, desperately confused. Finally, more by luck than navigation, he arrives at a sports field near the fence where a crowd led by his boss, a policeman with a drawn revolver, and the cameraman, confront a frightened deer. Panicked by the camera flashes, the deer races toward the fence. Impulsively, David releases the gate. The deer flees into the woods, and after a second's hesitation, David follows it, shuts the gate behind him, and does not look back.

Quite obviously, this story has a lot to do with Vonnegut's own experience as a public relations writer for General Electric. As in the novel *Player Piano*, the Ilium works substitutes for the G.E. plant in Schenectady, New York. Vonnegut disliked much PR work and felt a kinship with the journalists he and his colleagues were often called upon to mislead or give a company "spin" to in press briefings.[10] His reason for taking that job is essentially the one David offers in the story—the need for a steady job to support his family. Having escaped to Cape Cod from G.E. through his story writing, Vonnegut must have felt something like David shutting the gate behind him and heading into the woods. The flavor of this story resembles that of *Player Piano*, where Paul Proteus feels dehumanized by the vast impersonality and corporate culture of the Ilium Works. There exists the same note of nostalgia for a time when it must have been better, felt by Proteus in the novel when he enters Plant 58, a museum-like old building. In the story the old worker who has a fifty-year button and who points out that such length of service will not be possible any more, conveys the decline into impersonality.

The title underscores the central premise of the story, namely, the parallel between the plights of the deer and of David caught inside this frighteningly incomprehensible world. David's mounting confusion as he tries to find his way equates convincingly with the bafflement a wild creature must feel caught in such an alien industrial environment. But the story avoids such anthropomorphism by having the sensations all located in the consciousness of the man, while the deer itself makes only the briefest appearance at the end.

"Deer in the Works" provides another example of how some of Vonnegut's most successful descriptions, and dialogue, come in the depiction of people—and especially men—in the workplace. In behalf of the women characters, it must be noted that they frequently show a calmer wisdom and stabilizing influence in his stories, just as Nan exhibits better judgment than her husband's in this one. Another feature of this story characteristic of Vonnegut is his addition, when including "Deer in the Works" in *Welcome to the Monkey House*, of the simple sentence "It was summer" in the first paragraph. That conforms to his workman-like insistence that the first paragraph of a story should tell the reader "where" and "when."[11] It also lays the groundwork for the later sentence that refers to the "chilly gust from the air-conditioned interior" released every time applicants from the line outside are admitted.

The late nineteen-fifties saw a marked decline in Kurt Vonnegut's short story production. Seven stories published in 1954 dwindled to four in 1955, three in 1956, two in 1957, one in 1958, none in 1959, and one in 1960. After that came a spurt of story publication in the early nineteen-sixties, but by then the transition to books had begun. What caused this reduction in the rate of publication? Naturally, a number of factors contributed. One was the general decline in the magazine market, primarily because of the impact of television. Not only did some of the magazines that had been important markets for Vonnegut's stories, like the *Saturday Evening Post* and *Collier's*, eventually go out of business, some began to modify their formats, using fewer stories. The decline in readership under the impact of television led to a drop in circulation, which in turn led to a decline in advertising revenue. As advertising moved to television, the same money that had once helped fund short story writing now increasingly went to sit-com scripts and game shows. Vonnegut's publications in the early nineteen-sixties demonstrated that the short story market did not simply collapse overnight, but it did become progressively smaller and more difficult.

Vonnegut was also beginning to direct some of his writing energies elsewhere. He relates how at a party he ran into his old friend Knox Burger who asked why he had not written another novel. He replied that he had an idea for one, and he and the editor went into an adjoining room where he dreamed up on the spot the plot for what became *The Sirens of Titan*.[12] That novel appeared in 1959, the year in which there were no short stories, and despite the book's being written "very cheerfully and very quickly . . . Almost automatic," it obviously would have taken time and energy away from the writing of short stories (Bellamy and Casey, *Conversations*, 159).

The Sirens of Titan was a paperback original, and Vonnegut's discovery that he could obtain good advances for paperbacks turned his attention to that form. "I could get $3,000 immediately for a paperback original, and I always needed money right away, and no hardcover publisher would let me have it."[13] Knox Burger had by this time become an editor at Gold Medal Books, and Vonnegut entered into a contract there which led to the publication of *Canary in a Cat House* in 1961 and *Mother Night*, which was copyrighted in 1961 but which did not actually appear until February of 1962. With these publications, the transition to the longer form was well under way, and by 1965 two more novels (*Cat's Cradle* in 1963 and *God Bless You, Mr. Rosewater* in 1965) had followed, both in hardcover.

There were also events in Vonnegut's personal life that would inevitably impact upon his writing. On October 1, 1957, his father died. Then, in 1958, came the double tragedy of the deaths of his sister, Alice, and her husband, James C. Adams. Alice was close to death from cancer when word came that her husband had been killed in the crash of a New York commuter train. Vonnegut and his brother Bernard tried to keep news of James's death from Alice, but an ambulatory patient passed her a copy of the New York *Daily News* that headlined the story and listed the casualties. Alice died within forty-eight hours, leaving four children. Kurt and Jane took in the four children, and eventually adopted the three older ones (*Slapstick*, 11–14). The compound of emotional distress, dramatically altered family life, increased responsibility, and greater financial burdens produced by these events is hard to estimate.

As the demands on his finances increased and the short story market declined, Vonnegut also turned to other activities to supplement his income. In the mid-1950s he did free-lance public relations writing, including quite a lot for the K. Thomas Chirurgy advertising agency in Boston. This was an industrial account, so the work was familiar, being similar to that with which he had gained experience at General Electric. It was while he was leaving the agency's offices one day that he happened to see a truck loaded with what looked like large Easter eggs pass by. These were the early Saab automobiles, similar in size and general contours to the Volkswagen "Beetle." When the truck pulled into a service station, Vonnegut approached the driver, made inquiries, and soon became one of the first Saab dealers in the United States. He relates that they sold mostly as second cars, which in those days meant that they became the wife's car, and that their drivers had difficulty remembering that this was a two-stroke engine that required a mix of oil and gasoline, like a lawnmower or snow blower. The result was that all too often the oil was forgotten, with disastrous results. In the end the company decided to combine their dealerships with Volvo, which required much more expensive facilities. At that point Vonnegut gave up this particular venture. But it remains illustrative of the initiative he exercised in seeking ways to supplement the family income. At one point he even represented himself as a sculptor and sold a sculpture to a motel near Boston's Logan Airport for a thousand dollars.[14]

Regardless of what Vonnegut's aspirations for writing books might have been, it appears that circumstances contributed considerably to *when* that transition came about. Burger's happy suggestion nudged Vonnegut into writing another novel after a hiatus of over seven years, and then the rewards of paperback contracts led on to others. Perhaps, then, the decline in the short story market had some silver lining tucked away in its very gloomy dark cloud, in positively influencing the timing, if not the fact, of Vonnegut's turning again to the form in which he was to ultimately achieve renown. He was not through with the short story, however. As has been mentioned, more stories appeared in the early 1960s, plus the two collections, and the short story was to continue to play an important part in the manner and the content of his novels.

NOTES

1. Asa B. Pieratt, Julie Huffman-klinkowitz and Jerome Klinkowitz, *Kurt Vonnegut: A Comprehensive Bibliography* (Hamden, CT: The Shoestring Press/Archon Books, 1987), 1–2.

2. Richard Todd, "The Masks of Kurt Vonnegut," in William Rodney Allen, *Conversations with Kurt Vonnegut* (Jackson: University Press of Mississippi, 1988), 35. (Hereafter cited as *Conversations.*)

3. *Paris Review* Interview, *Conversations*, 189.

4. The teaser written across the heading illustration reads: "Go out with dames? Not Bert. He was . . . 'The Boy Who Hated Girls.' " This enticement seems even more off the mark than the title!

5. Stanley Schatt, *Kurt Vonnegut, Jr.* (Boston: Twayne Publishers, 1976), 127.

6. Kurt Vonnegut, speaking to an audience at Teikyo Marycrest University, Davenport, Iowa, April 4, 1989.

7. In the Introduction added to *Mother Night* in 1966, Vonnegut directly addresses various aspects of being of German stock in the era of the Third Reich and the Second World War. His prewar experience of Nazis "was limited. There were some vile and nasty native American Fascists in my home town of Indianapolis during the thirties, and somebody slipped me a copy of *The Protocols of the Elders of Zion*, I remember, which was supposed to be the Jews' secret plan for taking over the world" (v). He goes on: "So much for the Nazis and me. If I'd been born in Germany, I suppose I would have *been* a Nazi, bopping Jews and gypsies and Poles around, leaving boots sticking out of snowbanks, warming myself with my secretly virtuous insides" (vii). In his interview with the *Paris Review* he also mentions that when he was captured and tried out his few words of German, his guards "asked me if I was of German ancestry, and I said, 'Yes.' They wanted to know why I was making war against my brothers. . . . I honestly found the question ignorant and comical" (Allen, *Conversations*, 172).

8. Several of Vonnegut's novels contain writers who may be seen as representing the author or some aspect of him. Kilgore Trout stands out as an example. There is a writer in *Player Piano* who will *not* write what the market demands whose wife resorts to prostitution to support them, implying that for the writer to pander to market demand would be a form of prostitution, too. In *Mother Night,* the "Editor's Note" says of Howard Campbell, "To say that he was a writer is to say that the demands of art alone were enough to make him lie, and to lie without seeing any harm in it" (ix).

9. "I went down to the newspaper office . . . and looked to find what they had about Dresden. There was an item about half an inch long. . . . And so I figured, well, this really was the most minor sort of detail in World War II . . . Then a book by David Irving was published about Dresden, saying it was the largest massacre in European history. I said, By God, I saw something after all!" (*Conversations*, 175).

10. Conversation between the author, Marc Leeds, Ollie Lyon and Kurt Vonnegut, in the home of Mr. Lyon, Lexington, Kentucky, October 31, 1993.

11. In a 1980 interview with Charles Reilly, Vonnegut said, "When I teach now I frequently get annoyed when I get four paragraphs into a story and still don't know what city, or even what century, the characters are in. I have a right to be annoyed too. A reader has a right, and a need, to learn immediately what sort of people he's encountering, what sort of locale they're in, what they do for a living, whether they're rich or poor—all of these things make subsequent information that much more marvelous" (*Conversations*, 197).

12. Richard Todd recounts the following account of the genesis of *The Sirens of Titan*: "It began, Vonnegut said, at a party, when a publishing house editor asked, 'Why don't you write another book?' Vonnegut said, 'Well, I have an idea for one.' 'Tell me about it,' said the editor, and they went into a bedroom. 'I had no idea at all for a book,' Vonnegut recalls, 'but I started talking and told him the story of *Sirens of Titan* [sic]. Every mother's favorite child is the one that's delivered by natural childbirth. *Sirens of Titan* was that kind of book' "(*Conversations*, 35).

13. *Playboy* interview with David Standish, 1973 (*Conversations*, 106). In his interview with Robert Scholes in the same collection Vonnegut notes that payment did not have to wait on the completed manuscript. "In those days if you had published something you could go to a paperback house and give them one chapter and an outline and they would give you money which would pay your grocery bill, anyway" (129).

14. Vonnegut has recounted both the Saab dealership and the selling of the sculpture several times. My account of the Saab dealership relies on conversation with him. Richard Todd notes both ventures (*Conversations*, 35).

5

The Later Stories: 1960–1963

As Vonnegut returned to publishing short stories in 1960 it was mainly with some of the same magazines that he had been appearing in after *Collier's*, notably the *Saturday Evening Post*, but also *Cosmopolitan* and *Ladies Home Journal*. It was in the last-named that the sole story of 1960 appeared. "Long Walk to Forever"(August 1960, and *Welcome to the Monkey House*) is the largely autobiographical story that Vonnegut apologizes for in the Preface to *Welcome to the Monkey House* :

In honor of the marriage that worked, I include in this collection a sickeningly slick love story from *The Ladies Home Journal*, God help us, entitled by them. "The Long Walk to Forever." The title I gave it, I think, was "Hell to Get Along With." It describes an afternoon I spent with my wife-to-be. Shame, shame, to have lived scenes from a woman's magazine. (xi)

Vonnegut chooses the name Newt for the autobiographical figure in this story, a private in the Artillery who has gone absent without leave (A.W.O.L.) in order to come home to see Catharine, whom he had known since childhood and who has just become engaged. (In *Cat's Cradle*, Vonnegut again chooses the name Newt for a semi-autobiographical character. That Newt is a midget, resembling Vonnegut in being the youngest in a triangle of three children and in some other comically distorted respects.) Newt surprises Catharine and persuades her to go for a walk with him. She is resistant at every step, reluctant to be drawn into discussing her fiancé, protesting when Newt professes to love her, dawdling rather than keeping walking. But their old friendship runs deep, and Catharine seems vulnerable, impressed that Newt would risk so much to come back and evidently convinced of his affection. She bursts into tears of frustration, which she tells him express only rage, but one suspects more confused emotions. She denies ever loving him, saying that if she had, he would have seen it. " 'Women aren't very clever at hiding it.' . . . To her consternation, she realized that what she had said was true, that a woman couldn't hide love. Newt was seeing love now" (108). And Newt kisses her.

It is at this point that Catharine says, "You're hard to get along with," the phrase that no doubt formed the basis of the title Vonnegut says he would have given the story. She nevertheless remains resolved to go ahead with her planned marriage, and they sit under the trees of an orchard where Newt falls asleep. They awake to the chatter of a chickadee: *"Chick-a-dee-dee-dee"* (Vonnegut quite frequently uses birds and their calls in his fiction).

> "I love you," he said.
> "I know," she said.
> "Too late," he said.
> "Too late," she said. (108)

Catharine watches him walk away knowing that if he stops and turns around she will run to him. And that is just what happens.

Vonnegut did indeed serve in the Artillery at one time, as he describes hilariously in his *Paris Review* interview.[1] The actual events of this afternoon occurred before Vonnegut went to Europe in the autumn of 1944. One part of this story, certainly not autobiographically accurate, concerns the soldier's being A.W.O.L. Vonnegut says he was on "a spurious emergency leave" for some concocted family emergency, and "would never have had the guts to go A.W.O.L."[2] The real-life bride-to-be was Jane Marie Cox, to whom Vonnegut was married on September 1, 1945, after his return from the war. They had three children and also adopted three of the four children of Vonnegut's sister Alice. After she and Kurt were divorced, Jane remarried, to Adam Yarmolinsky, and died of cancer in December 1986. In her posthumously published book *Angels Without Wings*, she recounts (using the third person and fictitious names) the dramatic days following the deaths of Alice and her husband James Adams, the adoption of the children, and her subsequent battle with cancer.[3]

Since the author's comment on this story in the collection's Preface, it has become difficult to think of this story as other than autobiography. One cannot know, nevertheless, how precisely accurate other details of the dialogue or circumstances are, and it was not as autobiography that it was published. As fiction it seems a simple enough love story, full of youthful daring and anguish and rather posed dialogue. Romeo-like, Newt has dared severe punishment to woo his Juliet, who is already pledged to a young man as fully a model of eligibility as was Paris, and the romantic allusion is even pursued to the point of their meeting in an orchard. In general tone the story, like its icons, the glossy ladies magazine Catharine is reading and her silver pattern, seems very much a product of its time—and its place of publication.

By 1961 the number of magazine stories had risen back up to four a year. These included his last for *Cosmopolitan*, "Find Me A Dream," published in the February issue and not collected. This story has superficial similarities to "Long Walk To Forever," and at first glance even the illustrations (by B. Peak and Lorraine Fox) seem alike, each with a couple under trees, the young blonde woman looking down with an expression of reflective indecision and the young dark-haired man watching her with what might be suppressed longing. As was apparent in the earlier stories for these two magazines, the *Cosmopolitan* one tends to have more sophistication, both in its plot setting and in its technique.

That said, it perhaps needs to be recognized that the situation in "Long Walk" demands the kind of simplicity that Vonnegut insists on in its pared-down dialogue. The basic similarity between the two stories rests simply in the situation of a woman at the point of engagement to one man then encountering another man, with lesser prospects, and discovering she loves him instead.

"Find Me A Dream" is set in Creon, Pennsylvania, home of the Creon Works of the General Forge and Foundry Company which can claim to produce more sewer pipe in six months than China and Russia could produce between them in a year. At a country club dance, the leader of the band, Andy Middleton, has taken a break and, wandering outside by the first tee, finds a young woman crying to herself there. A little conversation establishes him as one of those rare men in Creon who is not "in pipe," and that the weeping woman considers the band wretched. Andy explains that the band could be better if they thought there was ever any hope that they could work their way out of Creon and if people ever bothered to listen to them. When Andy goes inside to fetch the young woman a drink he discovers that she came with Arvin Borders, works manager and the most eligible bachelor in Creon, and that she is "a small-time actress, the widow of a jazz musician, the mother of two very young daughters" and using her stage name, Hildy Matthews. Armed with this information he pries from her that the jazz musician had been a scoundrel who was shot dead by a jealous husband, and that Arvin Borders seemed to represent the untemperamental stability she and her daughters needed. But, like Catharine in the earlier story, she insists she loves this man: "one of the things I do best is love, . . . and right now I happen to love Arvin Borders" (110).

But soon thereafter Hildy turns her questions on Andy. She asks bluntly what he earns ("More than a school teacher, less than a school janitor"), learns that he lives in a big old house inherited from his family, and concludes that he is "quite well off when you think about it." And she reveals that after all the "wild and crazy" nights with the jazz musician she had wanted "a solid, sensible rich businessman," but then had to escape from all the pipe people, and that she thinks she could love Andy very much. With that she proposes, and Andy accepts. She concludes they are doing Arvin Borders a favor; the thing that had led to her being out there crying in the first place was having a woman tell her outright that it would ruin his career if he married a woman "like me." But for the clarinetist's career she thinks her love can do "a world of good."

Hildy's change of horses midstream appears more abrupt and seemingly improbable than Catharine's, and the burden the dialogue is asked to bear correspondingly the greater, yet it actually seems to come off every bit as naturally and convincingly. In part this stems from the characterization of Hildy as a "straight-ahead" person who has a no-nonsense directness about asking questions and expressing feelings. That may even have something to do with her being an actress and the expectations of extroversion that often adhere to that profession. Is she "Miss Temptation" years later, after the kind of marriage in which it is not hard to imagine Susanna might have found herself? But more important, she *is* vital, is a feeling, creative, emotionally engaged person in a society of hollow men. And there the rather heavily underlined symbolism of the repeatedly referred to pipe comes into play. The company men think of nothing else, and the life of this whole society, wives included, seems fixated with pipe, and just as empty. The bar with its forced conviviality is "The Jolly Piper" and the spiritless band "The Creon Pipers." Andy's "pipe" is the clarinet, however, an instrument capable of making beautiful sounds and expressing emotions. Hildy and Andy are kindred spirits, artistic souls in a barren world, so it seems likely they would warm to each other quickly, even without the help of the setting (moonlight on the first tee, as in "A Night For Love") and a couple of highballs.

The opening references to Creon's being beyond anything the Communists could ever hope to overtake in sewer pipe production, though made whimsically, nevertheless invite an expectation that this story will be another cold war expression of complacency in the superiority of the democratic and capitalistic American system. But it does not work out that way. For all that it is a romance, its setting implies strong reservations about the kind of company town, its inhabitants, and their values, that result from such capitalism. No one hears the music, a wife is assessed as a career asset, the men at the dance spend the evening, as Hildy says, "in the locker room, drinking, shooting crap, and talking sewer pipe, and all the women sit out on the terrace, talking about things . . . they've bought with money from pipe . . ." (109). It embodies the world Vonnegut repeatedly rejects in the Iliums, the other company towns, and the soulless mercenaries that populate them throughout his fiction. Dreams figure once more in this story. "Find Me A Dream" belongs in the tradition of fictions that debate "the American dream," where the ideals of individual fulfillment in a just society are subverted into the material dream of acquisition, of power, status and wealth. Andy's and Hildy's dreams that center on music, love and family struggle for survival in a society whose dreams are as empty as the pipe that sustains them.

In looking at the short stories of a writer who ultimately becomes more famous as a novelist, it is interesting to consider continuities or linkages between stories that might provide the basis for connection into a longer narrative. As was noted earlier, some of, or parts of, Vonnegut's novels are constructed from successions of episodes or mini-stories. The Helmholtz stories, with their continuing characters and setting, are the most conspicuous example of stories that show such potential for connection or combination into a longer narrative. Some that share very similar narrators—such as the various investment counselors—seem to offer this possibility. "Find Me A Dream" might conceivably be an epilogue to "Miss Temptation." And the next story to be published in 1961, "Runaways" (*Saturday Evening Post*, August 15), could, with some changes in genders, names, and such, easily have been shaped into an epilogue to "A Night For Love," where the offspring of rich and poor families run off together to be married.

"Runaways" (*Saturday Evening Post*, April 15, 1961) tells another story of star-crossed young lovers, complete with its own reference to Shakespeare's play when a radio announcer refers to them as "that Romeo and Juliet" couple. The runaways are Annie Southard, daughter of the Governor of Indiana, and Rice Brentner, the son of "an eighty-nine-dollar-and-sixty-two-cent-a-week supply clerk," as the press gleefully reports to the father's chagrin. They run away in Rice's "old blue Ford, with baby shoes dangling from the rearview mirror, with a pile of comic books on the burst back seat" (26). That description recurs in the story like an incremental refrain, initially perhaps implying the young love that connects them but increasingly representing the immaturity that in the end they themselves come to reject. After the runaway youngsters are intercepted and brought back, each is rebuked by parents in ways that predictably motivate them to flee again. Annie reads a prepared statement to the press, and immediately afterward rebels. " 'My own father, the governor of the state of Indiana,' said Annie, 'ordered me to lie. I'll never forget that' " (26). Rice, who to cap his other misadventures gets caught by his parents darkening his neophyte mustache with shoe polish, faces having to give up the old blue Ford. Pretending to be Bob Counsel, the eligible son of a rich man, in love with Annie and approved by her parents (Shakespeare's Paris once more), Rice calls Annie, arranges a meeting, and off they go again. This time the parents confer, and after some mutual recrimination, come to the conclusion that their children are growing up and perhaps should be given their heads. This time when the police stop the runaways, they are told they can come home as and when they like, and that their parents want them "to get married and start being happy as soon as possible" (56). All the radio news reports of their happiness leave them jaded. "They were beginning to look like department-store clerks on Christmas Eve, jangled and exhausted by relentless tidings of great joy" (56). By the time they get home Annie and Rice have decided that even though they love each other and might be happily married for a while, they are in Annie's words "too young for just about everything else there is that goes with love" (56).

While the plot line of this story remains simple and traditional, it is well told. The characterizations are brief and far from complete, but they are distinctive and capture the personalities effectively, mostly through what the characters say. Dialogue proves important in another sense in this story, for the failure of people to listen to each other becomes a major theme. In fact, the title could stand for the tendency of people to run away from others, from listening to them and hearing who they really are. Not only communications *between* the generations fail here. The young couple provides some amusing dialogue when they talk across each other all the time, even when both are talking about their parents' failure to listen to them. And while the dialogue reveals some of the stereotypical prejudices and rigidities of each generation and each class toward the other, no one has a corner on being right. Or wrong. There are no villains here. The governor, who initially seems to be tyrannical, snobbish, and concerned only with his political reputation, nevertheless makes some sensible arguments about the young couple's needing a little more than romantic love on which to base a complete, enduring relationship. When Rice's mother finally responds to the governor's attacks on how they have raised their son by ironically suggesting that perhaps they should have followed his example, he takes her point magnanimously. In the end, given permission by their parents, their lack of anything more to communicate about leads the young couple to decide to wait

The motif of communication continues in this story in other ways. There are press conferences when the runaways are caught, and there are news reports on the radio that the runaways listen for narcissistically and the parents with horror. The familiar topic of the search for identity is embodied in these responses to the news accounts. The governor is concerned for his political image, his wife with their social standing, Mr. Brentner with being typed before the world as "an eighty-nine-dollar-and-sixty-two-cent-a-week supply clerk," and the runaways with a confirmation of their image as romantic lovers defying all odds. The youngsters also rely heavily on the lyrics of popular songs to affirm their roles. Vonnegut inserts song lyrics into the story six times, with good effect. They are mostly about misunderstood young lovers escaping their parents and being sustained by love alone. They are usually ironically complementary to the situation. For example, when the runaways are given license to go their own way, this lyric confirms Annie's recognition of what their commitment would involve:

> "We certainly fooled them,

> "The ones who said our love wasn't true.

> "Now, forever and ever,

> "You've got me, and I've got you."   (56)

It is also evident that Vonnegut has fun parodying popular lyrics. The technique of using such interjected quotations is one that Vonnegut continues to develop, for purposes of commentary and for humor. The calypsos and quotations from the "Books of Bokonon" in *Cat's Cradle* may be the most conspicuous examples, but there are others, such as the short summaries of Kilgore Trout stories, poems, letters, "playlets," and even recipes interjected in various novels to similar effect.

"Harrison Bergeron" appeared in a new outlet for Vonnegut, *Magazine of Fantasy and Science Fiction*, the October 1961 issue. It was then reprinted in *National Review* (November 16, 1965, the source used here) and in *Welcome to the Monkey House*. The genesis of this story was an unpublished version called "Who Says It's A Parade" in which the protagonist's name was Ishmael. Despite its original place of publication, it is hard to see "Harrison Bergeron" as mainstream science fiction, although it is certainly dystopian in its portrayal of another society premised on an idealistic vision that has turned into nightmare. The events take place in the year 2081 when "everybody was finally equal." Nobody can be in any way superior to anybody else, as guaranteed by "the 211th, 212th, and 213th Amendments to the Constitution, and to the unceasing vigilance of the agents of the United States Handicapper General" (1020). The location of the story is the home of George and Hazel Bergeron. Hazel, judged to be average in every way, goes unhandicapped, but George is burdened with various bags of weight to lower his strength and an ear radio that frequently emits brain-shattering noises to disrupt his thoughts. The Bergerons' fourteen-year-old son Harrison has been taken away by the H-G men of the Handicapper General, Diana Moon Glampers, because he is a virtual superman.[4] That is revealed very shortly when the handicapped ballet the Bergerons are watching on television is interrupted by an announcement that Harrison Bergeron, athlete, genius and dangerous, has escaped. Moments later uproar ensues and there appears on screen a handsome giant who declares himself "the Emperor!" tears off his handicaps, selects and unburdens a ballerina to be his Empress, and proceeds to dance with superhuman grace and strength. As they kiss while suspended in an unimaginable leap, Diana Moon Glampers herself bursts upon the scene armed with a shotgun and blasts both dancers dead. George and Hazel return to watching the resumed program. Tears stain George's cheek, but the cacophony of a riveting gun in his ear radio ensures that he cannot remember why.

"Harrison Bergeron" represents vintage Vonnegut in being extremely funny while at the same time touching on several serious social issues. Much of its humor is visual. Most of the action, all of that involving Harrison, the dancers and Diana Moon Glampers, appears on the television set of the Bergerons. Harrison enters looking "like a walking junk yard," required to wear "a red rubber ball for a nose, keep his eyebrows shaved off, and cover his even white teeth with black caps at snaggle-tooth random" (1021). When he dances with the ballerina they defy "the law of gravity and the laws of motion as well," leaping to kiss the thirty-foot ceiling until finally "they remained suspended in air inches below the ceiling, and they kissed each other for a long, long time." It is then that Glampers enters with her shotgun. "She fired twice, and the Emperor and the Empress were dead before they hit the floor" (1041). The sheer implausibility and exaggeration of all of this—the handicaps, Harrison's size and prowess, the astronomical leaps—contribute to the comic spectacle. They also create humor by celebrating the very fictiveness of the story as fiction. Readers know these things cannot happen; the story in depicting the action in a representational manner actually subverts its claims to realism by the sheer exaggeration of what it shows. Thus rather than pretending to show what is real it exposes its fictionality. Having the dramatic events be on television within a story puts "reality" at two removes, giving emphasis to Vonnegut's technique.

If Vonnegut here reminds us, as he will many more times (in *Mother Night*, for example), that writers are liars who lure us into believing in made-up worlds, who bring us to tears over someone who exists only on a sheet of paper, he finds that both precious and dangerous. Its dangers are mainly those consequent on people's assumptions that a fiction is "true" (like Dwayne Hoover in *Breakfast of Champions*, who believes, based on a Kilgore Trout story, that everyone else is a robot) or a miraculous key to life. On the other hand, as is also said in *Mother Night*, the writer's lies can lead to truth—and they can certainly open an imaginative world of possibilities. It is that which Glampers tries to stop, and so "Harrison Bergeron" can be seen as, among other things, another statement by Vonnegut on censorship, an issue about which he has very strong feelings.

The "serious" topic that the story declares itself to be concerned with is equality. The achievement of a truly egalitarian society has occupied politicians and philosophers for centuries, but was there a particular social context giving it relevance in 1961? On the one hand, this was the era of the cold war, where Sino-Soviet Communist (and, for that matter, European democratic socialist) claims of egalitarianism were ranged against Western ideals of capitalism and individualism. And on the other hand, it was the pre-dawn of the Age of Aquarius, an era in which competitiveness and superiority were scorned, and where incidents occurred such as forcing a former beauty queen to wear granny-glasses, shear off her hair, and dress shapelessly before she could be accepted into a commune. In earlier stories—and subsequent fiction, too—Vonnegut has spoken out against striving for material acquisition, status, asserting superiority and other such aspects of competitiveness. On the other hand, the same stories show an admiration of those who strive, who take pride in something well done, or who are creative. This story clearly satirizes an obsession with equalizing; the predominant images are of the ludicrousness of the mental and physical handicaps, and the grimness of the inevitable reduction of the population to something close to its lowest common denominator. The implications of the kinds of bureaucratic and coercive oversight that would be required are also made frightening. Nevertheless, some suggestions of what makes the notion of equality appealing remain. Hazel's aversion to the old days when she could be made to feel like "something the cat dragged in" obviously is not very persuasive, but George's rejections of cheating for personal advantage and Harrison's promise to create a new monarchy and aristocracy are enough to allude to some of the problems with unfettered inequality.

But in the main, the topic of equality serves comic purposes. "Harrison Bergeron" may be a satirical fable, like George Orwell's *Animal Farm*, but the balance between comical rendering and moral message in the fable becomes almost reversed in the two stories. Vonnegut even appears cynical about what passes as average in America. "Hazel had a perfectly average intelligence, which meant she couldn't think about anything except in short bursts" (1020). The observation on the ballerinas continues the undercutting humor: "They weren't really very good—no better than anybody else would have been, anyway" (1020). Heavy irony emerges in the plodding Hazel's missing the point, as when she sympathizes with the stuttering announcer for trying "real hard" to do his best or suggests George might remove some of his weights in the evenings. Compounding the irony she says, " 'I think I'd make a good Handicapper General.' 'Good as anybody else,' said George." The range of sounds and the comic brutality of their effect provides another source of comedy. Remember, Vonnegut as a youth enjoyed the often painful comedy of comic teams such as Laurel and Hardy, Abbot and Costello and the Three Stooges. One of George's winces prompts Hazel to ask the cause. "Sounded like somebody hitting a milk bottle with a hammer," he replies. Another sounds like a twenty-one gun salute that leaves George "white and trembling" and leaves two of the ballerinas on the floor clutching their temples. The final one is a riveting gun.

> "Gee—I could tell that one was a doozy," said Hazel.
> "You can say that again," said George.
> "Gee—" said Hazel—"I could tell that one was a doozy." (1041)

The remaining story published in that year is "My Name Is Everyone" (*Saturday Evening Post*, December 16, 1961, and reprinted in *Welcome to the Monkey House* with the new title of "Who Am I This Time?"). The story once more uses the location of North Crawford, a fictional stand-in for Vonnegut's West Barnstable. And the narrator, again, sells and installs aluminum storms and screens—and the occasional bathtub enclosure. Another familiar ingredient is the theater, and in this appearance the salesman acts as director of the Mask and Wig Club's production of *A Streetcar Named Desire*. The club's star actor is Harry Nash, the self-effacing clerk in the hardware store. Given a dramatic role, Harry becomes a man possessed—by whatever character he portrays. Invited to try out for the play he asks, "Who am I this time?" The club's lack of a suitable young woman to convincingly fill the role of Stella gives promise of being solved when the narrator discovers Helene Shaw. She looks the part, but has no acting experience. She travels for the telephone company, visiting towns during the installation of new equipment, then moving on. Consequently she has little social life and welcomes being invited into the production. But she makes a wooden actress, and it proves that she has no experience of love to draw on for the role because of the transient life she has led. Harry has predictably come to life in "the Marlon Brando role," so in desperation, the director tries running the pair through a scene, to see if Harry's performance can get Helene into her role. The result astonishes onlookers, and through the rehearsals and the three performances the interaction between the two is electric. The wife of Harry's boss at the hardware store points out the problem that has been created, however; Helene has fallen in love, but the man she has fallen in love with will cease to exist when the play run ends. Helene soon discovers this, when Harry flees immediately after the first two performances and rejects her invitation to accompany her to the cast party after the third. But she devises a strategy. After the last performance she keeps him in hand until she can give him a copy of *Romeo and Juliet*. They leave reading lines to each other, Harry already eight years younger, "brave and gay." A week later they are married, by which time, Helene says, she has "been married to Othello, been loved by Faust, and been kidnapped by Paris." Asked about acting in another play she says, "Who are we this time?"

"My Name Is Everyone" represents another step in Vonnegut's willingness to depart further from the traditional norms of representationalism even in non-science fiction stories. Helene and Harry, in fact, come close to being robotized. Helene appears early in the story as "kind of numb, almost a machine herself, an automatic phone-company politeness machine." And Harry might belong in the storehouse in "Unready to Wear," a body waiting for an amphibian—in this case a role—to take him out. Once again the story explores the search for identity. It may be seen as a hyperbolic presentation of the idea Vonnegut frequently expresses, that people are prone to act as though they were in stories or plays, making themselves characters—and sometimes authors—within them. The narrator says that Harry's trouble was that as a baby he had been left on the doorstep of the Unitarian church (a situation straight out of fiction if there ever was one), he never found out who his parents were, and he now cannot function socially without a script. Harry's borrowing his characters has a double emphasis: he is always referred to as having assumed "the Marlon Brando role," an *actor's* presentation of a fictional *character* in a *movie* of a *play*. A further reminder comes in the description of what happens when the two rehearse: "What was about to happen was wilder than the chariot race in *Ben Hur*" (64). If Helene and Harry perform a hyperbolic demonstration of how people frequently act "to prepare a face to meet the faces that you meet," as T. S. Eliot puts it, then the playing of many parts to sustain a marriage may be seen the same way.[5] Interestingly, in the almost contemporary novel *Mother Night*

Vonnegut has his protagonist Howard Campbell agree to become a double agent largely because he cannot resist it as theater, while he also sustains his marriage to his wife Helga by enacting sexual roles as related in his *Memoirs of a Monogamous Casanova*. And this story comes hard on the heels of the runaways' acting out roles from the lyrics of their teen-favorite songs. A shadow over Harry and Helene's role playing as a road to lasting marital bliss is that it begins with reading from *Romeo and Juliet*, which Vonnegut has used twice before during this year as a signifier of impetuous and vulnerable romantic love.

So as in "Harrison Bergeron," this story has a story in another medium within it. Just as Harrison and the ballerina play out their romance on the video screen, Harry and Helene create theirs on stage. In each case this device not only calls attention to role playing to satisfy the need for identity, it influences style. It places an emphasis on visual presentation, since both stage and screen are visual, and the artifice of the situation invites comic exaggeration. Harry *almost* assumes the dimensions of Harrison, in fact, adding "fifty pounds to his weight and four inches to his height" and sounding "like a deep-sea diver coming upstairs in his lead shoes." Helene is left "limp as an eel. She sat down with her mouth open and her head hanging to one side" (64). There are visual vignettes, like Helene, when trying to hand one of the roses she has just been given to a Harry who has already fled, left standing alone in front of the curtain, "offering a rose to nothing and nobody." Which, to take the story literally and perhaps too seriously, seems about what she has, for Harry as a sequence of dramatic roles has no more substance than Grace McClellan's "stately mansions."

In 1962 Vonnegut once again published four stories. The first, "2BR02B" appeared in *Worlds of If* in January, and returns to the portrayal of a dystopian future world governed by a good idea gone mad. (Vonnegut will use "2BR02B" again as the title of a Kilgore Trout story in *God Bless You, Mr. Rosewater*.) The good idea carried to excess is population control. The population of the United States, for example, has stabilized at forty million. At the same time, as in "The Big Trip Up Yonder," a way has been found to stop the aging process. This has necessitated laws requiring that no child can be born until the parents can certify that someone else agrees to die. And to facilitate that, the Federal Bureau of Termination has established Ethical Suicide Studios—commonly known by such sobriquets as the "Catbox," "Easy-go," or "Sheep Dip"—with the telephone number "2BR02B," or "To be or not to be." These are staffed by efficient and welcoming young "gas chamber hostesses" who wear purple. This system results in a tightly ordered society where, despite the average age being one hundred and twenty nine, there are "no prisons, no slums, no insane asylums, no cripples, no poverty, no wars" and no diseases or aging.

The story opens in a waiting room of the Chicago Lying-in Hospital, populated only by a colorless and dispirited husband and, observing from above, a "sardonic" old painter on a stepladder. The painter is completing a mural of an immaculate and rigidly formal garden, populated by people in purple as gardeners. (Once again there is narrative in another medium within the story.) In the place of honor among them stands Dr. Benjamin Hitz, the Chief Obstetrician, the man responsible for the first gas chamber in Chicago. The painter speaks sarcastically about the ordered world of "The Happy Garden of

Eden," and regards the splattered drip cloth below as a better representation of life. The arrival of a woman from the FBT, who is to be included in the painting, interrupts the scene. Then Dr. Hitz himself arrives. He announces to the waiting husband that his wife as expected has delivered triplets, and asks if he has found three candidates for the Ethical Suicide Studios. The husband has but one, so he faces having to choose two of the triplets to die. But instead he produces a gun, shoots Hitz, the hostess, and then himself. The old painter, having watched silently from above, descends, picks up the gun, lacks the nerve to shoot himself, and instead calls "2BR02B." The answering hostess arranges an appointment, then delivers the story's ironic final lines: "Your city thanks you; your country thanks you; your planet thanks you. But the deepest thanks of all is from future generations" (65).

As in "The Big Trip Up Yonder," Vonnegut uses a kind of painful comedy to avoid a solemn discourse on the dangers of overpopulation while nevertheless calling attention to the issue and, through the distortions of hyperbole, some of the difficult choices it imposes. It remains one of the fundamental issues on which he continues to comment, to greater or lesser extent, throughout his career. In this instance, the imposition of population control has averted a disastrous situation where already drinking water was running out and people were eating seaweed. The negative aspects of population control receive particular bite here by the necessity to kill a baby if no volunteer for death can be found and by the references to the euphemistically-named Ethical Suicide Studios as gas chambers, calling up all the horrors of Nazi exterminations. The painter rejects the regulated paradise. He despises its imposed orderliness, as embodied in the mural, and prefers the splattered dropcloth. He may resemble his creator, who has spoken of seeing his role as a writer not to order chaos but "to bring chaos to order."[6] His vision may resemble that of "Jack the Dripper," Jackson Pollock, the abstract expressionist painter about whom Vonnegut has written.[7]

Some of the circumstances of "2BR02B" are repeated or extended in a Kilgore Trout story in *God Bless You, Mr. Rosewater* and in "Welcome to the Monkey House" some six years later, including what become Ethical Suicide *Parlors*. The hostesses wear purple there, too, and in each case the unnaturalness of this reversal of their human maternal functions is signaled by their unsexing. In "Welcome to the Monkey House," chemicals stop all feeling below their waists, while in this story they all develop facial hair—"an unmistakable mustache, in fact"—after a few years in the job. There are a couple of interesting details in this story. One is the inclusion of a popular song lyric with an interesting variation on the plaints of unrequited love in "Runaways." Here the lover tells his coy mistress that if she cannot reciprocate he will head for the suicide studio. In another amusing detail, Vonnegut uses the name of his Shortridge High School chum, Ben Hitz, who was later best man at his wedding, for one of the characters. Hitz stands seven feet tall, another instance of Vonnegut's exaggerated play with the height of his characters. He creates other seven footers, such as Harrison Bergeron, or Wilbur Swain of *Slapstick*, and some midgets, too, like Newt Hoenikker of *Cat's Cradle*.

"The Lie" (*Saturday Evening Post*, February 24, 1962, reprinted in *Welcome to the Monkey House*) has none of the exaggerated characteristics of preceding stories.   It represents a traditional story in style and technique, with only incidental humor.   It has familiar touches, in that themes such as the establishment of identity and the limitations of social status and wealth reoccur, and once again the woman proves to have steadier judgment, and a child undercuts adult pretense and pomposity.

Dr. Remenzel and his wife Sylvia, with their chauffeur, are taking their son Eli to the prestigious Whitehill School for Boys in North Marston, Massachusetts.   Remenzels have attended Whitehill for generations, their endowments resulting in scholarships and buildings bearing their names.   Eli sits hunkered down in the front seat of the Rolls Royce beside the chauffeur, and the more his parents talk about the school and its Remenzel tradition, or his mother reads from the bulletin, the further he sinks into his seat.   On the way they overtake a battered car bearing Tom Kilyer, who had been a classmate of Remenzel's on scholarship, now also taking his son to enroll.   Throughout the journal Dr. Remenzel repeatedly lectures first his wife and later his son on how they must not be so gauche as to use the Remenzel tradition or generosity to seek special treatment.   In the dining room at Whitehill they are greeted by the headmaster, Doctor Warren, at which Eli flees the room.   It soon emerges that Eli has failed the admissions test and then intercepted and destroyed the letter from Warren informing his parents.   Dr. Remenzel at once fumes that he is not a Remenzel for nothing, that a majority of the board of directors is in the room, and that he will get the decision reversed.   Tom Kilyer and his scholarship son have arrived in the midst of this, and Remenzel implies that if the school can find room for scholarship boys and foreign students it can find room for Eli. Sylvia, meanwhile, sees that their first concern should be for the son who has trapped himself in a dreadful situation.   When Remenzel rejoins them having been refused by the board, Eli tells his father that he can bear the shame of his failing but not of what his father has tried to do.   And the story ends with Remenzel's admitting that it was a bad thing to do and speculating that this will be their last visit to Whitehill.

There are some echoes of "This Son of Mine" in "The Lie," but only rather generalized ones.   Though Tom Kilyer and his son seem to provide the opportunity for a comparative father-son relationship, as Karl and Rudy Lindberg do to Merle and Franklin Waggoner in the earlier story, it never develops.   The Kilyers provide contrast; Tom was a scholarship boy, still does not seem to have succeeded financially, and his son has finished top in the admissions examination and will also have a scholarship.   They are the meek who are inheriting the earth of Whitehill traditionally owned by the Remenzels. More closely resembling "This Son of Mine" is Eli's reluctance, like Franklin's, to inherit the world and values of his father.   In both stories the fathers become overbearing in their expectation that the sons will, in effect, extend the fathers' lives, and make it all the more difficult for them to do so.   "The Lie," therefore, represents another examination of the father-son relationship.   Its other theme is implied in the title.   Obviously there is more than one lie; Eli has lied about the letter out of his dread of his father's reaction, and all of the father's protestations about what the Remenzels represent, their values, and how they must never exploit their rank for personal advantage turn out to be the big lie at the center of the story.   It is the boy who feels most shamed by that big lie, so once again it is the child who reveals the impostor. In fairness, Dr. Remenzel recognizes and apologizes for his mistake, and "The Lie" ends having made a moral observation, not creating a villain.

"Go Back to Your Precious Wife and Son" (*Ladies Home Journal*, July, 1962, and collected in *Welcome to the Monkey House*) reintroduces as its narrator the friendly salesman of aluminum storms, screens, and shower enclosures. He has just sold some Fleetwood Trip-L-Track combination storm and screen windows and a custom bathtub enclosure to Hollywood star Gloria Hilton. Actually, he has dealt with her fifth husband, writer George Murra. While installing the tub enclosure he overhears an argument in the living room below through the heat register. Gloria, hair in curlers, without make-up, and in her bathrobe—in short, looking nothing like her screen image—is telling George that he knows nothing about love and should go back to his precious first wife and son. The narrator is dismissed, but after he hears that Gloria and her maid have left in high dudgeon, he returns to the house to finish the job. A custom door for the tub enclosure with the star's face illustrated upon it and the eyes exactly where hers would be when she stood in the tub is no longer needed, so the salesman swaps it for one with the traditional 1950s flamingo on it from his home. George, meanwhile, feeling depressed about his marriages and the teenaged son who rejects him, entices the salesman into joining him in a drink. The two end up drunk, the salesman returning home muttering about loving Gloria Hilton, trying to install the custom shower door, and finishing passed out in the bathtub. When, later the next day, he returns to the star's house, George has his son there. But the son remains unforgiving and smart-mouthed. At the salesman's suggestion, George gives the boy a kick in the pants, which works, and before long George has his first wife on the phone forgiving him and every prospect of the family restored. The narrator returns to face his wife, full of trepidation. After a day of shopping, dining, and watching a movie alone she returns and goes up to take a shower. The narrator expects a further outburst and goes after her to promise he will change the doors back. He finds her, her body crowned with the face of Gloria Hilton, peeking through the eyes, laughing, "Guess who?"

This story falls into the category of domestic comedy, with a touch of the fathers-and-sons theme thrown in. Much of its success stems from the comfortable narration, which moves the story along easily, allowing just the right amount and tone of comment on the action, and the injection of humor. The narrator's role as the installer of bathtub enclosures allows for a useful balance of access to intimate detail and absence that permits speeding by nonessentials. His tendency to dwell momentarily on products and installations adds to his familiarity as a narrator and plausibility to the story, a technique carried over from some of the early science fiction stories with their attendant everyday furnishings. As a commentary on marriage—several marriages, actually—for a women's magazine, "Go Back" might have provoked mixed responses. The narrator is a man, much of the discussion of marriage takes place between two men (the "other man" being not just George, but Harry Crocker the plumber and the two sons as well), and a male view of marriage surely predominates. What else could it be when the husband comes home drunk in the small hours, mumbling of being in love with the local movie queen, passes out in the bathtub, and then seems surprised when his wife fails to make dinner for him the next evening? The movie star seems not to be forgiven for appearing without make-up, hair in curlers, schlepping in slippers and bathrobe, and not looking "any prettier than a used studio couch." George's frustration with Gloria is made understandable—even excusable—because her activities have kept him from writing for over a year. That she has been willing to move to the east coast to be near George's son evidently counts for little. On the other hand, perhaps the women readers did, or were expected to, get some satisfaction from seeing the actress looking like "the everyday housewife," the narrator's wife taking her day out in response to her husband's indulgence, and the Murras' marriage put back together again. Much about gender relations would have been viewed differently by a 1962 audience. In the main the story asserts that the glamorous marriage may not turn out to be so glamorous, especially when both its foundation and its flaw is the self-interest of each partner. The narrator's twenty-year marriage seems to be imbued with some healthy give-and-take and humor, so in true Vonnegut fashion pretension founders and homespun values prevail.

The remaining publication in 1962 does not qualify as a short story but deserves mention. It is a short satirical piece, in some ways reminiscent of some of the columns in the *Cornell Sun*, called "HOLE BEAUTIFUL: Prospectus for a Magazine of Shelteredness." It was published in *Monocle* (Vol. 5, no. 1), with an appended poem by Karla Kuskin. The satire is another expression of the current cold war fears. The proposed magazine's title obviously derives from *House Beautiful*, and its subject is fallout shelters and the activities surrounding them. It will be "the magazine of gracious survival." As a general public relations consultant the magazine would employ "a leading undertaker " who, "with his valuable experience in the field of putting people underground, will be helpful in overcoming the negative image that death has in this country" (46). Singing commercials might include "Hole is where the heart is" or "There's no place like hole." The publisher would be a separate corporation called Subterranean Publications, Inc., with offices in Mammoth Cave, Kentucky. "Cost per issue will be 50¢ in subways and $1.00 above ground." Because of negative connotations, the word "bomb" will never be used and instead it will be referred to as "the Big Fella." The editorial policy will be to oppose the government's community shelter program with the aid of the American Medical Association's attack on it as "socialized sheltering." The magazine would promote "Shelter Hopping Kits" designed to gain access to other people's shelters in time of attack by using various devices such as Cyklon-B gas or imitations of the pleadings of a loved family pet. A sample theater review focuses on the theater's emergency exits, lighting, and proximity to a fallout shelter. Editorials projected include "Unilateral Disarmament by the Russians— Does it Violate the American Sense of Fair Play?" (50). And so it goes on, irreverent and inventive, in the best comedic tradition of meeting society's worst fears head-on with laughter.

"Lovers Anonymous" appeared in *Redbook* for October 1963. Like "My Name Is Everyone" and the later "Hyannis Port Story" it uses the North Crawford setting, and once again the narrator works as a storm, screen and bathtub enclosure salesman. Herb White, the local accountant, has married

Sheila Hinkley, the girl whom every male now in his mid-thirties had dreams of in high school days. Sheila was a stellar student, and her admirers were all astounded when in her junior year in college she dropped out to marry Herb. A group of them spent the night of her wedding drinking, and proposed a "permanent brotherhood of eternal sufferers, to aid each other," which one mourner suggested should be called "the Brotherhood of People Who Were Too Dumb to Realize that Sheila Hinkley Might Actually Want to Be a Housewife" (70). They settle for "Lovers Anonymous." The group lives on, mainly because its members are mostly local small businessmen who meet at the lunch counter anyway.

The news that something is amiss in the White household, because Herb has moved into the ell (for non-northeasterners, a shed-like structure adjoining the house with connecting door) arouses the attention of the "L.A." members. The narrator, who has been installing Fleetwood combinations on the house and whose profession affords convenient opportunities for reconnaissance, can confirm this. Soon afterward Herb orders an expensive and total remodelling of the ell, including kitchen, bathroom and its own Fleetwoods. Then the narrator sees Sheila returning a large red book to the library, checks it out himself, and discovers it is *Woman, the Wasted Sex, or, the Swindle of Housewifery*. The book proves to have been the root of the Whites' problems. Both have read it; Sheila laments that her brains have "turned to mush," and Herb condemns himself for having subjected her to wife-and-motherhood and, vowing to give her freedom, has moved into the ell. Sheila reveals her belief that Herb feels happy for the first time, having been "a slave all his life, doing things he hated in order to support his mother, and then me, and then me and the girls" (148). Though it seems that each has greatly misjudged the feelings of the other in this reconfiguration of the household, it apparently works, and Sheila goes back to taking courses to finish her university degree. As for their relationship, Sheila says, "Love laughs at locksmiths." At the close the members of Lovers Anonymous are mocking the narrator for having given the infamous book to his wife, telling him he will have "a restless woman" on his hands. But he claims he has forestalled that with a magic bookmark—one of her old report cards.

"Lovers Anonymous" has the conversational ease and the comfortable small-town aura of other stories with these ingredients. An element of this story from the start is not the *battle* of the sexes, but a continuing exchange of jocular undercutting, of good-natured ribbing between them. In high school, the Lovers Anonymous have been awed by Sheila's looks but derisive and frightened of her intellect and career aspirations. They have not progressed a great deal since, and still make jokes accordingly. The drug store clerk may be right when she suggests that the narrator is the first one of the group to have opened a book in ten years! And their fear of the big red book is about what one might expect of this group of "good old boys." In examining gender relations in this story, however, Vonnegut treads a precarious line rather carefully. Much of that care manifests itself in the role given to his narrator. The narrator has some distinctly male chauvinistic views, which Vonnegut lets us see. Balancing that, however, the narrator sometimes sees that characteristic in himself and makes fun of it. When the drugstore librarian tells him that the book has been popular, he says, "That's as may be. Whisky and repeating fire arms were very popular with the redskins. And if this drugstore really wants to make money, you might put in a hashish-and-heroin counter for the teen-age crowd" (147). The hyperbole and the reference to another prejudice are so conspicuous and self-consciously used as to underline this as a knowing taunt, fully aware of the bias it appears to express. The seemingly blunt ending has the same effect. The narrator has read the book and it has had its impact. In spite of his pretending to view it as heretical and socially disruptive, he has passed it on to his wife to read (something he would surely never do if he seriously regarded it as he protests) but jocularly maintains the appearance of the unrepentant chauvinist with the jibe about his wife's report card.

Vonnegut obviously aims some of his satire in the other direction, too, as in the table of contents for *Woman, the Wasted Sex, or, the Swindle of Housewifery* :

I.   5,000,000 B.C.–A.D. 1865, the Involuntary Slave Sex.
II.   1866–1919, the Slave Sex Given Pedestals.
III.   1920–1945, Sham Equality—Flapper to Rosie the Riveter.
IV.   1946–1963, Volunteer Slave Sex—Diaper Bucket to Sputnik.
V.   Explosion and Utopia. (147)

While satirical, the table of content nevertheless reflects an awareness of serious issues behind the chapter headings. Characteristically, Vonnegut pokes fun in both directions, the sharpest jabs aimed where he sees most pretension.

Typically, then, the story turns around from what appears to be a predictable direction. What had the appearance of being the disintegration of the marriage everyone envied turns into a story of that marriage's taking a new and unexpected direction, one that promises to offer both partners freedom and growth, and thus a looser but stronger bond. Equally typical is the final segment with its return to the narrator, his wife, and the bookmark, with its flavor of the shaggy dog story ending.

Vonnegut sold another story to *Saturday Evening Post* in 1963, but it never appeared in that magazine. "The Hyannis Port Story" makes mention, favorably, of President John F. Kennedy, actually giving him a minor role in the conclusion. His assassination overtook publication of the story, and the magazine chose not to print it.[8] It was subsequently printed in *Welcome to the Monkey House* and is discussed in that section of this work. There were a few further stories in later years, such as the title story of the second collection. "Welcome to the Monkey House" was originally published in *Playboy* in January 1968. Better classified as "creative nonfiction" than as a short story, "The Big Space Fuck" nevertheless appeared in a short story collection, *Again, Dangerous Visions: Forty-six Original Stories Edited by Harlan Ellison.*[9] It was later included in *Palm Sunday* (1981). Both of these pieces are discussed elsewhere.

By this point—the end of 1963—circumstances had changed so much for Kurt Vonnegut that his short story writing career to all intents and purposes ended. The impact of television on the magazines' demand for short stories continued. Advertisers turned to television increasingly, and readers became viewers, the sitcom filling many of the functions of the short story. Magazines perished (*Collier's*, for example, went out of existence in 1956) and others changed their formats, using fewer short stories, or reduced the number of issues published in a year. This trend, which had begun to manifest itself in the mid-1950s, had reached its full measure by the middle of the next decade.

But the circumstances dictating change were not all negative. *The Sirens of Titan*, published in 1959, brought no immediate change in Vonnegut's fortunes, but it did begin to gather for him a following in an audience different from the magazine readership. The novel became a favorite of younger readers, mostly college students, who circulated dogeared copies (it was published as a paperback original). Those avid readers would form the "grass roots" of his following in later years. In 1961, Fawcett published *Canary in a Cat House* as a Gold Medal paperback, to be followed closely by *Mother Night* by the same publisher. As noted previously, Vonnegut had found that he could get a healthy advance on a chapter and an outline for these publications, so the turn to paperbacks was fortuitous. *Cat's Cradle*, written for the paperback market, made its first appearance in 1963 in hardback (Holt, Rinehart and Winston), however, with a Doubleday Book Club Edition the same year. And he then set about *God Bless You, Mr. Rosewater*, which would appear in hardback with the same publisher in 1965. So the transition to novels, prompted initially largely by necessity, was a significant outcome of the changes in the mid-1960s.

With the publication of the novels, recognition gradually began to come. Vonnegut's being typed as a science fiction writer, and how this led to his being ignored by reviewers and type-cast as tied to an inferior genre, has been noted many times. Vonnegut's own comments have tended to mellow from bitterness to ironic humor over the years.[10] Nevertheless, he had acquired reputation enough to be invited for a two-year residency at the University of Iowa Writers Workshop, where he was joined by other writers like Nelson Algren, Vance Bourjaily, Richard Yates and José Donoso and met influential academic critics like Robert Scholes. His interaction with this community proved very helpful to him in the development of his novel writing. It also led directly to the Guggenheim Fellowship which supported him in the research for and writing of his most famous novel, *Slaughterhouse-Five* (1969). His growing reputation also led to his writing reviews and other short nonfiction pieces for the *New York Times Book Review, The New York Times Magazine, McCall's, Life, Esquire*, and others at a creditable rate. Some of these items, mostly personal journalism pieces, were subsequently collected in *Wampeters, Foma, and Granfalloons* (1974), *Palm Sunday* (1981), and *Fates Worse than Death* (1991). The growing volume of work of this kind, in addition to the novels, provided the income and made the demands on his energies that replaced what had once been the role of short story writing. But what Vonnegut had learned through this form continues to manifest itself in the longer fiction, and the creative impulse that finds natural expression in the short, tight, crisp mini-story or parable, continues to find outlet in the novels, notably under the auspices of Kilgore Trout.

NOTES

1. *Paris Review* Interview, in William Rodney Allen, *Conversations with Kurt Vonnegut* (Jackson: University Press of Mississippi, 1988), 169–171.

2. Conversation between P.J.R. and Kurt Vonnegut, June 14, 1996.

3. Jane Vonnegut Yarmolinsky, *Angels Without Wings* (Boston: Houghton Mifflin, 1987).

4. Diana Moon Glampers, or at least the name, reappears in *God Bless You, Mr. Rosewater*, but as a totally different character. There she is timid, mentally retarded, and terrified of thunder.

5. T. S. Eliot, "The Love Song of J. Alfred Prufrock," *The Complete Poems and Plays, 1909-1950* (New York: Harcourt, Brace and World, 1964), 4.

6. Kurt Vonnegut, *Breakfast of Champions* (New York: Delacorte Press/Seymour Lawrence, 1973), 210: "Let others bring order to chaos. I would bring chaos to order, instead, which I think I have done."

7. Kurt Vonnegut, "Jack the Dripper," *Esquire* (December 1983), 549–553. Pollock and other abstract expressionists figure prominently in Vonnegut's novel *Bluebeard* (New York: Delacorte, 1987).

8. This account of the publication history of the story is confirmed in a letter from Jane Cox Vonnegut to Jerome Klinkowitz, cited in Asa B. Pieratt, Julie Huffman-klinkowitz and Jerome Klinkowitz, *Kurt Vonnegut: A Comprehensive Bibliography* (Hamden, CT: The Shoestring Press/Archon Books, 1987), 181.

9. Kurt Vonnegut, "The Big Space Fuck," in *Again, Dangerous Visions: Forty-six Original Stories Edited by Harlan Ellison* (Garden City, N.Y.: Doubleday, 1972), 246–250.

10. Kurt Vonnegut, "Science Fiction," in *Wampeters, Foma, and Granfalloons* (New York: Delacorte Press/Seymour Lawrence, 1975), 1.

6

The Collections: *Canary in a Cat House* and *Welcome to the Monkey House*

Vonnegut published two collections of short stories, *Canary in a Cat House* (1961) and *Welcome to the Monkey House* (1968). The former contains twelve short stories, all previously published elsewhere. *Welcome to the Monkey House* contains twenty-five, not all of which had been previously published, plus a preface. *Canary in a Cat House* had only one edition, the original Gold Medal Books edition by Fawcett Publications, a 160-pages-long paperback. The print order was for 175,000 copies, although it is doubtful that anything like this number was actually sold.[1] Once Vonnegut's reputation was established, this book became something of a collector's item. *Welcome to the Monkey House*, by contrast, appeared when Vonnegut's reputation was on the ascendant, following the accumulating successes of *Cat's Cradle* (1963) and *God Bless You, Mr. Rosewater* (1965), and its success was to be sustained by the immediately following publication of *Slaughterhouse-Five* (1969). *Welcome to the Monkey House* appeared first in hardback as a Seymour Lawrence/Delacorte Press edition of 300 pages, with a first printing of 5,000 copies. This was followed by a Dell paperback, with a first printing in January 1970 of 150,000 copies. By November of 1970 there was also a larger Delta paperback re-edition of the first edition, with a printing of 10,000 copies. British hardback (Jonathan Cape) and paperback (Panther) editions soon followed, and then publication in Japan, Czechoslovakia, Germany, Holland, and Sweden (*Comprehensive Bibliography*, 71–80). *Welcome to the Monkey House* has gone through numerous editions and continues in print at the time of writing, and it is the place where most people familiar with Vonnegut's short stories have encountered them.

Canary in a Cat House was the first of a two-book contract with Gold Medal, the second being the novel *Mother Night*. Its twelve stories, in order of placement, are: "Report on the Barnhouse Effect," "All the King's Horses," "D.P.," "The Manned Missiles," "The Euphio Question," "More Stately Mansions," "The Foster Portfolio," "Deer in the Works," "Hal Irwin's Magic Lamp," "Tom Edison's Shaggy Dog," "Unready to Wear," and "Tomorrow and Tomorrow and Tomorrow" (which had previously appeared with the title "The

Big Trip Up Yonder"). Since it is rare, the appearance of the book deserves mention. The cover illustration, by Leo and Diane Dillon, consists of a face that is actually a mosaic of small drawings illustrative of the stories in the collection. The predominant colors are green and blue, with a heavy black outline. The long narrow vertical that forms the face's nose shows a rocket ascending, illustrating "The Manned Missiles." Another panel shows black figures above whom is the slogan, "Live 200 years," alluding to "Tomorrow and Tomorrow and Tomorrow." There is a chess piece for "All the King's Horses," a stag's head for "Deer in the Works," and so on. The back cover illustration is of a black and white tiger-striped cat with a yellow canary inside it. A line passes through the cat's mouth down to two small black figures, as if the cat has *them* on a leash. There are also small black and white illustrations, approximately an inch-and-a-half square, at the start of each chapter.

The title of the collection owes itself to an image Vonnegut has made reference to more than once. It compares the writer in society to the miners' canary, taken into the pit to warn of lethal gases. In an address to the American Physical Society in 1969, Vonnegut said:

The most positive notion I could come up with was what I call the canary-in-the-coal-mine theory of the arts. This theory argues that artists are useful to society because they are so sensitive. They are supersensitive. They keel over like canaries in coal mines filled with poison gas, long before more robust types realize that any danger is there. (*Wampeters*, 92).

He makes essentially the same point in the *Playboy* interview, saying, "I have the canary-bird-in-the-coal-mine theory of the arts. You know, coal miners used to take birds down into the mines with them to detect gas before men got sick. . . . artists—all artists—should be treasured as alarm systems" (*Wampeters*, 238). The transposition of the coal mine into the Cat House perhaps adds a little prurient zest to the figure and sharpens its social focus. It may also look forward to the image of the cat's cradle in the novel of that name, where the implication is of a meaningless world arbitrarily assigned meaning, like the looped strings in the children's game. Either way, the point of the analogy seems clear, the artist compared to the coal miner's canary in a society that is compared to a Cat House. The blurb on the back cover announces, "Kurt Vonnegut, Jr./ Scarifying satirist by trade,/ Sings for his supper in a world/ He regards as a house of ill-repute/ Or worse—."

Vonnegut's recollection of the selection of the twelve stories is that they were what he thought were the most suitable ones at the time. The ordering suggests little, except that "Report of the Barnhouse Effect," which was his first story, remains first in the collection. "Tomorrow and Tomorrow and Tomorrow," which had been titled "The Big Trip Up Yonder" when it originally appeared in *Galaxy Science Fiction*, makes an appropriate ending. Its content examines an overpopulated future, and its new title, echoing Macbeth's final despair, leaves the collection pointing off toward times to come, though hardly optimistically. Apart from the last story's change of title, and minor stylistic changes in four others, the most significant departure from the original magazine appearance comes in the omission of the last sentence of "Hal Irwin's

Magic Lamp" ("Personally, I never forgave her for the Depression."), as noted previously.

To categorize the stories broadly, four ("Report on the Barnhouse Effect," "The Euphio Question," "Unready to Wear," and "Tomorrow and Tomorrow and Tomorrow") might be put in a science fiction category, three ("All the King's Horses," "The Manned Missiles," and "D.P.") relate to war or the cold war, and five ("More Stately Mansions," "The Foster Portfolio," "Deer in the Works," "Hal Irwin's Magic Lamp," and "Tom Edison's Shaggy Dog") are social or domestic in focus, and mostly humorous. This hardly represents Vonnegut as the "scarifying satirist" of the back cover, nor does it fully justify the popular contemporary classification of science fiction writer. His emphasis here, as throughout his career, is on human behavior, its broad social patterns and their individual enactments, and the inevitable consequences. The future, and hence much of the science-fictional, serves primarily to render hyperbolically the consequences of present behavior. Some of the stories could fit more than one of the broad categories used here; "The Manned Missiles," for example, might also fit in the science fiction group. None of the Helmholz stories appears in this collection, and "D.P." is the only one of the stories in which children have a significant role. While Vonnegut has no recollection of a specific reason for dropping "Hal Irwin's Magic Lamp" from inclusion with the other stories reappearing in *Welcome to the Monkey House*, that story does seem the logical choice for exclusion. Its plot more closely involves attitudes and values epitomized in a particular era, and its moral message may appear somewhat thinner and more obvious than those of the other selections. There are also passages relating to ethnic dialects and to a wife's household allowance, for example, which, in this decade of rapid social change, audiences for the later collection might have viewed differently. Overall, however, it is a collection that well represented Vonnegut's short fiction at that time.

Welcome to the Monkey House contains twenty-five stories plus the Preface. To repeat, eleven of the stories are ones that had appeared previously in *Canary in a Cat House*; that is, all of them except "Hal Irwin's Magic Lamp." The opening story, "Where I Live," serves as an introduction to the author's world of Cape Cod. It was initially published as "You've Never Been to Barnstable?" in *Venture—Traveler's World* for October 1964 (145, 147–149), although in the list of credits in the collection it is referred to as "So You've Never Been to Barnstable." As in *Canary in a Cat House*, the retitled "Tomorrow and Tomorrow and Tomorrow" ends the collection. Also retitled is "My Name Is Everyone," now called "Who Am I This Time." Other stories discussed earlier that are included in this collection are "Harrison Bergeron," "Long Walk to Forever," "Miss Temptation," "Next Door," "Go Back to Your Precious Wife and Son," "The Lie," "The Kid Nobody Could Handle," "EPICAC," and "Adam." Completely new is "The Hyannis Port Story," which, as noted earlier, had been sold to the *Saturday Evening Post* in 1963 but then not used because of the assassination of President John F. Kennedy, who figures as a character in the story. A not-quite-new inclusion is "Welcome to the Monkey House," which was originally published earlier the same year in *Playboy* (January 1968). The remaining, rather surprising inclusion is "New Dictionary," a review of *The Random House Dictionary* originally published in

the *New York Times Book Review* of October 30, 1966, as "The Latest Word."
(Once again the credits in *Welcome to the Monkey House* are inaccurate and
claim that it was previously published as "The Random House Dictionary.")

In the Preface to *Welcome to the Monkey House* Vonnegut introduces
himself by explaining that his name derives from the river Vonne in Germany
and that he is over six feet two inches tall and poorly coordinated, except when
he swims. He tells of the earlier generations of his family in Indianapolis, of his
older brother Bernard, the scientist, and of his tall, elegant sister Alice, a
sculptor, who died of cancer when she was forty. Vonnegut writes of Alice at
some length in the Prologue of his novel *Slapstick* (1976) where he speaks of her
as "the person I had always written for. She was the secret of whatever artistic
unity I had ever achieved. She was the secret of my technique" (15). In the
Preface to *Welcome to the Monkey House*, Vonnegut says that Alice always
denied that she was really an Alice, and he agrees. In *Slapstick*, which he
describes as "the closest I will ever come to writing an autobiography," the
brother and sister are Wilbur and Eliza Swain. Working secretly together, they
are capable of genius. Separated, and conforming to the conventional
expectations of their parents, they become "Betty and Bobby Brown" (88).
Perhaps Alice felt that name made her sound too much like a Betty Brown.

Also in this Preface, Vonnegut makes his often-noted denigration of his
short story writing: "The contents of this book are samples of work I sold in
order to finance the writing of the novels. Here one finds the fruits of Free
Enterprise" (x). He continues in this vein by describing his leaving General
Electric to become "a free-lance writer of so-called 'slick fiction,' a lot of it
science fiction" (x). And he adds that a college professor (a rare one, evidently,
since he drives a Mercedes-Benz 300SL!) assured him that "public relations men
and slick writers were equally vile, in that they both buggered truth for money"
(x). Much of the Preface retains this same comically exaggerated, self-
deprecatory tone, including his noting that a reviewer in *The New Yorker* had
described *God Bless You, Mr. Rosewater* as "a series of narcissistic giggles,"
adding, "This may be another" (xi). None of this denigration of the stories
should be taken too seriously. While there is no doubt that income was a strong
motivation in the creation of the stories—and how many artists can afford not to
be so motivated?—after *Player Piano* Vonnegut passes a number of years *not*
writing novels. Perhaps at this point, with his reputation at last being
established, Vonnegut could afford to speak airily of his earlier efforts. Clearly,
though, Vonnegut comes to regard the writing of the stories as a different and
lesser activity than the writing of novels.[2]

"Where I Live" describes the Cape Cod village of Barnstable and its
surroundings. Vonnegut fictionalizes the account by using the visit of an
encyclopedia salesman as the means of entry into his description of the
geography, people and way of life of the village. The salesman's presence
fades, but in his brief appearance he resembles the various salesmen Vonnegut
has used as narrators in earlier stories. "Where I Live" makes clear that this
writer, the creator of "slick fiction," science fiction, and "scarifying" satire,
remains at heart someone comfortable in Barnstable with its established middle-
American ways and enduring values. The people of Barnstable are not
conservative New England Brahmins—most have come from elsewhere in the

country—and their politics are varied, but they venerate the natural and social environment they have found, and resist the incursions of commercialism and trendiness. In fact, they sound much like the inhabitants of "Poor Little Rich Town." Like them, these residents have spent money on fire department equipment, and like the inhabitants of some of Vonnegut's fictional villages, they have their amateur dramatic society. Vonnegut draws on this setting for the backdrop to several of his stories, and his affinity for it reflects a part of his nature sometimes overlooked by those who would see him only in more radical terms.

"The Hyannis Port Story" makes use once again of the narrator who sells storm windows, screens, and bathtub enclosures. After a political lecture by a collegian named Robert Taft Rumfoord, he engages a man who has had hostile questions for the speaker on another matter. The boy's father, Commodore William Howard Taft Rumfoord, mistakenly believes the narrator has been taking his son's part and consequently invites him to the huge Rumfoord "cottage" in Hyannis to install storm windows. The Commodore, who takes that title from having been Commodore of the Hyannis Port Yacht Club in 1946, is independently wealthy and occupies himself with conservative Republican politics. Treating the salesman as a guest, the Commodore invites him to stay for cocktails and dinner and do his measuring in the morning. Their cocktails are interrupted by a call from the Secret Service to announce that the son has been caught aboard the President's father's yacht, "The Honey Fitz," and that he has been holding love trysts with an Irish fourth cousin of the President, a Sheila Kennedy, aboard various unattended boats in the harbor. Robert duly shows up with Sheila, announcing that they are engaged, which results in a predictably stilted dinner. Afterwards the Commodore, his wife, and the narrator retire to the balcony for their cognac. Rumfoord has mounted on the second floor balcony of his house, facing the Kennedy compound, a huge illuminated portrait of Senator Barry Goldwater, who was the most prominent exponent of conservative politics at the time and was to run for president in 1964. But after the events of this day the Commodore has decided not to switch on the lights of the sign. Then two cars draw up, and the voice of President Kennedy is heard calling to ask Rumfoord why he has not illuminated the sign, and if he would. He has Mr. Khrushchev's son-in-law with him who would like to see it. And he asks if the Commodore would leave it on. " 'That way,' said the President, 'I can find my way home' " (150).

Obviously, this story would have been very topical if events had permitted its publication as planned in 1963. Senator Goldwater presumably would have opposed President Kennedy in his seeking of a second term. Several other public figures—Adlai Stevenson, Walter Reuther, Pierre Salinger and Joseph Kennedy—come into the text, prefiguring the way Vonnegut creates a postmodern blending of fiction and history in some later novels, most notably *Jailbird* (1979). There are allusions to the fad, popularized by Attorney General Robert F. Kennedy, for fifty-mile hikes. In Hyannis there has been massive commercial exploitation of the craze for all things Kennedy: desserts named the *Jackie* or the *Caroline* or the *Teddy* or even the *Arthur Schlesinger, Jr.* the *PT-109 Cocktail Lounge*, and the *New Frontier* miniature golf course.

Once again the socially-comfortable salesman narrator proves an effective device, but the strength of this story resides in the characterization, and particularly the dialogue, of the Commodore. Vonnegut surely enjoyed creating blustering political reactionaries during this period. Other examples include "Pop" Cosby of *Cat's Cradle* and the more fully developed character of Senator Lister Rosewater in *God Bless You, Mr. Rosewater,* the two preceding novels. As with these two characters, Vonnegut refuses to make the Commodore merely a flat personification of politics he rejects. Rumfoord becomes a pompous eccentric, harmless as the cartoon figure of the clubroom capitalist in an overstuffed armchair, capable of loyalty, respect and decency. In futility, he fumes at a society whose changes he remains powerless to stop. He clings to a lost world, retaining the title of Commodore whose tenure ended two decades before, and wearing perpetually the blazer and whites of endless summers past. He derides motorboats as "stinkpots" and rues the day that anything but sail was admitted to the bay. He is all puff, and is even likened to a "gruff, friendly teddybear." Indeed, the Kennedys sometimes refer to the Rumfoords as *"the Pooh people."*

As with "Pop" Cosby and Senator Rosewater, it is the sheer excess of the Commodore's attitudes and outbursts that proves amusing—and even endearing. When the narrator, noting how many local places are named after Rumfoords, inquires why there are none named after Kennedys, he demands, "Why should there be? They only got here yesterday." "Day before yesterday?" the narrator asks. "What would *you* call nineteen-twenty-one?" Rumfoord responds (144). Later, the party on the balcony overhear the barker on a tour boat offshore end remarks to his passengers by saying, *"but you know how rich people are."* "Demoralized and bankrupt by confiscatory taxation," the Commodore hurls back (144). When he learns that his son has boarded a boat occupied by Adlai Stevenson and Walter Reuther, the Commodore explodes, "That's the last time I let my son go swimming without a dagger in his teeth. I hope he was opening the seacocks when beaten insensible by truncheons" (146). The final outrage comes when the Secret Service agent claims impartiality by saying he has also guarded Republican Presidents. " 'For your information, Mr. Boyle,' said the Commodore, 'Dwight David Eisenhower was *not* a Republican' " (147).

As in many of the earlier stories, the search for a sense of identity emerges strongly in this one. The Commodore identifies himself by his family name, and by perpetuating the title and uniform of his past Yacht Club role. He has no work, though his wife Clarice urges him to find some. The combination of overhearing the barker on the tour boat and discovering his son's engagement to a Kennedy shocks him into reflection. "The question is: Who am I?" he asks. His wife tells him he is "a lovable man," but, unconsoled, he asks, "what am I but what the man on the sight-seeing boat said I was: A man who sits on this porch, drinking martinis, and letting the old mazooma roll in." He concludes that he needs to find some kind of work, reassured by Clarice that they would both be happier then, since it is hard to admire a man who "actually doesn't do anything" (149). Significantly, it is at this point of recognition that President Kennedy calls out from below, leading to the turning back on of the illuminations which the Commodore, in his despondency, had left unlighted.

Vonnegut sometimes appears to take a qualified view of the Kennedys, certainly not liking the commercialization that came to Cape Cod in their wake, somewhat distrustful of the "brightest and best" that surrounded them in Washington and the decisions they made, and too skeptical by nature to approve the popular mythos that grew up around them. In "The Hyannis Port Story," however, he treats President Kennedy generously in his brief appearance, capturing well the urbanity and charm that were his hallmark. The president's final words in this story can be read in more than one way. He asks that the illuminated Goldwater portrait be left on so that "I can find my way home" (150). There is an obvious literal reading. It can also be seen as implying that the lighted face of his probable opponent in the next election serves as a reminder of where he must go, of his political home ground. And it concludes the story fittingly, underlining that Rumfoord has found his way home in coming to some conclusions about who he is and must be. Viewed retrospectively, given the context of the time in which the story was written, an inevitable poignancy arises from the memory of this president's finding his way home in a coffin on board Air Force One.

The Rumfoords also have a name familiar to readers of Vonnegut. There is Winston Niles Rumfoord and his wife Beatrice in *The Sirens of Titan*, the historian Bertram Copeland Rumfoord in *Slaughterhouse-Five*, and there are Rumfoords in *God Bless You, Mr. Rosewater* and *Cat's Cradle*. They are always wealthy, aloof and aristocratic, the bluebloods of their fictional worlds. Vonnegut seldom villainizes them; if they treat people badly, it is because they have been deprived, brought up in a narrow world that affords them little perception of what life involves for the less fortunate. The Commodore, nevertheless, comes off better than most.

Also set in Hyannis is "Welcome to the Monkey House," although by the time of its events the Kennedy compound has become a museum enclosed in a geodesic dome, its grasses, beaches and ocean replaced by appropriately painted concrete. This story returns once more to the topic of overpopulation, the problems associated with it and those entailed in eradicating it. The story originally appeared in *Playboy* of January 1968, only seven months before the publication of the collection, and there are aspects of it that seem designed to spike the attention of that readership. In the main, though, such sexual energy as runs through the story serves as the vital counterpoint to the moribund sterility of a society that suppresses sexual pleasure and encourages euthanasia. This world of seventeen billion people and Ethical Suicide Parlors with six-feet tall, sexily clad hostesses appears reminiscent of that in "The Big Trip Up Yonder/Tomorrow and Tomorrow and Tomorrow." The first difference is that in this story the world government has imposed compulsory ethical birth control, rendered through pills that numb the lower extremities.

Most women said their bottom halves felt like wet cotton or stale ginger ale. The pills were so effective that you could blindfold a man who had taken one, tell him to recite the Gettysburg Address, kick him in the balls while he was doing it, and he wouldn't miss a syllable. (29)

The pills do not prevent reproduction, they simply remove any sexual pleasure. "Thus did science and morals go hand in hand" (29).

The second difference from the world of "The Big Trip Up Yonder" is the emergence of an inevitable human resistance to these dehumanizing strictures of the world government. When Shakespeare's Malvolio strives to impose strict moral laws on Illyria, Sir Toby Belch challenges him by saying, "Dost thou think, because thou art virtuous, there shall be no more cakes and ale?"[3] The voice of irrepressible human vitality in this story emanates from Billy the Poet (surely artist as canary-bird), a "nothinghead," as those who refuse to take their pills are called. Billy is known to assume various disguises and abduct Suicide Parlor hostesses, deflowering them and introducing them into an underground culture of nothingheads.

The plot, then, has the sheriff come to an Ethical Suicide Parlor to warn the two hostesses, Nancy McLuhan and Mary Kraft, that Billy the Poet is on the loose. Past behavior suggests he will head for the suicide parlor, since his targets always have been the hostesses. The telephone rings and a voice delivers one of the brief, taunting poems that are Billy's trade mark. But the police are prepared and swoop down upon the caller. The sheriff races off to the scene of the arrest, Mary following. Nancy returns to the old man they have been about to terminate, but he pulls out a gun, strips off his disguise, and reveals himself as Billy the Poet. He smuggles Nancy out and leads her through sewer tunnels to the Kennedy Compound museum, which closes for the winter. There other nothingheads seize her and drug her. By the time she awakes the effects of her ethical birth control pills have worn off, and she finds herself in the cabin of Joseph Kennedy's yacht "Marlin" with Billy. She tells him that if he wants to take her he had better call his friends to hold her down, and that is what happens. Later she looks out from under her covers to see Billy quietly reading at the cabin table. When he confirms that he has done the same to the other hostesses, she asks why they have never killed or betrayed him. He explains that they are grateful, and that in time she will be, too. " 'What you have been through, Nancy,' he said, 'is a typical wedding night for a strait-laced girl of a hundred years ago, when everybody was a nothinghead' " (45). He explains that marriages often began that way, but that with time the bride could become "a sexual enthusiast." His intent is to bring an innocent pleasure back into the world, and to express his tenderness he leaves her a book of poetry open to the poem his grandfather had read his bride on their wedding night: Elizabeth Barrett Browning's *How do I love thee? Let me count the ways.* And he leaves her with a bottle that contains the *old* birth control pills that allowed pleasure but prevented conception. And on the label are the words, "WELCOME TO THE MONKEY HOUSE' " (47).

That inscription refers to the history of how the whole idea of the numbing pills began. A druggist named J. Edgar Nation had been taking his eleven children for a walk through the zoo and came upon a monkey playing with its genitals. He invented the pill to "introduce morality into the monkey house at the Grand Rapids zoo." Since the anti-aging pill that kept every one looking like twenty-two was boosting the population growth, Nation's ethical birth control pill was imposed on humans, too. The druggist's name is a portmanteau derivation from J. Edgar Hoover and Carrie Nation. Hoover, as the FBI Director of the time, was vigorous in his rigid moral judgments, despite some peculiar proclivities of his own, while Carrie Nation sought to purge the society of alcohol-induced sin.   Carrie's influence lives on in Nancy's teachers, for she believes that unrestrained licentiousness can be induced by just one glass of the worst drug of all—gin.

One of Vonnegut's targets, then, is

"the people who have been most eager to rule, to make the laws, to enforce the laws and to tell everybody exactly how God Almighty wants things here on Earth—those people have forgiven themselves and their friends for anything and everything. But they have been absolutely disgusted and terrified by the natural sexuality of common men and women." (46)

This world government has made the enjoyment of sex a moral wrong, rather than seeing excessive reproduction as an ecological problem. Given the place of publication and the presumed audience, the implication of Vonnegut's position would be that government actions that put *Playboy* in wrappers on high shelves but say nothing about population control are hypocritical, vapid and futile. There are echoes here of "Miss Temptation," with Cpl. Fuller's becoming the voice of his Puritan ancestors, crying out against sexual temptation. Vonnegut has consistently decried censorship and the self-righteousness that imposes controls on the individual human rights of others as surely as if they were hanging the weights on Harrison Bergeron.   Vonnegut is equally serious about the threat of overpopulation; in this story again, most people don't have jobs, most species of animals and plants have disappeared, and every aspect of a boring world is government controlled.   He warns vigorously against the propensity of those in power to misuse the need to respond to real problems by imposing   supposed solutions that are otherwise motivated   as well as ineffectual. J. Edgar Nation, father of eleven, with his pill that prevents pleasure but not conception, provides an example, and finding analogous "real world" examples among political and religious leaders does not require too great an imaginative stretch.

All of which looks past the fact that Vonnegut does also intend the story to be funny.   There is humor in Nation's name, of course, and in his being so offended by the monkey.   There is also humor in the uninterrupted reading of the Gettysburg Address, and perhaps in the hyperbolically stereotypical description of the hostesses: "Their uniforms were white lipstick, heavy eye makeup, purple body stockings with nothing underneath, and black-leather boots" (29).   Ethical suicides peak the week before Christmas; the President of the World is "Ma" Kennedy with offices in the Taj Mahal and a "THINK" sign on her wall; and people on the pill piss blue.   A small private joke is that the dummy captain of the "Marlin" in the museum is Frank Wirtanen, who in fact was its skipper and with whom Vonnegut sailed.[4]   In the tradition of the calypsos of *Cat's Cradle* and other stories where poems, recipes and quotations are inserted, there are Billy's irreverently humorous poems:

> *I did not sow, I did not spin,*

> *And thanks to pills I did not sin.*

I loved the crowds, the stink, the noise.

And when I peed, I peed turquoise. (35)

Other comic concepts include last suppers in the Howard Johnsons always adjoining Ethical Suicide Parlors, the Kennedy Compound Museum itself, and the observation that for all its other changes America had not adopted the metric system.

One change that America has undergone, however, much of it in the years since this story was written, has been in its views on gender. That is where this story remains troublesome. When Nancy is given a "truth drug" and asked how it feels to be a virgin at sixty-three (due to her anti-aging pills she looks twenty-two) she says, "Pointless." Being an overgrown Barbie doll administering ethical suicides might well seem pointless. But the passage implies that her still being a virgin causes her to feel pointless, purpose evidently residing in her being a wife and mother. And the fact of Billy's rape of Mary remains hard to dismiss. His judgment that his assault is no more revolting than a typical first night for a "strait laced" bride of that and earlier times may have some validity but provides little justification. Does Billy have any more right to do this than the world government has to make Nancy numb? He assures her that many wives endured such a first night but came to enjoy satisfying sex. But how many were inhibited in their marital sex forever by such initiations? And what of perhaps taking men, making them "nothingheads" and teaching then something of tenderness, rather than teaching women to endure their clumsiness? Even in comedy, there may be a little too much to laugh off here.

While not fiction, "New Dictionary" fits comfortably in this collection because it reveals quite a lot of the author and allows him to talk directly to his readers in the first person. Additionally, it makes mention of other writers, and, of course, it discusses language and its usage. As mentioned above, this review of the *Random House Dictionary* was originally published in the October 30, 1966, issue of the *New York Times Book Review.* It was written while Vonnegut was spending two years as writer in residence at the University of Iowa Writers Workshop, where he met writers Richard Yates and Vance Bourjaily, and critic Robert Scholes, all of whom he mentions in the review. The chattily informal style creates a personal immediacy as he discusses his own rummagings in dictionaries, his uncertainties of *principle* and *principal*, and the battered state of his own old *Webster's*, left him by his father. He provides a genuinely informative review of this dictionary, insightful comment on the nature and uses of dictionaries in general, and by his informal approach makes entertaining a topic with great potential for aridity.

Vonnegut talks about the differences between "prescriptive" and "descriptive" dictionaries, the former, he says, being like "an honest cop" and the latter like "a boozed-up war buddy." He gives examples of how the three editions of the Merriam-Webster treat the same usage, and then what the new Random House says. He uses the pronouncements on "*ain't*" and on "*like*" when used for "*as*" as test cases for comparing the relative prescriptiveness of dictionaries, quoting extensively for illustration. Then he goes on to talk about the biographical entries and the citation of famous works of art. He raises interesting questions about the former, noting the difficulties of determining which will be enduring names and of making selections. He asks, for example, why Joseph Kennedy, Sr., John F. Kennedy and Robert F. Kennedy are included while Edward Kennedy and Jacqueline Kennedy are not. Viewed from the perspective of decades on, his question seems even more apt than it did at the time. He also wonders why T. S. Eliot (born in America but becoming a British subject) is listed as a *British* poet, while W. H. Auden (born in Britain but adopting American citizenship) is listed as an *English* poet. And he looks at the authors and the works of art that are included, in contrast to those of seemingly equal claim that are omitted. All of this becomes quite engaging, and makes this review of a dictionary anything but dull. He avoids the reviewer's trap— perhaps especially dangerous when reviewing a dictionary—of being pompously sententious, even bringing humor to his task. And, placed as it is near the middle of this collection, the review confirms, in its frank first-rson voice, the sense of the person behind and within the stories.

One of the curiosities of *Welcome to the Monkey House* is the listing, under "Acknowledgments," of the following: "*The Atlantic Monthly:* 'Der Arme Dolmetscher' (originally published under the title 'Das Ganz Arm Dolmetscher.')" (Respectively these titles translate as "The Poor Interpreter" and "The Very Poor Interpreter.") Despite the acknowledgment, the story does not appear in the collection. The apparent explanation is that there was a delay in getting a release to reprint the story which led to a decision to go ahead without it, but that deleting the acknowledgment was overlooked. The story *is* present in the proofs of *Welcome to the Monkey House*, however.[5] The second point of interest is that despite what the acknowledgment says, the story was originally published in *The Atlantic Monthly* as "Der Arme Dolmetscher," not "Das Ganz Arme Dolmetscher."

There are also some points of interest in the headnote of the "Der Arme Dolmetscher" as it appeared in *The Atlantic Monthly* (July 1955). In the brief biographical note about the author it claims, "He is now working for General Electric in Schenectady and writing a novel in his spare time" (86). That note is clearly several years out of date, as by 1955 Vonnegut had left General Electric, moved to Provincetown and then West Barnstable, and had published the novel *Player Piano*. While the piece itself has autobiographical elements, it has been heavily fictionalized, and the account of capture by the Germans at the end differs radically from those given in the *Paris Review* interview (*Conversations*, 171).

Some officers overhear Private Vonnegut singing the first stanza from *Die Lorelei*, something he had learned by rote from his college roommate. The colonel and his executive officer are both Southerners, and become the objects of Vonnegut's usual contempt for officers. They refuse to accept that Vonnegut does not speak "Kraut," they pass up the proffered services of three Pennsylvania Dutch soldiers who do, and they apparently labor under the confused impressions that "the American Army had just licked the Belgians" and that the Belgian mayor would speak German. On the way to the Belgian burgomeister's farmhouse, the dolmetscher Vonnegut shares the truck with the three Pennsylvania Dutch soldiers. They try to give him a cram course in

German on the way, then leave him with an Army phrase book, many pages of which have been removed to serve as cigarette papers.

Soon left alone in his room in the burgomeister's house, the soldier desperately rehearses phrases from the guide book. They are all military expressions—"Where are your howitzers?" "Don't shoot!"—in semi-phonetic transcription: *"Vee feel grenada vairfair habben zee?"* for example. In the midst of a sleepless night he imagines a drama in which he is on the brink of seducing the burgomeister's daughter in phrase-book German when her father enters, draws a gun, but in doing so drops a map of the American First Army's positions. At this point Vonnegut produces a .45 and holds the spies captive just as a patrol of Pennsylvania Dutch soldiers arrive. In reality he produces no such heroics and hikes back to headquarters before dawn. He makes the excuse that he speaks only High German while the burgomeister speaks Low German. The officers respond that he will soon have a chance to use either since they are surrounded, and twenty minutes later the Germans arrive. Ordered to say something to them, he hunts through his phrase book for "Don't shoot!" In answer, the panzer commander produces *his* phrase book and demands, "Where are your howitzers?"

Vonnegut frequently has fun with spoken language in his writing, be it dialect, foreign phrases, made-up language, or miscommunication. The most famous example occurs in the novel *Cat's Cradle*, but there are numerous interjections of this kind. In "Dolmetscher" Vonnegut has fun with the officers' Southern drawls ("Heah's what's goin' to do most of youah interpretin' fo' ya," one says of a rifle), with the commands and questions in the book *and* their phonetic transcriptions, and with the imaginary drama's wacky dialogue concocted out of disconnected military phrases. The characteristic insertion of drama into the story looks forward to the inclusion of brief Kilgore Trout plots or "playlets" in the later novels. "Der Arme Dolmetscher" provides an amusing portrayal of military rigidity and confusion. Vonnegut appears as irreverent toward rank and as iconoclastically insubordinate as he had in Cornell's cadet corps, and as he was to prove to the Germans, too, when a prisoner of war (*Conversations,* 172).

There have been minor changes to some of the stories in *Welcome to the Monkey House*, in addition to the two title changes already noted. In "EPICAC" the main female character's name changes from Pat Callaghan to Pat Kilgallen, and the last sentence, rather than reading "Say nothing but good of those who have never been born" reads "Say nothing but good of the dead." In "Deer in the Works," as was noted in discussion of that story, Vonnegut has inserted into the first paragraph the new sentence, "It was summer." The many minor revisions often involve little more than corrections of typos. An example of these minor corrections might be seen in "Unready to Wear" (231 of the first edition, 100 in *Galaxy Science Fiction*). "I let her pick out one for me to watch whatever" in the original is corrected to "match" in the collection; "a good, homy, comfortable body" becomes "homey" and "taken out once a year but for" is corrected by the omission of "but." Sometimes new editions even result in the creation of new glitches! In the first paragraph of "Welcome to the Monkey House," for example, the sheriff, whose name is Pete Crocker, is naturally referred to as "he" in the *Playboy* original and in the hardcover first edition, but becomes "she" in subsequent Dell paperback editions.

The dedication of *Welcome to the Monkey House* is to Knox Burger, the editor of *Collier's* who accepted Vonnegut's first story, "Report on the Barnhouse Effect," gave him advice, and directed him to others who helped groom his early writing. It reads: "For *Knox Burger* Ten days older than I am. He has been a very good father to me." And there is an epigraph: " 'Beware of all enterprises that require new clothes.' THOREAU" The dedication is an appropriate one for this collection, which *almost* represents the culmination of Vonnegut's short story writing career. The epigraph is also apt. Short story writing delivered Vonnegut from public relations in the corporate world and the need to dress accordingly. The quote also accords with the kind of lifestyle Vonnegut portrays in the Preface and "Where I Live," and bespeaks the kind of irreverent independence that is the quintessence of his style.

OTHER COLLECTIONS

Vonnegut has published three other books that are collections of shorter pieces: *Wampeters, Foma, and Granfalloons* (1974), *Palm Sunday* (1981), and *Fates Worse than Death* (1991). All of these contain items that, besides their other interest, are enlightening about the author, his life and thoughts, and his writing, sometimes even in ways that bear upon his short story writing. It is those items that can be described as prose fiction that are of relevance here, however, and they are relatively few.

In the Preface of *Wampeters, Foma, and Granfalloons*, there occurs an example of the kinds of references that bear on short story writing. Recounting his many speaking engagements, Vonnegut says: "A writer can get more money for a bungling speech at a bankrupt college than he can get for a short story masterpiece" (xvi). He frequently laments the demise of the short story market, particularly because it has removed a nurturing ground for aspiring young writers. The selection of greatest interest in *Wampeters, Foma, and Granfalloons*, however, is "Fortitude," which first appeared in *Playboy*. Written in the form of a play, or more specifically, the script for a television or short film production, it represents fiction in a book composed mostly of what Vonnegut calls "New Journalism," including speeches, essays and reviews previously presented elsewhere.

"Fortitude" is set in a medical institution in upstate New York. The characters include Dr. Norbert Frankenstein, 65, "a crass medical genius," Dr. Tom Swift, his assistant, and Dr. Elbert Little, a genial general practitioner who is visiting. Their activities revolve around Sylvia Lovejoy, a billionaire's widow of one hundred. "*Sylvia* is no longer anything but a head connected to pipes and wires coming up through the floor" (46–47). The remaining character is Sylvia's "gorgeous beautician," Gloria. Much of Sylvia's fortune has been spent over the past forty-six years buying her eighty-seven operations which have left her nothing more than a head on a tripod, equipped with mechanical arms, connected to an array of artificial organs mounted in a separate room and monitored by Frankenstein and Swift. They can manipulate all of her senses and moods. The three settings comprise the control room, Sylvia's room, and the area just outside of it.

Sylvia whiles away her existence by writing countless letters, including the one inviting Dr. Little to visit, and talking to Gloria. When not chemically boosted into cheery moods, Sylvia often expresses a wish to die. She has asked Gloria's help, and she has asked Dr. Little to bring cyanide on his visit. Frankenstein relies not just on mood-altering to prevent this, but also makes it impossible for her mechanical arms to perform various suicidal acts. Gloria pleads that keeping Sylvia "alive" is inhumane and gets fired for her views, but not before she has smuggled a gun to Sylvia. The mechanical arms thwart Sylvia's attempts to shoot herself, and she asks Frankenstein how long he intends to make her go on living. He tells her that the equipment can go on for five hundred years, and is duplicated, so that after his death, his head can be set up beside her. They will be sharing the same organs, living closer than any normally married couple. At that Sylvia shoots him, but in the final scene the two heads awaken (to the strains of *Ah, Sweet Mystery of Life*) side by side on their pedestals and "perceive each other as old and beloved friends."

"Fortitude" presents another variation in Vonnegut's treatment of the pursuit of artificially extended life. Here there are none of the relative virtues of anti-aging pills or "super-anti-gerasone" forever preserving the looks and vitality of a twenty-two year old. Here is a near-eternity stuck on a tripod in one room, merely a brain recording sensations induced by others through artificial organs. It recreates the misery of the mythical Sibyl of Cumae, who wishes for eternal life and ends up suspended in a jar, desiring only to die. The play exposes the nightmarish potentials in the common human wish to extend life and in such medical science as transplant surgery, artificial organs, xenographic transplants, and mood altering drugs. And it raises another very relevant issue—cost. At one point, Dr. Little speaks of people who cannot be cured "at any price," then catches himself and adds, "at any price within their means." Frankenstein has only one, very rich, patient. Little, the "Family Doctor of the Year," has many and lives modestly. The reservation that exotic procedures become the privilege of the rich, and drain personnel and resources from the more basic needs of the majority, emerges powerfully in this story. Obviously, Vonnegut's choice of names signals his message. Dr. Frankenstein is a caricature not just in name, keeping a monstrous creation alive. Behind its macabre humor, this drama invites questions about medical science and projects situations that daily assume more relevance.

Palm Sunday has the subtitle, *An Autobiographical Collage*, and like *Wampeters, Foma, and Granfalloons* it consists of a collection of disparate items which do indeed tell much about the author when assembled. Of most direct interest to this study is "The Big Space Fuck," a short story that previously appeared in *Again, Dangerous Visions: Forty-six Original Stories Edited by Harlan Ellison*.   In that publication a long and rather self-indulgent introduction by Ellison precedes the story. Among other things Ellison observes that this story may be the first ever to use "fuck" in its title. He also speaks of meeting Vonnegut through Knox Burger when the latter was editor of Gold Medal books. Ellison says Burger asked his opinion of Vonnegut's short stories because he was considering putting together a collection (*Canary in a Cat*

House), and asked him to help package the book, so that it was he who contacted Leo and Diane Dillon to do the artwork. He also wrote the blurbs for the cover. The story itself undergoes two changes when reprinted in *Palm Sunday* . First, its dates are moved forward a decade, so that 1977 and 1979 in the first two paragraphs of the Ellison edition become 1987 and 1989 in *Palm Sunday*. Secondly, the addition at the conclusion of the story in the Ellison collection, "*Afterword:* And so it goes" (272), does not appear in *Palm Sunday*.

"The Big Space Fuck" resembles a Kilgore Trout story, partly in its content, and partly in its having the rather off-the-cuff, unfinished quality that they often possess. America in 1987—here an imaginary future, remember—is distinguished by two developments. First, children can now sue their parents for the way they had been raised. Second, rife overpopulation, with the pollution resulting from it, threatens continued human habitation on Earth. The Great Lakes, for example, are so polluted that they are inhabited by giant lampreys thirty-eight feet long. Perhaps a third development should be noted; words like "fuck" and "shit" are now socially acceptable, and even the president uses them regularly. As a consequence, a project to send a space vehicle to the Andromeda Galaxy carrying eight hundred pounds of freeze-dried human sperm, as a gambit to perpetuate the human species, bears the official title "The Big Space Fuck." The spaceship is named the *Arthur C. Clarke*, and the launch date is July 4.

Dwayne Hoobler and his wife Grace are watching the launch in their modest home in Elk Harbor, Ohio, on the shores of Lake Erie—home of the man-eating lampreys. Dwayne works as a guard at the state prison and in his spare time makes birdhouses out of Clorox bottles, even though there are not any birds anymore. The arrival of the County Sheriff, an old friend, interrupts their watching of the space launch, bringing the bad news that he has come to subpoena them. Their daughter, Wanda June, having become twenty-one, has accused them of ruining her life. When she was four, she claims, she drew crayon pictures on the walls to please her mommy, who instead was angry and spanked her, after which she hates arts materials. This, she charges, has deprived her of "a brilliant and lucrative career in the arts" (231). She claims her father deprived her of an advantageous marriage by being "half in the bag" when suitors arrived and often naked to the waist when he answered the door. Wanda June's motivation, it emerges, stems from her being arrested for shoplifting and needing to prove that everything she did was her parents' fault.

In the meantime, Senator Flem Snopes of Mississippi, chairman of the Senate Space Committee, gives an interview on television wearing a codpiece in the shape of a rocket embroidered with "U.S.A." and a Confederate flag. Such dress is in vogue. And outside, even the giant lampreys are finding the lake too polluted and are oozing their way out of the mud. The sheriff departs and walks straight into the jaws of one. The Hooblers rush out to see the cause of the screaming and share a similar fate. Meanwhile the television goes on with its countdown.

As suggested at the outset, plot is not the strength of this story, and it remains fragmentary and abruptly finished. But it has brash humor, brisk pace, and amusing allusions. Vonnegut uses the name Hoobler elsewhere, various of this ilk turning up in *Breakfast of Champions* (1973) and *Deadeye Dick* (1982), just as Snopses recur in William Faulkner's novels—Vonnegut's borrowing

Flem Snopes is a gesture of recognition. Wanda Junes appear in *The Sirens of Titan* (1959), *Happy Birthday, Wanda June* (1970), and *Hocus Pocus* (1990). Another kind of allusion is in the reappearance of chronosynclastic infundibulae, also from *The Sirens of Titan*. Here they are described as time warps through which the *Arthur C. Clarke* must pass, ensuring that "the ship and its load would be multiplied a trillion times" in time and space.

There is topical humor in the daughter's suing the parents, reflecting social trends toward deflecting responsibility to others. There is ironic humor in Grace's being amused by Dwayne's and the sheriff's "wit" in calling each other "you old motherfucker," "shitface," and so on. There is the amusing determination of whose "jizzum" will be selected for transmission to Andromeda, IQs of over 115 being required except of athletes, musicians and painters. (The Director of the New York Philharmonic can contribute a full quart, despite being sixty-eight. The younger Dwayne does not qualify, there being no priority for birdhouse builders.) And there is the encouragement of population control by giving to any woman who has an abortion a table lamp or bathroom scale. Finally, there is the fatalistic, rather bitter, but characteristically Vonnegutian humor in the realization "beginning to dawn on even dumb people that [Earth] might be the only habitable planet human beings would ever find" (230).

The other fictional contribution to *Palm Sunday* is *Jekyll and Hyde Updated*, which Vonnegut explains came about when he served on the New York State Council for the Arts with Lee Guber, the Broadway producer. Over the summer of 1978, Guber asked Vonnegut to write a modern version of Robert Louis Stevenson's *Dr. Jekyll and Mr. Hyde* for the musical stage (260). The actual title he gives to the resulting script is *The Chemistry Professor*. Vonnegut sets his musical on the campus of a college that suddenly faces bankruptcy. The students, led by their student body president, Jerry Rivers, set about producing a Broadway show to raise funds. Simultaneously, the chemistry professor seeks some dramatic project to bring fame and grants to the college. The two efforts collide, so that there are on-stage and off-stage Jekyll and Hyde plots intermeshing. Vonnegut indicates where there would be musical and dance numbers inserted into the script. Since this piece represents a distinctly different genre from the short story, it need not be pursued here. It is worth noting in passing, however, that "Jerry Rivers" is how Vonnegut frequently refers to his ex-son-in-law, talk show host Geraldo Rivera.

The remaining book in this group, *Fates Worse than Death*, like *Palm Sunday*, is subtitled *An Autobiographical Collage*. It, too, is a collection, although the selections are integrated into their commentary. This results in complete chapters that *contain* speeches or essays produced previously, rather than separate selections with perhaps brief introductions, the format generally followed in the earlier works. None of the inclusions in *Fates Worse than Death* actually qualifies as short fiction, although the book will reward those interested in this form with what it reveals of Vonnegut and for what he has to say about some other exponents of the form, notably in Chapter V.

NOTES

1. Asa B. Pieratt, Julie Huffman-klinkowitz, and Jerome Klinkowitz, *Kurt Vonnegut: A Comprehensive Bibliography* (Hamden, CT: The Shoestring Press/Archon Books, 1987), 28–29.

2. In 1971, in response to an interview question from Laurie Clancy, Vonnegut enlarges on his remark about the distinction between short story and novel writing: "Well, it forced me to write for magazines and the sort of fiction they wanted was low-grade, simplistic, undisturbing sort of writing. And so, in order to pay the bills I would write stories of that sort. I would try to accumulate enough capital to allow me to write a book. In effect, I was scrambling pretty hard writing lousy stories for years in order to pay the bills. It wasn't all bad— nothing ever is all bad—I did learn how to tell a story, how to make a story work, so that the thing has a certain flow and suspense and so forth. It is mechanical and it's somewhat worth knowing. Because I went through that apprenticeship I did learn how to tell a story. But every book I ever wrote I wrote with great seriousness, no cynicism at all and no large financial hopes each time. The reason I was living, so far as my professional life went, was in order to write books, simply books I wanted to exist. The short stories were going to make my money and after I had accumulated enough I would write as good a book as I could. There's no cynicism in my book writing whatsoever." Laurie Clancy, "Running Experiments Off: An Interview," in William Rodney Allen, ed., *Conversations with Kurt Vonnegut* (Jackson: University Press of Mississippi, 1988), 52.

3. William Shakespeare, *Twelfth Night*, II. iii. 116–117.

4. The real Frank Wirtanen figures in "Brief Encounters on the Inland Waterway" in *Wampeters, Foma, and Granfalloons*, where Vonnegut recounts crewing for him on Joseph P. Kennedy's yacht *Marlin* on a journey from Hyannis Port to West Palm Beach. The name is used again for the "Blue Fairy Godmother" who is the spy under Howard Campbell's control in *Mother Night*.

5. I am indebted to Asa B. Pieratt, who has examined the proof copies of all of Vonnegut's books, to date without publishing his findings, for this information.

7

The Novels: Stories, Mosaics, and Jokes

While Kurt Vonnegut has been at pains to characterize the writing of short stories and of novels as very different activities, th fact must remain that the two come out of the same creative genius and that, just as the apprenticeship in journalism sometimes manifests itself in the short stories, so the short fiction writer's education shows itself in the novels. Sometimes the apparent carryovers from the earlier form to the later, though seemingly closely related, are superficial and have less to do with the heritage of short story writing than with Vonnegut's evolving postmodernist style. *Hocus Pocus* (1990), written as a memoir made up of fragments written on scraps of paper, has chapters composed of many short segments separated by a line across the page. Each of these fragments, or short passages, hardly represents a complete short story. How different is this form from the short chapters of *Cat's Cradle* (1963), or from the segments of *Slaughterhouse-Five* (1969), intermixed in un-chronological order? Perhaps the more apt description of these techniques is one used by Vonnegut himself, where he speaks of his novels' resembling mosaics, wherein each tile is a joke: except that not every segment in these fragmented novels *is* a joke, and that this analogy works better with some novels than with others. [1]

There do appear to be discernible carryovers, however, despite these difficulties in arbitrarily separating what might be classified as resulting from one influence and what from another. The underlying and perhaps dominant factor at work may be Vonnegut's evident preference for working with short units. His remark about building a mosaic out of tile-jokes accords with that. So does his often declared method of working, where he contrasts himself with "swoopers" who draft out the whole work then go back and revise, saying that he revises one page at a time, and when he has that to his satisfaction, sets it aside and begins the next page.[2] This, doubtless to his regret, does not mean that he does not frequently then discard a whole segment of manuscript and start over, but it does demonstrate again a tendency to think and create in smaller units. Most of his books tend to be segmental or episodic in some form, and such evidence as he offers tends to confirm that they are composed in that manner (*Conversations,* 48–49).

This study naturally cannot proceed to an analysis of each of the novels in terms of its apparent connections to the short fiction. Instead, *Player Piano* (1952) will be discussed because it is the first novel and concurrent with Vonnegut's early ventures into the short story market, and therefore perhaps the one where the most evidence of similarity in technique, form and content might be predicted. After that, other novels will be cited where they appear to reveal most evidence of a technique or content echoing what appears in the short fiction. The main emphasis in the body of this chapter, then, will be on showing how, in these fundamental components of Vonnegut's longer fiction, the characteristics evident in the short fiction continue to manifest themselves.

The structure of *Player Piano* appears at first to be one of the least obviously affected by a short story writer's technique. That is, there are not the immediately apparent features such as its being constructed out of numerous very short chapters or fragments like *Cat's Cradle* or *Hocus Pocus*, although the chapters nevertheless are noticeably short. Indeed, the rather derivative nature of this novel, standing as it does in the tradition of such other dystopian novels as Aldous Huxley's *Brave New World,* invites consideration of the novel's form only in those terms. Vonnegut himself has been quite frank about this, acknowledging "I cheerfully ripped off the plot of *Brave New World,* whose plot had been cheerfully ripped off from Eugene Zamiatin's *We*"(*Conversations,* 93). Within the rather traditional linear, chronological exposition of the novel, however, the organization of the narrative has some interesting characteristics which perhaps show the influence of short story writing.

Since Vonnegut seeks to make a fairly wide-ranging social commentary in *Player Piano,* he faces the challenge of creating broad or multiple plot situations and categories of characters to permit his plausibly portraying many aspects of life. He needs to do this in a way that minimizes the danger of the reader's becoming confused and distracted. At the same time he needs to preserve the impressions, first, that these many levels of life interact and influence each other, and second, that a degree of chaos or unpredictability is an inevitable part of life, one that the manager-engineers have tended to overlook. This he manages ingeniously by writing a plot and a series of subplots. These interact, and there are many switches between them, sometimes leaving one situation suspensefully "in the air" while he switches to another. But the reader is guided in this process by a labeling of the plots. The main plot naturally concerns the protagonist, Paul Proteus. The central symbol in this plot is the *p*layer *p*iano of the title, prototype of all the subsequent automated duplications of human motions that have led to the displacement of countless workers. The central plot, then, bears the "PP" stamp. Around this plotline weave the subplots, all designated by the letter "H." Paul Proteus's world of managers and engineers is a suburban Nirvana on the same side of the river as the great Ilium Works. Across the river from it lies Homestead, the alternate world of those displaced by machines, the breeding ground of revolution against the "Second Industrial Revolution." Typifying its inhabitants is Edgar R. B. Hagstrohm, whom the computers find absolutely average in every respect and therefore redundant. Also in Homestead lives Rudy Hertz, the machinist whose movements Paul Proteus and colleagues had duplicated for their first automated manufacturing machine. When Paul tries to find an alternative world to these two, he considers retiring to the Gottwald Farm, whose caretaker, the farmer Haycox, bluntly undercuts Paul's dreams of escape. Another subplot involves Private Elmo C. Hacketts, who has joined the Army to escape the make-work "Reeks and Wrecks." Intruding into these worlds from Washington comes Dr. Ewing Halyard, the State Department official who squires the Shah of Bratpuhr. Halyard's subplot has its own comic substance but serves mainly to enable the Shah to fulfill his role as the outside observer, the commentator from another culture who, through the prism of his own rather comical perspective, presents an undercutting assessment of things in this automated Utopia.

The effect of having the five "H" plots is to make each its own manageable unit, not altogether unlike its being a separate short story with a focus on its own central character, situation, and even moral, though each then becomes chopped up and interspersed into the main plot. What might be the "message" of each subplot, were it a separate short story, is interjected into the main plot, with its consequent impact there. For instance, as Halyard conducts the Shah on his visits to everyday Americans, he has to combat the visitor's propensity to regard the likes of Hacketts and the Hagstrohms as "Takaru"—slaves. But Halyard comes face to face with that prospect himself when it is found that he has never completed his P.E. requirement at college, thus is not entitled to his degrees—or his job. His plight tends to vindicate the view of the Shah, and the bleak judgment of the novel on what the technological world has done to the status of average citizens.

In another subplot Paul Proteus wishfully thinks he can evade the choices confronting him by escaping into a world that seems to embody the characteristics of an idyllic past. He considers resigning and moving to the Gottwald Farm, but Haycox assumes a role not unlike that of the down-to-earth, common sense drugstore owners in "Miss Temptation" or "The Powder Blue Dragon." He scorns all the Ph.D.s of this new age, and declares himself "a doctor of cowshit, pigshit and chickenshit." Haycox holds to the bygone values Paul hopes to enjoy by evasion, but enacts them by his membership in the rebellious Ghost Shirt Society, just as ultimately Paul must do himself.

Several of the more striking vignettes within the novel almost take on the characteristics of short stories within themselves. The episode of the stray cat that Paul Proteus finds actually serves to foreshadow his own fate. Paul wishes to keep the cat, a redeeming embodiment of the natural world in the sterility of the automated plant, but a robot cleaning machine relentlessly tracks down the terrified creature and swallows it up. Miraculously, however, the cat emerges alive from the machine and sprints for the fence. It reaches the top, only to be killed by the electrified wires. "She dropped to the asphalt—dead and smoking, but outside" (21). This emblematic little story of animal life swallowed up in a world of machines and dying for its freedom parallels Paul's own course in the novel and foreshadows the failed Ghost Shirt rebellion. It can also be seen as foreshadowing "Deer in the Works," published three years later. That story embodies many of the same conflicts of values, but concludes happily with both animal and man outside of the fence alive and bound for happier worlds.

Another equally emblematic vignette that takes on the quality of a story within a story involves the player piano itself. On one of his forays into Homestead, Paul encounters Rudy Hertz, the original lathe operator whose movements he had duplicated. The bar where they meet has a player piano. An excited Rudy watches it enthralled, saying, "You can almost see a ghost sitting there playing his heart out" (38). It is a heavily ironic moment. The player piano serves as the prototype of all those machines where the operator's movements can be punched onto a roll, or keypunched into a card, or programmed into a computer. The ghost he sees might well be himself, but his excitement with the musical machine puts him on a par with the barber who ends up inventing the machine to replace himself. Rudy's response predicts the closing scenes of the novel where the Ghost Shirters cannot resist tinkering with and fixing the very machines they have just wrecked. The ghost that haunts Paul as he watches Rudy with the player piano is the ghost of Rudy himself, of all the men he has reduced to such pitiful lives by replacing their meaningful occupations, and even of himself, robotized by the company life. The point is underlined when he arrives home, ashen, and his wife exclaims, "Darling, you look as though you've seen a ghost" (38). That could be the clinching final line of a short story easily constructed out of these events.

There are other vignettes, far less central to the plot but with all the makings of a short story, such as the one involving Alfy, the bar shark, who wins his money by betting that he can identify songs being sung on television with the sound turned off. Of course, the phenomenon of excerpts from novels becoming freestanding short stories, or stories being expanded and becoming parts of novels, has precedents. There are examples such as William Faulkner's "The Spotted Horses" and *The Hamlet*, or Evelyn Waugh's "The Man Who Loved Dickens" and *A Handful of Dust*, and many more. The two writers instanced, like Vonnegut, are accomplished exponents of both forms. What seems to be involved is the short story writer's capacity to create rapidly a character who necessarily will remain two-dimensional but nevertheless vitally engaging, and a self-contained situation with its own satisfying outcome, even within the context of a longer work.

Apart from these apparent connections with short story writing in the structuring of the novel, there are a good many echoes of other kinds. The element of contrivance in the names used in some of the stories reappears, not just in the "PP" and "H" names but others, too. The conscience-stirring preacher is Lasher; the technocrat engineer-managers at the top are Teutonic—Kroner and Baer; the unkempt nonconformist who stirs resistance is the Celt, Ed Finnerty. Ilium, a fictionalized rendition of General Electric's Schenectady, reappears several times in Vonnegut's fiction, as does a computer named EPICAC.

Recurrent themes abound, too. The familiar search for identity remains prominent, as Paul asks who he is, why he hesitates to assume the mantle of his father, why he cannot generate the necessary enthusiasm to assure his promotion to manager of the Pittsburgh Works, why he feels nostalgia in the old Plant 58 and discontent with what he has achieved, and why he cannot tell his wife he loves her with more conviction. He struggles with whether his anxieties actually stem from the world he inhabits and the life he leads, or from something psychological. Here Vonnegut enjoys the time and space in which to develop the inner searchings that in the short fiction must be signaled more abruptly and flatly. Part of Paul's search involves a fathers-and-sons motif once more. People expect him to follow his father's lead; in his trial, Paul feels challenged by the proposition that he is motivated not altruistically out of social concerns, but to enact a personal rebellion against the figure of his father. Similarities emerge between this theme's treatment here and in "This Son of Mine" four years later.

Other instances of characters' searching for their identities abound. Alfy, the television watcher, creates an occupation and hence a sense of a role, an identity, from this pastime. Reminiscent of Harry in "Unpaid Consultant," who invents his make-believe job as an adviser to the catchup industry to keep himself busy and assume an air of importance, Alfy goes further by actually making money in his occupation. Mrs. Hagstrohm feels utterly pointless in her automated home, with nothing to do but watch television, so she lets the washing machine remain unrepaired so that she can wash clothes in a tub and feel some purpose in that. Paul's wife, Anita, resembles aspects of various women in the short stories. In part she derives her sense of identity from Paul and his position, so she feels deeply threatened when his emotional crisis undermines his performance in his role. Indeed, she has engineered that identity for herself by pretending pregnancy and forcing the marriage. Being of a modest background and with no academic performance to give her status in this society, the social role that determines her identity depends entirely upon him— or, as it turns out, his replacement. In this she perhaps resembles Falloleen in "Custom-Made Bride," or those company wives of Creon Pipe in "Find Me A Dream." But she also resembles other women from the short fiction, such as Grace McClellan in "More Stately Mansions," in her reliance on determining what she should be from glossy magazines. In another twist on the identity theme, the President of the United States has been an actor, something that seemed comically improbable at the time of writing.

Vonnegut's concern with the responsible oversight of technological and scientific innovations becomes a recurrent theme in both the short fiction and the novels, and needs no belaboring. Obviously, it re-emerges as a major theme of *Player Piano*. Perhaps less obvious is the question of how accurately its development can be classified as science fiction. Vonnegut has said that he did not think of himself as writing science fiction in this novel, simply as writing of the technological world that surrounded him.[3] Since it depicts technology projected to a state of sophistication and ubiquity beyond what existed in 1952, and places it in a future time, the novel nevertheless invites the science fiction categorization. Bantam obviously thought so when they reissued it in 1954 as *Utopia 14*. Two characteristics that it shares with the handling of science fiction in the short stories are, first, that it often highlights contrasts between the futuristic and objects of the past, and second, that the treatment frequently involves humor.

Player Piano constantly evokes the past. Its shrine, Plant 58, the original building, has adz-hewn rafters carved with initials of former workers and photographs of company sports teams of long ago. The camaraderie of those times for which Paul yearns contrasts with the present, the Works now being so automated that an entire shift can leave work in one station wagon. Haycox and his Gottwald Farm embody the same nostalgic quality, as underlined by Anita's seeing the place only as a repository of usable antiques. The juxtaposition of these objects with the advanced technology has a similar effect to, say, the listing of the old furniture in the room right before the professor demonstrates *dynamopsychism* in "Report on the Barnhouse Effect." The undercutting comments of the Shah of Bratpuhr, whose culture appears medieval, contribute to the contrasting effect. As for the humor, it surrounds the enormous EPICAC XIV, Bud Calhoun's conversations with his talking car, the constant propensity to over-complicate (like inventing a machine to go through the fence rather than just using wire cutters), the Shah's getting caught up in a mass of similarly dressed Shriners, and even Ed Finnerty's wry conclusion, "If it weren't for [the people] earth would be an engineer's paradise" (313).

Vonnegut obeys many of the basic lessons for short story writing that he recalls being taught. For example, that the protagonist should "want" something, that there should be a decision to be made.[4] With Paul there are several, such as whether to go for the Pittsburgh job, whether to quit, whether to join the Ghost Shirts or whether to become a spy, but they all hinge on the same general question of what he will choose to be in relation to his society. There is also the admonition that an object, such as "a gun over a fireplace," should not be noted if it will not play some role in the story.[5] Illustrating that rule, the rusty old pistol in the glove box of Paul's car becomes the piece of evidence that traps him. Vonnegut also speaks of the importance of conflict to a story, and that surely abounds (*Conversations*, 189). One interesting embodiment of it reminiscent of a short story occurs with the enactment of the central conflict of man versus machine in a chess game between the robot "Checker Charley" and Paul Proteus. It echoes the way that the life and death conflicts of the cold war are played out in a game of chess in "All the King's Horses."

A character who does not appear in *Player Piano* nevertheless serves as the vehicle for a topic that Vonnegut will treat with increasing frequency. The topic is the role of the writer, with emphasis upon the conflict between artistic integrity and the need for income, and the character is the writer known only as Ed. The Shah encounters Ed's wife working as a prostitute because her husband has failed as a novelist. The novel that could have won him promotion was rejected for being twenty-seven pages too long and being too intellectual. Books are marketed at less cost than seven packs of chewing gum by twelve book clubs, the favorite topics being dog stories or tales "of the old days on the Erie Canal." Ed disdains such subjects and thus fails to gain promotion to "fiction journeyman" or the next level up, "public relations." Halyard notes the dubious ethic of a man who would rather have his wife become a prostitute than become a public relations man himself. " 'I'm proud to say,' said the girl, 'that he's one of the few men on earth with a little self-respect left' " (234). Ironies abound here, of course, with Vonnegut jibing at what the market demands of writers in his own world. He appears to have his shot at both public relations writing and those who would disdain those who do it out of need. Writers who prostitute themselves by public relations writing or publishing pornography or slick fiction make frequent appearances, culminating in the *alter ego* figure of Kilgore Trout. The situation in *Player Piano* has some of the same thematic ingredients that will be repeated in "Deer in the Works," except that there the writer would compromise by becoming a public relations writer while his wife rejects that as selling out.[6]

That there should be these many connections between the short stories and this novel, written early in Vonnegut's career and while his short fiction writing was gathering momentum, may seem hardly surprising. Perhaps the more interesting question is to what extent it continued, and it what ways it manifested itself. Reference to other novels suggests that there continue to be connections. Among the most obvious are the repeated names, topics, jokes and locations, but in fact these may be less significant than apparent, and in any case hardly rare or distinctive, in that such reappearances are found in the work of other writers. What remains a distinguishing feature of much of Vonnegut's fiction is its form, notably in the structure of such novels as *Cat's Cradle*, *Slaughterhouse-Five* or *Breakfast of Champions*, and there the apparent connection with the short stories has more significance. The short story influence manifests itself both in the basic structure of some of the novels, to greater or lesser degree, and also in the imbedding of short fictions, most obviously the Kilgore Trout stories, within the larger structure.

The Sirens of Titan (1959) may appear among the least influenced structurally by short story technique, if the expectation is that this influence shows itself in segmentation into smaller, more nearly self-contained units. This novel, which, as we have seen, Vonnegut speaks of as having been spontaneously conceived and easily written, has a flow and continuity that seem relaxed in comparison with *Player Piano*. That quality stems largely from its linear construction; one episode leads on to another in natural succession. The novel often has been described as a "space opera," a kind of sci-fi soap opera set in space, where the plot moves by relocating from one planet to another, each with its own circumstances and cast. Though having the segments placed sequentially rather than intertwined simultaneously, as in *Player Piano*, eases the movement of the novel and makes the transitions between plots less abrupt, the separating out of topics into their own settings still takes place. Thus the stories of Rumfoord and his manifestations from the chrono-synclastic infundibulum, of "The Church of God the Utterly Indifferent," of the Martian army and its invasion, or of the caves of Mercury and the harmoniums, all have a good deal of self containment. Their nature suggests that in writing this novel, Vonnegut might have subtracted episodes or added more with relatively little difficulty.[7] His experience with characterization in short fictions facilitates his easy and rapid casting of new characters as the location shifts. Finally, there is another step in the evolution of the story-within-a-novel in the form of Unk's diary.

Cat's Cradle (1963) contrasts with *The Sirens of Titan's* linear continuity, being chopped up into 127 chapters, yet in its different way it, too, moves easily and quickly. In fact, much of its movement and tempo resembles that of the short story. The characters are quickly and sometimes stereotypically drawn, there is a minimum of description, and the dialogue is snappy. If the mini-chapters can hardly be described as short stories in themselves, they usually have integrity in completing a step or stage in the narrative, and each little episode moves quickly to a punch line—sometimes a joke, sometimes an ironic, shaggy-dog ending. If any novel fits Vonnegut's description of the mosaic of jokes *Cat's Cradle* does, but it also appears closest, in narrative technique, to the story-writer's style.

Slaughterhouse-Five (1969) certainly has the characteristic of being fragmented or segmented, most of its actions taking place in three distinct time periods which are then chopped up, intermixed, and shuffled out of chronological order. This is certainly a novel where Vonnegut's declared goal of wanting to make chaos out of order shows itself. The novel can be shown to be very carefully organized, in fact, but the apparently random shiftings in time and place have the effect of denying the kind of rational sequencing of events that linear narrative usually provides. Vonnegut does not want logical sequence to supply the impression of cause-and-effect to make rational an event that he can only see as absurd and chaotic. The structure of the novel, then, would seem to owe more to Vonnegut's conception of how this subject should be narrated than to any conscious or unconscious carryover from the short story writing.

Breakfast of Champions (1973) has twenty-four chapters plus an epilogue, but dividing the chapters are spaced subdivisions indented with arrows. These shorter segments sometimes have only one paragraph, though frequently they are longer. Often they contain one of the simple line drawings that made this novel distinctive, if not notorious, when it appeared. The segments are often like jokes, with a closure that makes them self-contained. For example, when a salesman complains that his boss's dress code makes him feel as if he works for Watson Brothers funeral home, the employer responds: "Listen, Harry, . . . Burn your clothes and get new ones, or apply for work at Watson Brothers. Have yourself embalmed while you're at it" (46). Sometimes that punchline is separated by its own indentation, like a final couplet of a sonnet. After the illustration of a rattlesnake comes the description:

The Creator of the Universe had put a rattle on its tail. The Creator had also given it front teeth which were hypodermic syringes filled with deadly poison. [New indent] Sometimes I wonder about the Creator of the Universe. (159–60).

The closure can be dramatically curt. At the end of one of the longer segments comes the conclusion:

Celia Hoover was crazy as a bedbug. My mother was, too. (181)

Other segments contain summaries of Kilgore Trout stories, like *Plague on Wheels* or *Now It Can Be Told*. These allow Vonnegut to tell or summarize a story within the larger fiction itself, often in such a way that it emphasizes a point being made in the surrounding narrative. In the case of *Now It Can Be Told*, the story actually influences the course of the novel. One of the central characters, Dwayne Hoover, takes literally this story's premise that all other people are actually robots and goes on a rampage which changes the plot.

In being reminiscent of the short fiction these devices may have invited some of the stern negative criticism that descended upon this book. Perhaps the punchlines and the breezily summarized Trout tales smack too much of the "slick fiction" that he had himself denigrated. In his Preface, Vonnegut says "I feel lousy about it" of this book, and also that it represents a fiftieth birthday present to himself and an attempt to clear all the inhibiting junk out of his mind (4–5). It is dedicated to Phoebe Hurty, the woman who got him the job of writing Block's advertisements for the *Shortridge Echo* and who taught him "to be impolite" (2). If its spirit matches those occasional circumstances, its technique fits well a novel whose main character is the pulp fiction writer Kilgore Trout. Even more, coming as it does in 1973, its manner seems appropriate to the times. It reflects a society riven by recent and continuing divisions over civil rights, America's war in Asia, equal rights for women, and political assassinations. It was a time when the traditionally assumed, sonorously propounded tenets of American society, and its icons, no longer seemed to fit or answer. Vonnegut asserts his need to clear his head of them and find a new culture. In this context, the snappy, irreverent, even flippant tone proves the only way to handle sober images that no longer signify meaning to most Americans—like "E pluribus unum" or the eye in a pyramid on the dollar bill—and also to address without bathos the pain and tragedy afflicting the society that the novel depicts.

The book's manner of appearing breezily off-hand about serious, often distressing issues extends to the use of the Kilgore Trout stories. Take the example of his story called "This Means You." It depicts the Hawaiian Islands at a time when every "bit of land on the islands was owned by only about forty people," who put No Trespassing signs everywhere. The other million inhabitants have difficulty existing without constantly invading private property. The federal government mounts an emergency program and fits every person not owning property with a harness attached to a helium balloon (73). By floating aloft they can continue to exist without constantly being on someone else's property. Like many Trout stories, this one is a cross of joke and parable directed, as they often are, at social issues such as the perennial Vonnegut topics of inequality and overpopulation. "Gilgongo!" takes aim at the extermination of species by depicting a planet where there is too much creation, and the extermination of a species is celebrated. "Gilgongo!" in the language of the planet means "Extinct!" (87). Typically, Trout's story delivers its message by a comically exaggerated inversion of a situation. Like the Fool in Shakespeare's *King Lear*, Trout is amusing but "a bitter fool" whose barbed humor drives home the moral message of his creator. But more of Trout later.

Slapstick (1976) follows a somewhat similar organizational format to *Breakfast of Champions* in having its chapters divided into shorter segments. These are visually separated by a line of three black diamonds. These segments again vary in length but have an element of self-containment even when only one line long. In those cases they usually comprise a kind of punchline to be delivered after the end of the preceding segment has sunk in. In other words, the breaks often become a way of controlling the timing of the jokes—or of delivering the final thought on a more serious point. A number of the segments in this book end with "Hi ho." Some have found this objectionable as being flippantly dismissive of the very issues the novel has raised. While the expression works less successfully than the "So it goes" that punctuates with increasing poignancy each successive death in *Slaughterhouse-Five*, it does voice the weary resignation to the absurd workings of the chaotic universe of this novel. There are no Trout stories in this novel because the bizarre events Wilbur Swain relates, of "The Albanian Flu" and "The Green Death" and Chinese who can change their size and variable gravity, are themselves like a series of Trout stories. In fact, one of the central premises of this book, the idea of governmentally created artificial extended families, began as a Kilgore Trout story.[8]

   Deadeye Dick (1982) is another of the novels written in short segments, this time divided by a line of three circles. The divisions cause less sense of fragmentation in this case. Rather they work like one step beyond a paragraph break, marking off units in an unfolding narrative rather than involving shifts of setting or juxtapositions. Replacing Kilgore Trout stories as a way of interjecting another form and fresh content are "playlets." The protagonist, Rudy Waltz, deals with his worst memories by visualizing them as plays. Thus there are four extended scenes inserted as plays, complete with stage directions, *dramatis personae,* and dialogue. The other amusing interjections in *Deadeye Dick* are the recipes, which usually occupy a short segment each. One for Haitian banana soup begins with two pounds of goat or chicken. Other ingredients are added, all simmered until the meat is tender. Then: "Take out the meat. What is left is eight servings of Haitian banana soup. *Bon appetit!* " (41). Such interjections, like some of the briefer Trout summaries, seem intended primarily to lighten the narrative, like Shakespearean comedy's introduction of a clown or a song.[9]

   Hocus Pocus (1990) is the remaining example of a novel that uses the segmented construction. Its forty short chapters are composed of fragments written by Eugene Debs Hartke on scraps of paper in the prison library. They are numbered so that the editor ("K.V.") can assemble them in order, but he has retained lines across the page to indicate each new scrap. In a note that may actually reflect upon Vonnegut's own method of composition, the editor observes that Hartke might have begun without the thought of writing a complete book, but continuing "from scrap to scrap, as though each were a bottle for him to fill. When he filled one up, possibly, no matter what its size, he could satisfy himself that he had written everything there was to write about this or that" (7). As in the other novels written in this mode, the narrative advances segmentally, with the freedom to interject asides, to pause to generalize or explain, to draw a moral, or to introduce historical background. Some of these segments, perhaps especially the ones that give historical background, resemble short stories in recounting an event or a character's role in an aside that plugs into the main narrative. On the whole, though, the chief influence of the short fiction appears to be in the manner of thinking and composing segmentally, rather than in stylistic similarities.

   As noted earlier, there are many connections between the short fiction and the novels in areas of content such as themes, characters (or names), settings, or concepts. If anything, this self-referential characteristic in Vonnegut's fiction becomes even stronger as his canon grows, and the recurrences from one novel to another add considerably to those between the short fiction and the novels. To list all such reappearances in the novels of contents first seen in the stories would be tedious, and in the discussions of the short fiction many of the more noteworthy subsequent incarnations already have been noted. They indicate that whatever distinction Vonnegut draws between his writing of the two forms, there was cross-fertilization, as it were, between them in the creative process. As themes such as overpopulation and its related phenomena like resistance to aging, food shortages and pollution continue to concern him, so devices such as Ethical Suicide Parlors, anti-aging pills, or prophylactic numbing of the lower body return to serve him well. Some names, like Hitz, O'Hare and Wirtanen, recur as continuing jokes with the real persons whose names have been borrowed. Others, like Rumfoord or Ilium or EPICAC, come to stand for a particular conception, conveniently transported from one text to another. From short stories to novels, however, there are some, but fewer, of the kinds of trademark repetitions that have come to characterize Vonnegut's books. Yet the beginnings are in the short stories, where the recurrence between stories of characters (Helmholz, the storms salesman, the financial adviser), places (Ilium, North Crawford), themes (fathers-and-sons, population, failed dreams) and plot devices (song lyrics, secret fortunes, dystopian futures) prefigures the recurrences in the novels.

In *Breakfast of Champions* Vonnegut laments that the story reads like something by "Philboyd Studge" (4). In *God Bless You, Mr. Rosewater*, Eliot Rosewater, having praised science fiction writers for being the only ones who write about what really matters, admits that they "couldn't write for sour apples" but dismisses "the talented sparrowfarts who write delicately of one small piece of one small lifetime" (13-14). Vonnegut also speaks in an interview about the speed at which pulp science fiction writers wrote, having no time for characterization (*Conversations,* 93) All of these references to writing style are humorously exaggerated and not to be taken as serious commentary on his own style. Yet there resides in them an element of truth, in that most of his novels do not slow for the kind of elaborate description of setting or building of characterization that many more traditional, classic or "high-culture" novels do. In an interview he tellls Bellamy and Casey, "The reason novels were so thick for so long was that people had so much time to kill. I do not furnish transportation for my characters; I do not move them from one room to another; I do not send them up the stairs; they do not get dressed in the mornings. . . . You can fill up a good-size book with this connective tissue" (*Conversations,* 162). There are later novels—*Bluebeard* especially, and *Deadeye Dick*—with rich and full characterization of the protagonist, building through the entire novel. But much of the time in the novels the characterizations and settings are not elaborated with minute physical description. The emphasis, conveyed also in the frequent use of short sentences, paragraphs and chapters, falls on advancing the action and making a point. And just as some of these same characteristics in his short stories point back toward his training in journalism, so these features of his style in the novels resemble the techniques learned in writing short stories.

Whether there is a cause-and-effect relationship that produces this resemblance is not easy to say. Obviously such a personal matter as style involves habits of thought and expression evolved from an early age. Isolating elements and asserting that "he does this because of thus and so" in most cases proves a risky business. In a more generalized way, however, it may be argued that Vonnegut's novels exhibit a distinctive style, and that it can be reasonably expected that this style has been evolved over his years of learning and practice in writing for newspapers and magazines. When similarities of style and technique, and even fairly minor details of content, continue to appear in the novels, it may be reasonable to speak of influence. It needs to be born in mind, however, that the writing of the novels does not simply *succeed* the writing of the short stories; there is considerable overlap. Indeed, even a cursory examination of unpublished manuscripts from the nineteen-fifties and -sixties reveals that many story components were tried in one genre only to emerge ultimately in the other. Publication of *Player Piano* comes only two years after the first short story, and although there then follows a lengthy hiatus before the next novel, three more are published in years when Vonnegut continues to publish short stories. One might argue, then, for the shared characteristics in both forms evolving out of the same experience. Whether influence or shared evolution hardly matters ultimately. The essential point remains that relationship exists. As a consequence, to regard the short stories merely as some sort of bastard offspring, or to set them aside as inconsequential hack-work, risks ignoring a component of Vonnegut's art important in itself and intrinsic to the whole.

NOTES

1. Interview with David Standish for *Playboy*, 1973, in William Rodney Allen, *Conversations with Kurt Vonnegut* (Jackson: University Press of Mississippi, 1988), 91. Hereafter cited as *Conversations*. Vonnegut says, "My books are essentially mosaics made up of a whole bunch of tiny little chips; and each chip is a joke." In his interview with Laurie Clancy in 1971 he explained, "I build jokes. I find sections of my book constructed like jokes and then they're not very long and I suddenly realize the joke is told, and that it'd spoil the joke if I were to go past. The tag line is where the joke paid off and so I'll make a row of dots across the page to indicate that something's ended and I'll begin again and it'll essentially build as another joke" (*Conversations*, 48–49).

2. Vonnegut has spoken of this technique in public and in interviews such as that in 1974 with Joe David Bellamy and John Casey (*Conversations*, 158).

3. "In the beginning I was writing about what concerned me, and what was all around me was machinery. . . . So the first book I wrote was about Schenectady, which is full of machinery and engineers. And I was classed as a science fiction writer." (Laurie Clancy interview, *Conversations*, 51).

4. In his interview with the *Paris Review* in 1977, Vonnegut recalls, "When I used to teach creative writing, I would tell students to make their characters want something right away—even if it's only a glass of water" (*Conversations*, 189).

5. Vonnegut recounts that "one of the rules to tell a good story in so short a space was 'put nothing in the story which doesn't either, one, reveal character,

or, two, advance the action.' " William Rodney Allen then adds the amplification, "If you have a gun over the mantelpiece early in the story, it needs to be fired sometime in the story" (*Conversations*, 268).

6. Vonnegut comments on how the analogy with prostitution arose in his own life: "When I was supporting myself as a freelance writer doing stories for the *Saturday Evening Post* and *Collier's*, I was scorned! I mean, there was a time when to be a slick writer was a disgusting thing to be, as though it were prostitution" (*Conversations*, 4).

7. In fact, parts of the subplot about the robotizing of humans for the Martian army are paralleled in an unpublished short story manuscript, "Robotville and Mr. Caslow."

8. In 1973 Vonnegut outlined at length the artificial extended families plot as a Kilgore Trout story in his *Playboy* interview with David Standish (*Conversations*, 83–85).

9. Again in the *Playboy* interview, Vonnegut describes various shifts of tone or subject as being like Shakespeare's "bring[ing] on a clown or a foolish innkeeper . . . equivalent to bringing on the clowns every so often to lighten things up" (*Conversations*, 94).

8

Other Voices: Kilgore Trout

One of the manifestations of Vonnegut the short story writer that occurs in the novels—as was seen in the previous chapter—is the interjection of stories or other short texts by writers who appear as characters. Various reasons for these inclusions suggest themselves. Most simply, they may assist in the characterization of their authors. On a rather more complex level, when their authors appear as surrogates for Vonnegut himself, or for aspects of him, they may make comment on the writer's craft. Sometimes they do indeed appear to be for light relief, "sending in the clowns," as he puts it. Frequently they are useful for lending another perspective. Particularly in the earlier novels, Vonnegut has been fond of bringing an outside observer onto the scene to provide just such another point of view. The Shah of Bratpuhr in *Player Piano* and the Tralfamadorian Salo in *The Sirens of Titan* serve that purpose. Those two make their observations in the dialogue, but in other instances the commentary comes in written inclusions. They enable Vonnegut to have another voice, in effect. He can say things in a different manner or from a different perspective from that established in the novel's narrative voice. And, importantly for a writer who reaches far in his social commentary, they enable him to get at other topics that may lay beyond the compass of his setting.

Ed, the writer whose wife appears in *Player Piano,* has been mentioned previously. He will not compromise his standards to write what the book clubs want—dog stories or adventure tales. His novels are rejected as too long, too intellectual and too anti-machine. Thus he fails to qualify for the grade of "fiction journeyman," let alone the higher rank of "public relations." Consequently, his wife turns to prostitution, and seems to regard that as a lesser compromise than would be her husband's recourse to popular fiction. Obviously Vonnegut makes fun of his own situation here, since he has been both fiction journeyman and public relations writer at this stage. Even more, however, he takes aim at those who denigrate such honest labor, viewing it as morally on a par with prostitution. The introduction of Ed and his wife into this novel, then, enables Vonnegut to indicate the dangers he sees implicit in the purely commercial dictation of what will be published in an increasingly philistine society. And in the typically two-edged fashion of his satire, he can puncture the elitist "high art" denigration of popular fiction writers.

The central character of *Mother Night*, Howard Campbell, personifies more of the moral ambiguities surrounding the writer. A playwright, he embodies Vonnegut's assertion that people tend to make dramas or fictions of their own lives. He does this first by making a diary of the variety of roles he and his wife Helga invent to keep their sex life vital, called *Memoirs of a Monogamous Casanova*. In time the *Memoirs* become not a diary but a fiction self-consciously created, a real-life drama performed for the writing. Eventually the manuscript is plagiarized and published throughout Eastern Europe, with lurid illustrations, and Campbell feels mortified that the record of his precious love has become pornography. Implicit within this plot are the questions often asked of (and by) writers about their making use of their real life-relationships and acquaintances as fodder for their fiction. More tellingly, perhaps, it parallels the main part of the novel's plot wherein Campbell becomes an American spy and a Nazi propagandist. The fiction he makes of his own life, pretending to be a Nazi propagandist until it becomes hard to say that that is not his primary role, shows the same slide into making the fiction the reality. Hence the moral that Vonnegut says the novel asserts: "We are what we pretend to be, so we must be careful about what we pretend to be"(v).

Campbell writes romantic plays, and his quest for the "authentic hero" makes him unable to resist playing that role himself, hence his acquiescing to become a spy. Looked at less heroically, he cannot resist the role playing, the deception. In the "Editor's Note," Vonnegut writes of Campbell: "To say that he was a writer is to say that the demands of art alone were enough to make him lie, and to lie without seeing any harm in it" (ix). But Campbell's lies are not harmless. While he professes that he thought the propaganda he writes so ludicrous no one would believe it, people do, and apparently they act on it. That raises the question of what responsibility the writer must assume for people's responses to what he or she creates, be it propaganda, public relations copy or fiction. Vonnegut raises that question repeatedly in various guises.

Campbell's role as the central narrative voice makes him the reverse of the outside observers. And yet, Campbell does remain an outsider, a detached observer of the Nazi German scene in which he also participates. This detachment continues in his isolated existence in postwar America, and even in his observations of his guards and fellow prisoners in an Israeli jail. The novel's warnings emerge through both Campbell's detachment and his commentary. His detachment warns of the danger in maintaining an unspoken, inner reservation from the things going on around us. His commentary warns against simplistic and categorical thinking. It rejects equally the bigotry of the neo-Nazi White Christian Minutemen, the popular assumption that Nazis were *different* and went around "trailing slime," and Bernard O'Hare's vengeful conviction he has God on his side. All of this, however, depends upon the intensity of a first person narration and a sustained central role for its full impact. Hence Campbell's dual role.

Writers also occur within *Cat's Cradle*. John, or Jonah, the narrator, embarks upon writing *The Day the World Ended*, which seemingly turns out to be *Cat's Cradle* itself. The other writer is Bokonon, priest-philosopher-charlatan, who writes his *Books of Bokonon* whose tenets and calypsos are quoted frequently. He declares that all of his truths are *foma,* or shameless if harmless lies, once again raising the issue of the ethics of the writer. Bokonon sums up his philosophy in a calypso that also illustrates his style:

> *I wanted all things*
>
> *To seem to make some sense*
>
> *So we all could be happy, yes,*
>
> *Instead of tense.*
>
> *And I made up lies*
>
> *So that they all fit nice,*
>
> *And I made this sad world*
>
> *A par-a-dise.* (109)

The Bokononist calypsos and sayings work so well because they are contextualized by a fancifully contrived setting and a charming linguistic environment that includes the Bokononist vocabulary of such things as *wampeters* and *vin-dits* and the San Lorenzan dialect that turns "Twinkle, twinkle, little star" into "Tsvent-kiul, tsvent-kiul, lett-pool store"(78).

Bokonon's functions in this novel are various. In part he serves to underline one of the messages of *Mother Night*, that people are willing to make fictions of their lives and indeed to live by fictions. This novel begins by echoing the opening of Herman Melville's *Moby Dick*, underlining its own fictionality. John announces his intention of writing *The Day the World Ended*, which this novel then depicts. Bokonon, like Campbell, writes fictions that dupe people into behaving in certain ways. That is an aspect of the writer's craft which Vonnegut continues to illustrate with his fictional authors, and to which he sometimes refers directly. In his *Films for the Humanities* interview, for instance, he laughingly points out that just by putting words on a piece of paper a writer can reduce a reader to tears.[1] Here he goes further, the anthropologist Vonnegut showing the willingness of people to believe almost anything and adopt it as a doctrine that makes "this sad world," if not "a par-a-dise," at least "seem to make some sense." That vision, of course, emanates not just the anthropologist Vonnegut but from the descendant of German free thinkers.

Bokonon's *foma* express the self-conscious fictionality of this book, the self-reflexivity of a text that talks about made-up texts. Its religion's founder, Bokonon, thumbs his nose at his creator, like a character declaring independence of his author. Indeed, Bokonon has made himself up, virtually becoming his own author. Born Lionel Boyd Johnson, he has created his new name, religion, and role. Bokonon and his religion are the vehicles to *Cat's Cradle's* becoming Vonnegut's first truly postmodern novel. Outside of its own fictionality, however, the novel relates to the real world of Haiti, with its "Papa" Monzano a caricature of the actual island's dictator, "Papa Doc" Duvalier, and its religions a parody of symbiosis of Roman Catholicism and Voodoo there. Bokonon remains above all the source of the majority of this novel's humor and breezy irreverence. Like Vonnegut's subsequent favorite writer-character, Kilgore Trout, Bokonon is a debunker, a demystifier, a mocker, an alternative voice through which Vonnegut can find the freedom to be as iconoclastic as he pleases.

The appearance of Kilgore Trout has to await the next novel, however, and *God Bless You, Mr. Rosewater* features another writer-within who should be noted first. This is the disreputable Arthur Garvey Ulm. A struggling writer, Ulm tells the millionaire Eliot Rosewater that he wants to be free to tell the truth, relieved of financial dependence. The ever-naive and hopeful Eliot writes him a huge check on the spot, whereupon Ulm spends eight years only to eventually produce for a book club an eight-hundred pages long pornographic novel called *Get With Child A Mandrake Root*. It begins:

I twisted her arm until she opened her legs, and she gave a little scream, half joy, half pain (how do you figure a woman?) as I rammed the old avenger home (69–70).

Ulm becomes the inverse of *Player Piano's* Ed, not a writer who refuses to write marketable trash out of economic need, but who does so as an expression of his financial independence. The image of writer reduced to pornographer persists.

In Kilgore Trout the writer becomes reduced to what Vonnegut says the critics regard as *lower* than the pornographer; the science fiction writer. In fact, one of the measures of Trout's low esteem is that his stories are often used as fillers in pornographic publications. Trout varies in his successive incarnations throughout Vonnegut's fiction. His most consistent characteristics are that he writes science fiction stories at an astonishing rate, that he appears a disheveled older man, and that he remains impecunious and generally unknown. Other constants are that he was born in Bermuda, the son of Leo Trout, an ornithologist who studies the Bermuda ern, and that he in turn has a son, also named Leo or Leon. The son has run away and generally despises him, and three marriages have failed, so that he lives alone.

In *God Bless You, Mr. Rosewater*, Trout emerges as the favorite author of Eliot Rosewater, whose praise lavished on science fiction writers has been noted previously. At one point Eliot, obsessed with the polarities of deprivation and wealth he observes, tells a science fiction writers' gathering: "I leave it to you, friends and neighbors, and especially the immortal Kilgore Trout: think about the silly ways money gets passed around now, and then think up better ways"(17). Trout certainly would not be daunted by such a task; his stock in trade is to stand back and take a deconstructive look at something long accepted. His story *2BR02B*, a title Vonnegut had used himself three years previously, sounds like a mix of Vonnegut's plots: it features an America where machines perform all the work, the only people with jobs have three Ph.D.s, there is overpopulation, and Ethical Suicide Parlors stand next to Howard Johnsons. One customer plans to ask God, "What in hell are people *for?*" (16). That question underscores the search reiterated in *God Bless You, Mr. Rosewater* for meaning and substance in the lives of so many.

Another Trout story in *God Bless You, Mr. Rosewater*, recounted by Eliot, is *Oh Say Can You Smell?* It presents a country out to eliminate all odors and conducting research to that end. Finally the country's dictator ends the search at a stroke, not by one chemical to eliminate all odors but by eliminating noses (164–165). While essentially a joke, the story also takes aim at the senior Rosewater's conservative politics that seek not to eliminate social inequalities but the sufferers' perceptions of them. Another story, the briefly summarized *The First District Court of Thankyou*, deals with ingratitude. It depicts a court where people could take those they felt had not been properly grateful for a good deed. Those convicted had the choice of thanking the plaintiff publicly or a month in solitary confinement on bread and water. Eighty percent chose the latter (173). Recounted in more detail, *Pan-Galactic Three-Day Pass* tells of an interstellar expedition to the outer rim of the Universe. The Tralfamadorian commander of the expedition calls its only human member to tell him he has some bad news from back home. The earthling asks if someone has died. The commander responds, "What's died, my boy, is the Milky Way" (185). Eliot's reading of this story precedes his vision of Indianapolis enveloped in a Dresden-like fire storm. The story has a typical Tralfamadorian distancing perspective, wherein disasters, as can be seen in *Slaughterhouse-Five*, are viewed in the enormous context of all time and space.

Most interesting of the inclusions in *God Bless You, Mr. Rosewater* is Trout's novel *Venus on the Half-shell*. Fred Rosewater furtively picks this off a news stand when he thinks his daughter is not watching, and reads on the back cover "an abridgement of a red-hot scene inside. It went like this:

Queen Margaret of the planet Shaltoon let her gown fall to the floor. She was wearing nothing underneath. Her high, firm, uncowled bosom was proud and rosy. Her hips and thighs were like an inviting lyre of pure alabaster. They shone so whitely they might have had a light inside. 'Your travels are over, Space Wanderer,' she whispered . . . (119).

The quotation actually goes on for twenty three lines. After that the back cover photograph of Trout is described as "like a frightened, aging Jesus, whose sentence to crucifixion had been commuted to imprisonment for life" (120). The unique aspect of this passage is that it offers an extended glimpse of a Trout story in his own words.

There is a further point of interest about this story, in that another writer, Phillip Jose Farmer, took up this extract and published a novel of the same title using the name Kilgore Trout. In a 1980 interview with Charles Reilly, Vonnegut said this about it:

Venus on the Half-Shell was written by Phillip Jose Farmer. . . . I have never met him. He kept calling me up, though, and saying 'Please let me write a Kilgore Trout book.' He was delighted by the character and, as I say, he was a respected writer himself, so I finally said, 'Okay, go ahead.' There was no money involved, by the way; I didn't get a cent of royalties. . . . So he published it, and I wound up getting abuse from all over the place — accusations that I was ripping off college kids' money and whatever.[2]

Later in the same interview, Vonnegut has more to say about what obviously became for him an embarrassing and potentially damaging situation.

This Framer wanted to forge on and write a whole series of books 'by' Trout—and I understand he's capable of knocking out a pretty decent Vonnegut book every six weeks. I hardly know Mr. Farmer. I've never met him and most of our contacts have been indirect, so I asked him, please, not to do it. And I asked my publisher, please, not to publish any more of his Trout books because the whole thing had become very upsetting to me. I understand he was really burned up about my decision. I heard he had made more money in that one 'Kilgore Trout year' than he had ever made before—in case you're too polite to ask, I didn't get any of the money (*Conversations*, 222–223).

Thus did the fictional writer almost come to life, as it were, and in something like the kind of confrontation that occurs at the end of *Breakfast of Champions* where a bewildered Kilgore Trout comes face to face with his creator, Kurt Vonnegut. Trout has another fictional meeting with his maker in an interview in *Crawdaddy* for April 1, 1974. This was actually conducted by Greg Mitchell but is set up so as to look as if done by Trout. Vonnegut does acknowledge that Trout has his origins in an actual writer—the science fiction writer Theodore Sturgeon. This was even noted in Sturgeon's obituary in the *New York Times*. "I was so pleased," Vonnegut said, in conversation with Hank Nuwer. "Sturgeon got a nice big obituary in the *Times*, . . . it said in the middle of it that he was the inspiration for the Kurt Vonnegut character Kilgore Trout"(*Conversations*, 263).

By the end of *God Bless You, Mr. Rosewater*, Trout has been brought in to assist in the recovery of Eliot Rosewater from his breakdown. Charged with putting into words what Eliot has been trying to do, and to establish his sanity, he argues that Eliot had tried to show that people are worth treasuring just because they are human beings, not for what they do or have. Hew says that Americans, to the contrary, have been trained to hate people who will not or cannot work—including themselves. People need uncritical love, and Eliot has been that rare thing, a person who could give it. The ultimate praise Eliot's father can bestow upon Trout is, "By God, you're great! You should have been a public relations man!"(197). So the marginalized science fiction writer comes to the rescue of the beleaguered saint whose indiscriminate compassion has convinced people of his insanity. It is particularly in these closing scenes of the novel, where Trout assumes the burden of explaining Eliot's role and hence enunciating the moral message of the book, that he serves Vonnegut best as an alternative voice. Vonnegut avoids the didacticism that would overload another form of direct pronouncement by putting the words in Trout's mouth. Surrounded by comic circumstances and spoken by this undercut figure, the words are relieved of the hard edge of direct statement that might otherwise invite resistance to their import.

In *Slaughterhouse-Five*, Kilgore Trout makes his appearance as the tyrannical supervisor of newspaper delivery boys, a necessary job since he makes no money from his writing. His stories are read, however, and once again by Eliot Rosewater. One of the stories Rosewater reads is *Maniacs in the Fourth Dimension*, about people whose mental illnesses could not be treated because the causes were all in the fourth dimension. Its appeal to the disturbed Rosewater is predictable. He also delights in its claim that vampires, werewolves, goblins and angels all existed, but were in the fourth dimension. "So was William Blake, Rosewater's favorite poet, according to Trout. So were heaven and hell"(90).

The moral of Trout's second story seems more clear, especially in context. Called *The Gutless Wonder,* it tells of a humanoid robot who is despised for his halitosis. The narrator finds the story remarkable for being written in 1932 and predicting napalm. The robot pilots an airplane and drops napalm on people without conscience. Despite this, the curing of his halitosis assures his acceptance into the human race. Bombing people may be socially acceptable, but bad breath never. In the context of this novel with its central event the fire bombing of Dresden, this story's moral is obvious. Once again Trout enables Vonnegut to offer a parable that underlines one of the messages of the novel.

The remaining Trout story in *Slaughterhouse-Five, The Gospel from Outer Space*, tells of a visitor from outer space who makes a study of Christianity. In particular he seeks to learn what made it so easy for Christians to be cruel. He concludes the problem lies with careless narration in the Gospels. They were meant to teach mercy, even to the humblest people. They have failed by inviting the interpretation that killing Jesus was wrong because he was "the Son of the Most Powerful Being in the Universe." That leaves the impression that there remain some people it is all right to kill, namely those not well connected. The space visitor leaves Earth a new gospel in which Jesus "really *was* a nobody," though he preached the same philosophy. At his crucifixion God thunders from the sky that he is "adopting the bum as his son," and decrees: *"From this moment on, He will punish horribly anybody who torments a bum who has no connections!"*(92–95). Here, too, Trout's voice supplements Vonnegut's. This novel depicts the mass slaughter of Dresden, dwells on the horrors of the thirteenth-century Children's Crusade, recounts one death after another, and chronicles the persecution of the frequently Christ-like Billy Pilgrim. Just as with *God Bless You, Mr. Rosewater*, it is a novel in which a serious, direct statement of the ethics implicit in it would seem didactic and false. Trout's simple, humorous, hyperbolic stories deliver the message effectively without changing the author's narrative stance in the novel.

Breakfast of Champions sees Kilgore Trout being given an even larger role in the novel as a character. As a consequence, a greater number of his stories occurs; more, in fact, than need to be recounted here. Trout makes no copies of the stories he sends off, mostly to "World Classics Library," which uses them to bulk pornographic books and magazines while paying him "doodley-squat." The stories, which usually have no female characters, appear with "salacious pictures" and are often retitled. Hence "Pan Galactic Straw-boss" becomes "Mouth Crazy." It is another over-population story, in which a bachelor produces endless offspring by mixing shavings from his palm with chicken soup and exposing them to cosmic rays. Instead of the society's taking a stand on overly large families, it bans the possession of chicken soup by single people (21).

"The Dancing Fool" gives vent to some of the frustration Trout-Vonnegut must feel when, Cassandra-like, their warnings go unheeded. Zog, from the planet Margo, comes to Earth to tell humans how to cure cancer and end war. He belongs to a species that communicates by means of tap dancing and farts. As he lands he sees a house on fire and rushes in, tap dancing and farting furiously to warn the occupants. The owner brains him with a golf club. Some plots are simply opportunities for brief comic jibes. In "Hail to the Chief" an "optimistic chimpanzee" becomes President. He wears a blazer with a presidential seal on the pocket. Wherever he goes bands strike up "Hail to the Chief." The chimpanzee is delighted and responds by bouncing up and down.

One summarized plot interests because it appears to prefigure the later novel, *Galapagos*. Trout's novel, *The Smart Bunny,* features a rabbit with the intelligence of Einstein or Shakespeare. She lives like other rabbits so finds her brain useless, regarding it simply as a tumor. She heads for the town to have the tumor removed, only to be shot on the way. The hunter and his wife also conclude that the rabbit has a tumor, is diseased, and therefore do not eat it. In *Galapagos* huge human brains are judged as excessive as the massive antlers of the Irish elk, a creature brought to extinction by over-specialization.

The Trout fiction that has greatest impact in *Breakfast of Champions* remains his novel, *Now It Can Be Told.* The premise of the book is that the reader is the only human; all others are robots, put there by the Creator of the Universe so that he can watch the human's responses. Dwayne Hoover reads this and, taking it as gospel that the robots can neither reason nor feel, dementedly sets off on a rampage. Trout's story splendidly complements major ideas within *Breakfast of Champions*. There are twin themes linked to the notion of people as robots. One envisions people as being robot-like in that they are chemically controlled. This grows out of Vonnegut's own experience in taking anti-depressant pills and discovering that those chemicals can manipulate his mood. The other sees people as being robot-like in the way they are treated. They are made functions of their jobs, doing "women's work," for instance. And often people act as though they shared Dwayne's Trout-induced obsession, viewing the world solipsistically and making other people merely projections of their own visions of reality. Trout's piece of "solipsistic whimsy" makes graphic in its hyperbole the consequences of such attitudes.

In *Breakfast of Champions*, Vonnegut says he is getting rid of all of his characters, and tells Trout he is being set free, leaving him imploring, "*Make me young! Make me young! Make me young!*"(295). But it is not the end of Kilgore Trout. *Jailbird* announces, "Yes—Kilgore Trout is back again. He could not make it on the outside"(ix). Once again another writer uses Trout's name. In *Jailbird,* Kilgore Trout becomes one of two pen names used by Dr. Robert Fender. His story "Asleep at the Switch" is recounted at some length. It depicts a large reception center at the Pearly Gates "filled with computers and staffed by people who had been certified public accountants or investment counselors or business managers back on Earth"(184). In a parody of the parable of the talents, these officials give all new arrivals a thorough review of how well they have handled the business opportunities offered them on Earth. Repeatedly they point out each newcomer's missed chances, to the refrain of, "And there you were, asleep at the switch again." The ghost of Albert Einstein emerges as the hero of the story. The auditors tell him that if he had taken a second mortgage and bought uranium commodities before announcing $E=Mc^2$ he could have been a billionaire. And so on. Finally, Einstein gains admittance into heaven carrying his beloved violin. But Einstein recognizes the fallacy in the procedure.

He calculated that if every person on Earth took full advantage of every opportunity, became a millionaire and then a billionaire and so on, the paper wealth on that one little planet would exceed the worth of all the minerals in the universe in a matter of three months or so. (187)

So Einstein writes God a note, arguing that the auditors must be sadists, misleading new arrivals about their opportunities. God commands an archangel to tell Einstein to be quiet or he will have his violin taken away, and he hushes.

This story obviously parodies the notion of a final accounting, and perhaps also mocks that particular set of preachers who make a large part of their appeal the notion that God *wants* people to get rich. It certainly recognizes the ironic fact that whatever kind of accounting people might expect to make in a next life, a good percentage *act* as if they were to be audited on their financial opportunism. Another point to be made about this story is the way it appears to be triggered simply by the phrase "asleep at the switch again," an expression that seemed to be enjoying a revival at the time. Many of Trout's stories apparently spring from this same kind of spontaneous response to an object, a saying, or a particular event, as also revealed in *Breakfast of Champions*. Trout becomes one of the ways that Vonnegut keeps alive the mischievous, adolescent irreverence, seen in his earliest writing and manifest again and again in his later work, that questions all assumptions and authorities.

One of Fender's other stories, supposedly to appear in *Playboy* under his alternative *nom de plume*, Frank X. Barlow, concerns a planet that runs out of time. Aptly named Vicuna (the animal of that name also may be running out of time), the planet disintegrates as its inhabitants mine time from its very substance. Eventually the Vicunans have to leave their bodies and, like the amphibians of "Unready to Wear," go off as spirits in search of bodies. The central character, a judge, gets to earth. What Vicunans did not realized was that, having entered through the ear of a human, they were unable to leave again. The judge sees what appears to be a happy old man in a quiet place, only to discover he is a criminal in a minimum security prison. The judge finds himself forever locked in the head of a man who aimlessly and interminably repeats a silly scatological childhood rhyme. It seems an apt punishment for a judge who has condemned the convicted to be stood up to their necks in a pond of excrement as deputies aim powerful speedboats at their heads. An interesting detail of this story is that Vicunans say "ting-a-ling" in place of "hello," "good-bye," "please" or "thank you." In a draft manuscript of the later novel, *Timequake*, Kilgore Trout does the same thing.[3]

The Barlow story fits *Jailbird's* subject matter of trials, convictions and prisoners, but it also relates to this novel's return to that favorite Vonnegut theme of social inequality. Like the Trout story, it underlines the question of the distribution of resources among people. The Vicunans' exhaustion of time itself makes this a parable about human time running out with the exhaustion of resources. That the Vicunans once had bonfires of time when they still regarded it as limitless sends an obvious message about human consumption of things like fossil fuels. The holes that open up in Vicuna as they consume time might be analogous to the holes in Earth's ozone layer.

Perhaps the clearest example of how Vonnegut uses Trout stories as parables, that is allegories or near allegories that illustrate a religious or philosophical moral, occurs in his employment of one called "The Planet Gobblers." Originally cited in a commencement address at Hobart and William Smith Colleges on May 26, 1974, and collected in *Palm Sunday*, the story appears only as summary. In it humans are cast as like "interplanetary termites," who arrive at a planet, use everything up, but always send space ships on to the next planet. They were like a disease, "since it was not necessary to inhabit planets with such horrifying destructiveness. It is easy to take good care of a planet"(209). In his address, Vonnegut quickly goes on to draw out the lesson from Trout's story. "Our grandchildren will surely think of us as the Planet Gobblers. Poorer nations than America think of America as a Planet Gobbler right now"(209). And he goes on to make willingness to change the concluding call of his address.

Kilgore Trout has a major role in the novel *Timequake,* as seen in manuscript form in 1996. His son, whose ghost narrates the novel *Galapagos*, still is depicted as having been killed in a Swedish shipyard in 1975. Since that time, Kilgore Trout has thrown away his handwritten stories within hours of finishing them. He has been writing an average of a story every ten days since he was fourteen, so by the novel's setting of 2000 A.D. he has written about twenty five hundred. He is now an eighty-four-year-old homeless person, one of the "sacred cattle," as he calls them. Like Barlow's Vicunans in the story from *Jailbird*, Trout uses "ting-a-ling" as a general purpose greeting, just one of many echoes in this novel from previous ones.

Another Trout story for *Timequake* is called *The Sisters B-36.*[4] It tells of three sisters, two pleasant and one evil, on a matriarchal planet named Booboo. One good sister paints, the other writes. The third, a scientist, can only talk about thermodynamics, so bores people to death. In an obvious parody of the way people learn and form biases, Trout explains that Booboolings are programmed by what they are told in words when young. Booboolings are thus trained how to look at pictures or respond to ink marks on paper, and develop circuits that Earthlings would call "imagination." So the bad sister, "Nim-nim B-36," invents television. Booboolings no longer need imagination, and only the older ones can appreciate pictures and writing. This makes the two nice sisters feel awful, as she wished, but still no-one likes Nim-nim B-36. So she invents the landmine, barbed wire, the machine gun, the flame-thrower, the computer, and automation. Then Booboolings kill each other readily, feeling nothing because they have no imaginations. "They couldn't do what the old-timers could do, which was see touching stories in faces. So they were unmerciful."

Quite clearly this story speaks, like a parable, to the extraordinary rate at which young people kill each other on American streets. It addresses the vital role that writing and other arts play in the development of the imagination, and the crucial importance of that facility to the culture and the individual. It decries the negative impact that television has had on society. And it returns to two even older themes in Vonnegut's work; pacifism, and the failure of the public to respond with understanding to scientific knowledge. It is vintage Trout, a comic little science fiction story loaded with implication.

Many Trout stories occur in drafts of *Timequake*. In one rather gory tale called *Disgusted Chemicals* various elements lament the horrors societies have inflicted upon the bodies of which they have been part, and come up with a scheme to make all diseases both incurable and fatal. In another, *Bunker Bingo Party*, Hitler pleads, "I never asked to be born in the first place." Trout also leaves an unfinished memoir of the timequake, the central event of this novel, called *My Ten Years on Automatic Pilot*. In one story, ironically told as a lullaby, the crew of a bomber assigned to drop a third atomic bomb, this one on Yokohama, decide not to do it and return to base. At their court martial a fissure opens in the Pacific floor and swallows the island—bomber, crew, courtroom and all. The humor in this story comes in the depiction of the reactions on base as the bomber lands with an atomic bomb slung beneath it giving only eighteen inches clearance from the runway.

Dog's Breakfast tells of a scientist, Dr. Fleon Sunoco, who questions whether the human brain, which he describes as a dog's breakfast or a blood-soaked sponge, is really capable of the greatest human accomplishments. Then he discovers a miniature pink radio receiver in brains taken from extra-intelligent people. He sets about writing up his discovery, convinced he is a cinch for a Nobel Prize. He writes with a fluency he has never known before, until he stops to ask himself where his new-found loquacity, or even his discovery, comes from. It has to be from a receiver in his own brain. He is, in Trout's (or Shakespeare's) words, "hoist by his own petard!" Horrified, Sunoco jumps from the window. Ironically, as a result of his own research, he cannot even be sure that his suicide is his own idea.

Most of the Trout stories in *Timequake* appear only as humorous plot summaries. Two such are *Empire State,* about a meteorite the size of the Empire State Building heading toward Earth, and *Dr. Schadenfreud*, about a psychiatrist who forbids his patients to talk about themselves and who, if they do, will scream, "Who cares about *you*, you piece of shit?" Incidents or phrases from these stories are referred to throughout the novel. Vonnegut uses them to make a joke, to underline a point, or as a kind of refrain.

As in his earlier appearances, Trout supplies *Timequake* with much of its humor and a great deal of its energy. Vonnegut has consistently used Trout's quirky, rapid plots and blunt colloquialisms to inject vitality and pace. They contribute to tone with their often slapstick humor, their outrageousness, and their naive but penetrating observations. Their frequently bizarre science fiction settings help establish mood in novels where Vonnegut unleashes the chaotic to destabilize habitual, unquestioned assumptions about society, the universe, life. From seeming to be a kind of *alter ego* who epitomized what Vonnegut feared he might have become—an unknown hack writer reduced to odd jobs, pornography and ignored science fiction—he has come to embody the questioning mind, the forever adolescent mischief, the irreverent iconoclasm, and the egalitarian conscience that are the quintessence of Vonnegut himself.

NOTES

1. *Kurt Vonnegut: A Self-Portrait*, produced and directed by Harold Mantell (Princeton, N.J.: Films for the Humanities, 1976).

2.   Interview with Charles Reilly, in William Rodney Allen, ed., *Conversations with Kurt Vonnegut* (Jackson: University Press of Mississippi, 1988), 213.

3. The Barlow story, untitled appears on 54–58 of *Jailbird*. *Timequake* was seen by the author in manuscript form in 1996 by kind permission of Kurt Vonnegut. The manuscript cited is what Vonnegut later calls *Timequake One*. The eventual text differs; the stories, most of which reappear, remain illustrative.

4. This story was recounted by Kurt Vonnegut to Peter Reed and Marc Leeds in 1993, and appears in Vonnegut's own summary in their interview. See Peter Reed and Marc Leeds, eds., *The Vonnegut Chronicles* (Westport, CT: Greenwood Press, 1996), 41–42.

9

The Short Fiction and the Canon

Kurt Vonnegut's short fiction followed much the same course of critical evaluation as the early novels: initially overlooked, later sometimes disdained. Being published in glossy magazines, the stories were not reviewed as they came out. Their evaluation rested with the editors and readers of those magazines, who registered their appraisal in higher payments and continuing demand. As popular fiction the stories, like the earlier novels, were not given serious attention, especially if they smacked of science fiction. The stories qualified for review when they appeared in *Welcome to the Monkey House*, because here they constituted a book by a major publisher and because by this time Vonnegut was gaining some recognition. And some reviews were distinctly unfavorable. The *Newsweek* reviewer called *Welcome to the Monkey House* a "pseudobook" in which too many of the selections were "mere contrivances or tearjerkers."[1] Richard Rhodes, reviewing the collection for *Book World,* complained that the stories were "written to sell" and that "they carry along a burdensome weight of disguise."[2] Perhaps Vonnegut's own introduction of these stories as "the fruits of Free Enterprise" written to support his writing of novels opened the door to such responses.

Before proceeding to any evaluation of the stories individually or collectively, however, it helps to consider the standards by which they should be judged and the context in which they are viewed. Vonnegut himself, while several times being dismissive of the stories as a commercial enterprise, has also made the point that there is nothing criminal or immoral about writing "slick" fiction or even science fiction—though some have attacked him as if there were. Many novelists have followed the same course, certainly. The British satirist Evelyn Waugh, now rather a venerated figure, was sometimes dismissed as a popular lightweight in his early years. He wrote dozens of reviews, essays, gossip columns and short stories throughout the first decade of his career, again from financial need, and many of them were poorly received and some even disdainfully rejected by editors. F. Scott Fitzgerald has been criticized for squandering his talent in hastily-written short stories for the magazines. But whereas for Vonnegut the short story writing was part of a continuing development of his skills, for Fitzgerald this work came mostly late in his career as a capitalization on an established reputation. As James Lundquist observes, "Vonnegut's short stories are no worse than many of the slick stories of the same type written by Fitzgerald; and in some ways, perhaps as expressions of sentiment genuinely felt by the writer, they are better."[3]

In such discussions of this body of work, much of the assessment appears predicated on the *type* of fiction rather than on the quality of the fiction within its given genre. The fact that these stories are popular fiction for general public audiences, rather than "literary" stories of the type found in the quarterlies, was often at the heart of their dismissal. The argument against that point of view is decades old now, of course. Forms of popular fiction once marginalized have come to wider acceptance, and beyond that, appreciation. In the case of Vonnegut, the extremely influential essay by Leslie Fiedler, "The Divine Stupidity of Kurt Vonnegut," found his work important *because* of its grounding in popular fiction. In brief, Fiedler argued that the "High Art" novel reached a point of no return with James Joyce, taking itself out of the mainstream and becoming the province exclusively of an elite, intellectual audience. The novel found its new strength in a return to popular forms. These always had been the repository of myths, of the aspirations and needs widely shared in their culture. During the dominance of the High Art novel, Fiedler argued, popular fiction had continued "underground." As the High Art novel became increasingly esoteric and remote, popular fiction was able to re-emerge as a mainstream form. Vonnegut, Fiedler saw, was of the mainstream precisely because of his background of writing short stories for wide-circulation magazines, experience that facilitated his ability to write to a wide audience in his novels, too.[4]

That leads to the other necessary consideration, not simply the merits of the stories in themselves, but their importance to Vonnegut's larger canon. It has been evident that much of the methodology he developed in writing short stories played an important role in the creation of the novels. Not only does he continue the same techniques to make his writing accessible to a large audience—and to have impact on that audience—but the myth-making function that Fiedler speaks of begins in the stories. The fables or parables planted in the novels in Trout stories and other vignettes trace their origins to the short fiction. They may sometimes be sugar-coated in the short fiction, lacking the "black humor" bite so monotonously attributed to his novels, and may lack the depth and complexity of development available in the longer form, but the essence is there. The story "Adam" acknowledges in its title the mythic dimensions implicit in its plot. The short story itself inevitably remains too restricted a form to enunciate myth, but it can invoke it, allude to it, present it in emblem. The unheroic journeyings of the protagonists in the novels, perhaps above all of Billy Pilgrim in *Slaughterhouse-Five,* are needed for Vonnegut's propounding of myths for his times. Nevertheless, the stories speak to the anxieties, hopes and wants of his age, as classical myths did for an earlier age, and lead to the invocation and reinvention of some of those earlier myths that takes place in the novels.

The fact to be born in mind, too, remains simply that this *is* how Vonnegut evolved as a writer. He began by writing short stories, and later was writing short stories at the same time as he was evolving as a novelist. Manuscripts reveal that often ideas were tried in one form then used in the other. The writing of short stories, the strategies and skills, the themes and topics involved are as intrinsic to his overall development as is his apprenticeship in journalism. The experience gained in journalism and short fiction inevitably contributes significantly to the shaping of his longer fiction, to why the novels are as they are. It may be argued that the fact that both journalism and short fiction employ short units, economy and concision has influenced the novelist's style, where those characteristics are frequently evident. Those literary traits, learned in short fiction, fit with Vonnegut's minimalist tendencies. They accord with his approach of reducing things to their simplest terms, demystifying or deconstructing them, often by adopting the perspective of a child, outsider, or irreverent adolescent. Vignettes, jokes, and short, simple stories often then become an appropriate medium.

The methods shaped by his development through journalism and short fiction writing also lead to his finding expression in a mode that accords with his times. His honed prose, the short sentences and paragraphs and chapters, the segmenting of the story with the segments shuffled, the intermix of fact and fiction, often contribute to a montage effect also seen in pop art. The technique accords with the era of the soundbite and MTV—accessible, emphatic, expressionistic. The shuffled segments, the mix of journalistic reportage from an exterior "reality" with short moralizing stories and jokes, and the direct personal intrusions (all techniques traceable to his earlier writing) make Vonnegut's movement into postmodernism a natural evolution. Not that these are characteristics to which Vonnegut himself might consciously aspire. He speaks of traditional influences in the shaping of his prose; admiration of R. L. Stevenson and George Orwell, the advice of Littauer, Burger and Wilkinson, or even Aristotelian models for the well-made story.[5] Vonnegut recognizes, as he has often said, that reading is not an especially easy activity, that the reader has no obligation to finish a text, and that the writer owes the reader respect. These are all facts to be born in mind if the writer wants that reader to entertain the ideas presented. Thus the awareness of an audience, essential in his writing of his wide-circulation short stories, continues to influence the formulation of a voice and a style appropriate to those contemporary issues he addresses. The resulting fiction can be experimental, innovative and often provocative, but remain accessible, entertaining and morally grounded.

For Vonnegut, as for any writer, one of the more testing challenges faced in achieving propriety of style to subject has been the finding of a "voice." One sees him struggle with that in some of his high school and college writing even, sometimes seemingly torn between needs for journalistic detachment and first-person immediacy. Occasionally the result emerges as a rather self-conscious use of an editorial "we" in an informal narrative, such as a visit to the infirmary or a bar. Many years later Vonnegut was to recount what a relief it was to him to be told by those writers and critics who were his colleagues at the Iowa Writers Workshop that it was all right for him to speak in the first-person in his novels, something he said his journalistic training had told him he should not do.[6] The first instance of his doing that occurs when he adds his introduction to the 1966 Harper and Row edition of *Mother Night*. That novel, like the later *Slaughterhouse-Five*, deals with the Second World War and his being German-American. The latter novel especially invites both a distanced, objective view of historical events and an immediacy that conveys the personal trauma of individuals caught up in those events. In *Mother Night* he achieves some of that balance by employing a first-person narrator reflecting on events that mostly occurred years before. The new introduction, however, adds a personal connection to the story that makes a significant difference to the novel's overall impact. In *Slaughterhouse-Five* the technique becomes more complex. A third-person narrative voice follows a protagonist who has mythic dimensions but who remains quasi-autobiographical in experiencing events like those Vonnegut himself went through. But Vonnegut then brackets this account with his own first-person description of writing the novel, and by interjecting himself at various points in the novel through assertions like "That was me."

In solving the problems of voice, Vonnegut appears to draw upon his experience with the short stories. There he shows an increasing confidence in the use of a persona to provide a narrative voice. The personality of the narrator gives flavor to the story. In some, such as the first, "Report on the Barnhouse Effect," having a narrator within the story seems a necessary device to lend authenticity. That is, having Barnhouse's assistant write the report provides the necessary perspective of someone "on the inside" who would know all the facts—and who could provide the twist at the end of the story. But while some biographical information about the narrator emerges, such as his experience in the military making him sympathetic to Barnhouse's views, his personality does not flavor the narrative significantly. It remains a report. In some later stories, however, the narrator influences the tone of the story, even when not a major participant in the plot. The personality of the narrator shows through in asides that comment on the action, in the kinds of similes or images used and in the diction. The easy conversational voice of narrators such as the storms-and-screens salesman or the investment counselor, both of which are used several times, impart a comfortable and persuasive immediacy that contributes much to the success of those stories.

In the novels, Vonnegut has applied the same technique increasingly. The first two, *Player Piano* and *The Sirens of Titan*, were objectively narrated from the third-person omniscient perspective. *Mother Night* introduces first-person narration, though by a person not just a narrative voice but the central character. There is an editor's note in the original edition of the novel, signed "K.V.," but this, too, remains a persona, purporting to be an editor commenting on Howard Campbell's story. But the 1966 introduction, in which Vonnegut speaks for himself, autobiographically, begins a technique that he will use more frequently and more extensively. In effect, he makes *himself* like those comfortable narrators of the short stories. In successive books he speaks about himself, his family, his life, his beliefs, his feelings, and he establishes a persona for himself. It establishes a point of view from which the novels will be told, and permits him the same kind of comfortable informality in the narrative voice, the same context for asides and observations and exclamations, even simply sighs, available to those earlier narrators. The effect, of course, has been cumulative, growing incrementally as book follows book. One consequence is that he can slip out of first-person narration in the body of the novel but retain the same informal voice, the same easy style, even in using the third-person.

There are other devices for manipulating narrative voice that continue from the short stories into the novels. One previously noted involves his use of a commentator, or even a storyteller, within the text but separate from the main narrative voice. Naturally, the short stories afford little room for this technique, since it could be too digressive and might threaten the unity of the story. But it exists in embryonic form in the commentators like the drugstore clerks in "Miss Temptation" and "The Powder Blue Dragon" who intrude their wisdom. They interject another voice, typically sensible and somewhat derisory, in a way that emerges more elaborately in the novels in the likes of the Shah of Bratpuhr in *Player Piano* or Salo in *The Sirens of Titan.* Part of the function of Kilgore Trout, as he emerges in later novels such as *God Bless You, Mr. Rosewater* and *Breakfast of Champions,* is to extend this role. These commentators—or as they become in Kilgore Trout's case, secondary storytellers—permit Vonnegut the chance to interrupt the main narrative in another voice. That voice remains plausibly contained within the novel, so that it can be an outside perspective without being an obvious authorial intrusion.

These various techniques involving narrative presences result in the creation of a kind of contention or dialogue within the narration itself. For example, the voice of the "editor" in *Mother Night* warns at the outset that writers, playwrights or propagandists like Howard Campbell are liars, so that his narrative cannot be trusted. Campbell's story immediately becomes suspect, the more so for being written in prison seemingly as a confession but also as rationalization. The reader encounters a kind of double narrative which frequently seems to contain two truths that are mutually contradictory. The reader's waiting for a single, absolute version of the truth may be answered no more than Campbell's hope that his "Blue Fairy Godmother," Wirtanen, will resolve unequivocally for him whether he has been criminal or hero. While nothing quite this complex emerges in the short stories, the use of the interior commentators may point toward it. There are instances of a more familiar technique, the use of an unreliable narrator, that also point in this direction. An example might be the narrator of "Any Reasonable Offer," who turns out to be pulling the same confidence trick as the couple his story exposes.

In writing of these various narrative voices, the impulse to refer solely to the masculine pronoun arises, because the author and the surrogates are invariably "he." The roles of women, the attitudes toward them, their relationships with men, as these things appear in Vonnegut's fiction, constitute too large a subject to be usefully explored here. But that subject needs to be given some consideration. It is relevant to the assessment of the short fiction and to consideration of the connection between the stories and what develops in the novels. Vonnegut has been questioned about his portrayal of women, particularly in the earlier fiction, any number of times. In 1977 when asked about women in his books he replied, "There aren't any. No real women, no love." He goes on to answer that he has tended to avoid it because, once introduced, that element makes it hard to get the readers' attention back to anything else.[7] Actually, a number of the stories do have a "love interest." "A Night for Love," "Long Walk to Forever," and "Find Me a Dream" deal directly with romantic relationships, while in others like "Runaways," "Go Back to Your Precious Wife and Son," "Custom Made Bride," and "The Package" gender relations occupy a significant role. Women and man-woman relationships appear more central to many of the stories than they are to any but the later novels like *Galapagos* and *Bluebeard*. The issue, however, may be *how* they appear.

In *Welcome to the Monkey House* two stories perhaps illustrate the problem: the title story, "Welcome to the Monkey House," and the semiautobiographical "Long Walk to Forever." Vonnegut includes the latter rather apologetically, calling it in his Preface "a sickeningly slick love story from *The Ladies Home Journal*" and adding, "Shame, shame, to have lived scenes from a woman's magazine" (xi). The title he had planned for it, he says, was "Hell to Get Along With," which would create a rather different expectation in the reader than the present title. He says he included it "In honor of the marriage that worked," and that sentiment no doubt goes far to account for its inclusion. Another reason could be that it has a soft, romantic tone, an easy pace and a hopeful ending that contrast to some of the other stories in the collection. In addition, it adds to the creation of a sense of the author, the autobiographical element that Vonnegut has consistently pressed toward, already introduced by "Where I Live."

As noted in the discussion of "Long Walk to Forever," one problem imparted by the Preface is that forever after it becomes hard to look at the story other than as autobiographical. And when viewed that way, it feels somehow too personal, with that touch of embarrassment one feels when a politician or an athlete refers to him-or-herself in the third person. It is a gentle story of a young man's discovering the depth of his feeling for a young woman he has grown up knowing only after she has committed to someone else. It seems evident that the realization he brings her to, that she actually loves him more or rather than the other man, is an accurate one. Yet there remains something bothersome about it, or rather, about the way it is presented. His persistence, and the element of what might be called "emotional blackmail" in revealing that he has gone A.W.O.L. in order to see her, are part of it. But the implication that the young woman lacks choice, that she is almost biologically controlled, remains troubling. Catharine says that if she loved Newt he would have seen it—"Women aren't very clever at hiding it." And then later, "Newt was seeing love now." Soon after that "Newt kissed her. He kissed her again because she wanted him to." Finally, Catharine knows that "if he called to her, she would run to him. She would have no choice"(52–53). All of this may be accurate description of what happened, even of what the woman felt, but there remains an awkwardness in having these feelings described this way by the man who elicits them. And to overstate it to make the point, there lingers over this portrayal the notion of the woman in love's being a poor thing who cannot help herself.

"Welcome to the Monkey House" presents different difficulties in the portrayal of women. The cartoon characterization of the voluptuous hostesses of the Ethical Suicide Parlors may irritate some readers, although it is done with a self-conscious hyperbole that undercuts itself and preserves its humor. But the role of Billy the Poet proves troubling. It, too, must be intended to be humorous. His appearance and his poems are ludicrous. The whole vision of the Kennedy Compound theme park to which Billy and the "nothingheads" take Nancy is comic. Yet the notion that Billy brings Nancy, and other hostesses, to a realization of the beauty of human sexuality by way of rape resists humor. Part of the intention behind Billy's explanation to Nancy of what has passed may seem benign enough. It makes the point that all too often, in the past and even at the present, a woman first experiences sex as painful and demeaning because of the ignorance and inexperience of the man, if not both. That is a judgment with which at least the readers of *Playboy*, where the story first appeared, would doubtless concur. But does that give Billy the right to demonstrate it? And while he argues that many brides have survived such an ordeal and come to enjoy sex, what of the counterargument that such an experience could traumatize a person into rejecting sex forever? The fact that Billy's act strikes a blow against a governmental tyranny, or occurs in a comic story, fails to dispel doubts of Billy's presumption of the right to rape and "educate" the woman.

Both of these stories suffer in part because of changed social attitudes. At the time of their writing, the one may have looked more simply a rather touching love story and the other actually broadminded and taking the woman's part. Other stories suffer in the same way, though less conspicuously. The physical descriptions of Susanna in "Miss Temptation" might well encounter resistance in a readership of a later generation, and so would some of the male attitudes, despite the vindication of Susanna's point of view in the story. "More Stately Mansions" depicts a woman who becomes a slave to women's magazines and obsessed with home decorating fashions, which may seem to make her both brainless and trapped in a narrowly stereotyped female role. On the other hand, the woman is *sick*, homemaking was the primary role of most married women at the time, and the story actually makes the case for being sorry that the only outlet afforded such a woman's creativity comes from glossy-magazines. In other stories, women in lesser roles quite often come off poorly, as either dim or shrewish, though sometimes, as in the collection's "Deer in the Works," as inately more wise and stable than the men.

The women in the early novels are similar. The characterization of Anita in *Player Piano* does not invite empathy from the reader. She appears "pushy," possessive and duplicitous. Another glossy-magazine follower, she seems shallow and calculating. Yet her portrayal shows her as much a victim as a manipulator. She has narrowly escaped a dreadful life in Homestead, and she has applied intelligence resourcefully to survival and to advancing her husband's career. Her efforts frequently seem mechanical, prompting Ed Finnerty's barb that she could be replaced by something made out of foam rubber and stainless steel, which places her on a par with the chess-playing robot Checker Charley. Yet for all the obvious strikes against her as a character, she clearly deserves some sympathy. She tries to understand a husband floundering psychologically, and in her own way she attempts to make the best of what she is and the role in which she finds herself. Sadly, Finnerty comes even closer to the truth than he realizes in saying she could be replaced by a machine; in the world of this novel, most people have been replaced by machines, and are reduced to being automatons themselves. Society would make Anita the Company Wife Machine. The novel recognizes the sad fact that there are all too many such roboticized women in the Schenectadies of 1950s America. So the novel's objective may be enlightened, but the portrayal of its main female character nevertheless remains one that feminists of a later decade in particular find disquieting.

Inevitably, the presentations of many of the female characters in the short stories reflect attitudes that are current in the society of the time. That may be the more true in that these stories are written for a broad, general audience. Many of those attitudes sit less comfortably with succeeding generations, so that even when being sympathetically presented, some of the female characterizations will come to be seen as somewhat sexist. Again, the intent frequently appears to be the reverse. The short story "Custom-Made Bride," for example, sets out explicitly to decry the husband's designing a "Falloleen" out of Kitty Cahoun. "Miss Temptation" attempts to show Susanna as an ordinary young woman who wants to be treated and respected as such, not as a sex object. There are similar examples in the novels. The "heartbreakingly beautiful" Mona Aamons Monzano of *Cat's Cradle*, for instance, resembles Susanna in being a stereotypical embodiment of men's fantasies who wants to be an "ordinary" young woman. Largely through sheer exaggeration, Vonnegut undercuts the imagery of titillation that surrounds her, and he makes Mona soberly sensible in the face of the narrator's ill-timed sexual overtures, but some readers still find the slick fiction descriptions of her appearance hard to get past. Similarly, Beatrice in *The Sirens of Titan* emerges by the end as a wise, forgiving, charitable woman, but the earlier depiction which makes her preserved virginity an emblem of her meanness of spirit remains troubling. With the beautifully sensitive treatment of Sylvia in *God Bless You, Mr. Rosewater,* the reservations begin to be dispelled. Sylvia becomes the embodiment of love and compassion finally overcome by the excesses imposed on her by the husband who cannot then give her the conjugal love she needs. By *Breakfast of Champions* Vonnegut flatly denounces the robotization of women in the expectations and roles male society imposes on them, such as the designation of "women's work." A more complete conception of women characters emerges in later novels. In *Galapagos* and *Bluebeard,* for example, women prove wise, strong and whole, while the men appear blundering, weak, and maimed.

Catharine seems to lack free will and acts almost as if biologically controlled. Anita appears almost robot-like in the mechanical fulfillment of her role. Their characterizations raise another topic that emerges in the stories to reach fruition in the novels: the conception of people as robots, or humans in various ways mechanized or dehumanized. The reverse also appears, namely, humanized machines, sometimes with the purpose of emphasizing the former idea by contrast. In some instances the stories lean in this direction in a fairly traditional way—people so obsessed or restricted that they become one-dimensional. Sherwood Anderson of *Winesburg, Ohio*, with his "grotesques," used that style of characterization. Grace McClellan of "More Stately Mansions," absorbed by her decorating mania, or Harry Nash, the living void who finds identity only in dramatic roles in "Who Am I This Time?" are essentially of this type. Other characters become dehumanized by circumstances rather than by being themselves uni-dimensional: those reduced to a catatonic state by the euphio in "The Euphio Question"; the American prisoners turned into chess pieces in "All the King's Horses"; the eternally unaging generations of "The Big Trip Up Yonder." "The Manned Missiles," in which the two astronauts become endlessly orbiting satellites, or "Unready to Wear," with humans become "amphibians" who occasionally employ bodies, make the dehumanization more literal. Some of these stories, and also "Welcome to the Monkey House," with visions of circumstances that leave people feeling deprived of their humanity and wondering "what are people for?" come close to reducing humans to robots. "EPICAC," on the other hand, shows the computer with human capacities for love, poetry, grief and mortality.

These stories set the stage for the extended treatments in the novels. Robots duplicate human movements and replace workers in *Player Piano*. Salo, the Tralfamadorian robot in *The Sirens of Titan*, takes further the development of human emotions begun with EPICAC, once again leading even to suicide. (Unlike EPICAC, Salo can be resurrected!) The humans recruited to the Martian army are made robotic by the insertion of antennae in their heads, an idea first used in an unpublished story, "Robotville and Mr. Caslow"). The ultimate treatment of this often-included topic comes in *Breakfast of Champions*. There humans are turned into robots in the vision Dwayne Hoover borrows from Kilgore Trout's *Now It Can Be Told*. He takes literally the story's premise that everyone else is a robot. More generally, people are depicted as being robot-like in that their behavior is biochemically controlled. Introduce a certain drug or undergo a change of body chemistry and dramatic swings in mood and behavior can result. People also can be reduced to robots effectively by the solipsistic perceptions of others. When people are stereotyped by function, for example, they are made no more than a machine that performs that task, and such reductions invariably become demeaning. Thus in *Breakfast of Champions* people refer to "*women's work*" and "*Nigger work*," a girls' swimming champion becomes "pure tuna fish," and the author himself becomes "a writing meat machine." When Dwayne decides his mistress Francine Pefko must be a robot and calls her "a fucking machine" it seems no more or less than how he has regarded her before. Nowhere else in the novels are these ideas treated so specifically, but the notion that human beings are robot-like in lacking free will, because of body chemistry, fate, or events beyond their control, returns frequently.

In *The Sirens of Titan*, Malachi Constant declares his lack of free will when, as the returning Space Wanderer, he declares, "I was a victim of a series of accidents, as are we all" (253). From the start, Malachi, whose name means "constant messenger," seeks a message to deliver, something to give meaning to his life or, ultimately, identity. In spite of his name Constant, his identity changes repeatedly, from playboy to space traveler to the Martian soldier "Unk" to the prophesied "Space Wanderer," and so on. Paul Proteus of *Player Piano* also undergoes protean changes in his search for identity. Harry Nash's changes in "Who Am I This Time?" come from borrowed dramatic identities. These three almost allegorical treatments of characters who strive to determine who they are, to find an identity, are among the most explicit examples of Vonnegut's persistent pursuit of this theme. It is tested repeatedly in the short stories, as has been noted in the discussions of "The Foster Portfolio," "The Powder Blue Dragon," "Unpaid Consultant," "The Hyannis Port Story," and others. It remains a central preoccupation in the life journeys of the protagonists in the later novels, finely elaborated in a character like Rabo Karabekian in *Bluebeard*. Such a universal topic needs no further rehearsal here, especially since it has been raised in connection with individual stories, but it should be kept in mind how consistent the developments in the novels remain to their origins in the short fiction.

An aspect of the identity theme that does deserve further note in passing is how the search for self-identity relates to the father-son relationship. Vonnegut's own circumstances are worth recollecting in this respect. His relationship with his own father was not particularly close, especially as his father increasingly retreated into himself as the Great Depression overtook his profession. In turn, Vonnegut had a son of his own and then adopted three more who were orphaned when his brother-in-law and sister died. These various circumstances would presumably make that relationship a particularly preoccupying one in his life.

In the short stories, aspects of the father-son relationship occupy central places in "Adam," "This Son of Mine," "Runaways," "Manned Missiles," and "Go Back to Your Precious Wife and Son," and a lesser role in other titles. Its treatment in the early novels remains similar. Paul Proteus feels challenged to follow in the footsteps of his father, but comes to wonder himself whether his public rebellion in fact represents a psychological uprising against his parent's ghost. Malachi Constant, too, is challenged by his father's accomplishments. The Hoenikker family in *Cat's Cradle* looks like a comic replay of the Vonneguts, with the preoccupied father, two sons and a daughter. In *God Bless You, Mr. Rosewater*, Eliot's reaction to his father and the Rosewaters' patriarchal tradition profoundly influences his behavior. And in *Breakfast of Champions*, where Vonnegut intrudes as author and character, he addresses his relationship with his father directly. In that novel, he becomes the literary father of his creation, Kilgore Trout. That old science fiction writer has Vonnegut's father's legs and his voice, so that the father-son relationship between the author and Trout remains ambivalent. Perhaps Trout also represents a kind of literary parent, the prolific writer of science fiction who never achieves recognition and thus personifies Vonnegut's worst fears of what he might have become.

In natural accord with the advance of Vonnegut's age, the focus of the father-son relationship seems to shift with the passage of time. The short stories, like the early novels, look from the perspective of the son or at the relationship as the son grows toward independence. In the later novels, the perspective is more likely to be that of the older man, like Walter Starbuck of *Jailbird*, or old Kilgore Trout himself, with unforgiving offspring who reject him. Kilgore Trout has a son, Leon or Leo, and their abrasive relationship comes up in later books. In *Breakfast of Champions*, where Vonnegut's father exerts a strong presence, the mother remains remote: "My mother stayed far, far away, because she had left me a legacy of suicide" (294). Mother-son relationships are scarce throughout—another aspect of the portrayal of women—although in later novels, notably *Galapagos* and *Bluebeard*, women assume strong maternal roles in relation to other characters. Fathers-and-sons, however, stands as one of the main identity-defining relationships in Vonnegut's fiction.

The short fiction reveals a propensity to take stories based on mundane events to the edge of realism, and conversely to endow science fiction with a touch of the everyday. Both sides of this technique continue into the novels, eventually contributing enormously to the characteristic Vonnegut style. Illustrations of this technique have been noted in discussing the stories. In

"Custom-Made Bride" a domestic situation goes to extremes in the design of the house and in the transformation of "Falloleen." In the brief "Mnemonics," the memory-inducing visions are fantastic. The Jekyll-and-Hyde transformations of Herbert Foster in "The Foster Portfolio," or the wild scenes at the end of "A Present for Big Nick," test the bounds of credulity. As was observed earlier, these stories often suggest a heritage in the traditional tall tale. At the same time, the science fiction stories incorporate the mundane, as embodied in the furniture in "Report on the Barnhouse Effect." Several stories, however, seem to stand between the two worlds of the mundane and the fantastic. "The Manned Missiles" sets a space catastrophe in a context of the all too understandable emotions of the fathers and their daily worlds. "EPICAC" mixes the traits of science fiction and love story. And "The Euphio Question" uses a domestic setting and a cast of homespun characters in a story of interstellar radio waves.

These combinations show up in the novels. *Player Piano* has future setting and technology, but its domestic scenes, its sales retreats, even its haircuts, are pure nineteen-fifties. *The Sirens of Titan* is more purely science-fictional, and *Mother Night* the reverse. But then comes *Cat's Cradle*. While this novel has its *ice-nine* and its vision of the end of the world, it remains hard to think of it simply as science fiction. Nor is it simply realistic fiction with some science fiction ingredients thrown in. Its self-conscious combination of the two, its inclusion of the *Books of Bokonon* and John's *The Day the World Ended*, and its recognition of its own fictionality, like loops of string purported to signify a cat's cradle, mark it as Vonnegut's first postmodern novel. From that point on, the freedom of this technique, so matched to his world view, has characterized his approach to his novels. Thus the interplay of science fiction and realism in the stories leads on to the postmodern mixes of genre and technique evident in most of his later books.

Another characteristic of the science fiction in Vonnegut's stories is frequent humor, as noted previously. Of course, humor becomes a dominating feature of almost all of his writing, even in a story as bleak as "Adam" or a novel as dark as *Mother Night*. Most of the short fiction, responding to the market demand for "happy" stories, does not have this "black humor," so prevalent later. There are hints of it; the drooping gun barrels and zapped aircraft in "The Barnhouse Effect," the crowding generations and delights of solitary confinement in "Tomorrow and Tomorrow and Tomorrow," for example, are humorously rendered and point toward the painful comedy to come. A different humorous treatment of science fiction appears in "The Euphio Question," both in the chaotic scene that ensues from the euphio experiment and in the twist at the end, where the machine is being turned on in the hearing room. The gentler humor of the poetry writing, love-sick EPICAC balances the sentimental pathos. "Tom Edison's Shaggy Dog" fits a different genre, but the intelligence-measuring machine that discovers the secret brilliance of dogs is the touch of science fiction whose introduction into this tall tale underpins its main joke.

The novels abound in humor conveyed through science fiction—or science fiction with a comic bent. The very description of Salo in *The Sirens of Titan* is comic, and some of the Tralfamadorian messages attributed to Earth's great monuments are hilarious: Stonehenge spells out *"Replacement part being*

rushed with all possible speed" (271). In *Cat's Cradle*, surely one of
Vonnegut's funniest books, the comic concept of *ice-nine* that makes water
freeze at room temperature is at the heart of the plot. The Tralfamadorians and
the time/space traveling to which they subject Billy Pilgrim provide much comic
relief in *Slaughterhouse-Five*. And in some later books it falls to Kilgore Trout
to infuse humor into the novel through his outlandish science fiction plots.

Frequently the humor in the novels differs from that of the short stories in
being more like a Camusian humor of the absurd, or the kind of humor
sometimes associated with the gallows or the trenches. The short stories,
however wry their humor, generally sustain a level of optimism that precludes
such bleak laughter. The novels, with their frequent scenes of war, depression,
and apocalypse, are invariably punctuated with jokes and other light moments.
But the short stories can only hint at the kind of bitter humor epitomized by
Slapstick, whose tone Vonnegut sets by prefacing the novel with an account of
how his sister Alice used that expression—"Slapstick"—on hearing of the death
of her husband hours before she herself died of cancer. These autobiographical
ruminations in the novels, naturally not available in the short stories, often
contribute to the darker tone—and humor—as Vonnegut reflects on such things
as depression, suicide and loneliness.

The dystopian—or anti-Utopian—vision in much of Vonnegut's fiction also
accounts for some of the pessimism found there. That is one subject in which a
darker tone does emerge in the stories, although there, as often in the novels, too,
it may be treated with humor. "Welcome to the Monkey House," "2BR02B,"
and "The Big Trip Up Yonder" ("Tomorrow and Tomorrow and Tomorrow") all
present dystopian visions of worlds where anti-aging drugs exacerbate the
existing overpopulation. The resulting scenes, of a planet jammed with
geriatrics who appear to be in their twenties and who are lured to ethical suicide
parlors, bring comedy to a situation whose threat is already becoming a reality.
"Harrison Bergeron" mocks Utopian dreams of a fully egalitarian society.
"Deer in the Works" points toward the novel *Player Piano* in depicting the
dehumanizing aspects of a technological-industrial Utopia. In both the
bewilderment inflicted upon their denizens produces comical and sad scenes.
While stories like those mentioned call attention to the future dire consequences
of "progress" in science, technology, medicine and social management, others
take a dystopian approach to more limited, domestic situations. Such stories as
"The Package" and "Hal Irwin's Magic Lamp" debunk dreams of happiness
found in the domestic Utopias of the fully-gadgeted house and car in the
trendiest suburb. Since *Player Piano* was the most contemporary with stories
dealing with these topics, it is scarcely surprising that both levels of social satire
have their most direct treatment there. But the preoccupations of the dystopian
stories—overpopulation, technological displacement of humans, science
unchecked, authoritarianism, existence robbed of meaning—continue to persist,
and to be treated even more overtly with bitter yet resigned humor.

The other technique that contributes conspicuously to the tone of
Vonnegut's writing is the propensity toward short units of prose. The curt
sentences, paragraphs, chapters, even books themselves, earn repeated mention
as the feature that characterizes his work. Aspects of Vonnegut's stylistic
evolution have been discussed in earlier chapters and need no reiteration here,

but it does seem important to note this characteristic when trying to reach some summation of the place of the short fiction in the larger canon. It does appear that organizing thought in tight, successive "bullets" comes naturally to Vonnegut, and that this habit underlies his manner of composition. But his training as a newspaper journalist, writing short paragraphs that break up those long, narrow columns, and short, direct sentences that do not lose the reader, must also play its part. The requirements of short story writing would continue the same emphasis. His ability to compress without seeming to skimp in those stories remains impressive. "Mnemonics," for instance, takes less than a page of *Collier's*, while remaining quite rich in images. The novels are broken up into short chapters, and the chapters themselves into shorter segments. In fact, the devices used to separate these segments, varying from ellipses to arrows to single dots, and always new in each book, make quite an entertaining study themselves. Yet Vonnegut proves capable of quite lyrical prose, while the conversational manner frequently used also tends to alleviate the jerkiness one might expect from such compressed sentences.

The style, however pronounced, proves adaptable. Just as the range of stories became remarkably wide, so do the variations of tone and subject in the novels. The clipped prose and the variant narrative voices work effectively in novels as different in mood as *Mother Night* and *Cat's Cradle*, and facilitate the rapid shifts within one text, such as those between a sober historical account and its parody via a Trout plot. The range of the stories may have implied the readiness to experiment that would emerge over the course of the novels. Vonnegut describes his technique as being like that of the scientist who asks, "What if?" Sometimes, he admits, it is more like the inquiring adolescent's reluctance to accept the laiddown explanations. His plots can be shaped by questions like, "What if water froze at room temperature?" "What if gravity varied, like the wind?" "What if humans were secluded in a confined environment? How would they evolve?" "What if the universe stopped expanding and started to contract?"

Vonnegut experiments freely with technical innovations. The shuffling of chronology in *Slaughterhouse-Five*; the coexistence of the author as external creator and internal character in *Breakfast of Champions* and elsewhere; the invention of dialect, language and even religion, notably in *Cat's Cradle*; the inclusion of playlets, mini-stories, poems, recipes, calypsos, songs and drawings; the refrains and repeated exclamations; all are stamps of the Vonnegutian, some of which have been there since high school. The evolving form of Vonnegut's novels, and perhaps the security gained as his stature grew, give him the freedom to experiment with such things more conspicuously as the novels progress. Less uncommon devices, like the carrying of names, locations, objects, events or catch phrases from book to book, can also be traced back through the stories to the journalism, though employed with increasing sophistication and incremental humor. Other writers have certainly used such features, but few with such conspicuous emphasis or to such comedic ends. They contribute to the daring, the sense of literary recklessness in a willingness to risk much for the accomplishment of effect, that characterizes Vonnegut's work. Some have been frustrated by this manner, but for those who enjoy him it constitutes a major part of his appeal. [8]

The stories, then, possess fewer of the signature tags that have come to be associated with the novels. They also allow less room for the didacticism that emerges over the course of the novels. Vonnegut leaves his most overtly opinionated writing to his nonfiction, but some of the novels, perhaps most obviously *Breakfast of Champions*, speak directly, and in the first-person, on issues.[9] In some novels the directness comes in the introductory pages, and if there are other messages to be delivered they come from the mouths of characters or through the parables of Kilgore Trout. In whatever form of expression he chooses, Vonnegut makes unusually outspoken declarations about a range of social issues. He questions orthodoxies that many view as cornerstones of American culture and citizenship. Seeing him as pacifist, atheist, socialist, profane and unpatriotic, the more extreme have regarded him as someone to be censored. Perhaps only "The Big Space Fuck" among the short pieces would elicit such hostile response. Yet the values that form the basis of Vonnegut's more didactic passages have been implicit in the stories all along.

Where, and what, are those values? Near the top of the list surely would be "common decency," what he has espoused as perhaps more important than, and not necessarily dependent upon, love. In *Slapstick* he says that he wishes couples who are supposed be in love would say when they fight, "Please—a little less love, and a little more common decency" (3). Others might characterize this as a wish for more *caritas*, less *Eros*. The passions of romantic love remain suspect as erratic and inconstant: he extols a more universal blend of compassion and respect, governed by good sense. This requires breaking from solipsism and the effort to imaginatively recognize the otherness of others, the capacity of which the young Booboolings are deprived in Trout's "The Sisters B-36." The stories constantly validate this seemingly modest but all too rare quality. In the four stories that feature him, George Helmholtz appeals because he embodies it, beyond even his ambitions for his bands. It sustains the relationship between Turley and Milly Whitman in "A Night For Love," transcending the romantic memories of Milly's earlier moonlight encounter with Louis Reinbeck. It emerges only after much hurt and conflict in the relationship that develops between Beatrice Rumfoord and Malachi Constant at the end of *The Sirens of Titan*. Vonnegut applies it to conjugal relationships and to the whole broad range of human social interaction. The primacy of common human decency in his thinking sets the dominant mood throughout his writing. Where the note of resignation, frustration or occasionally cynicism arises it most often has to do with his perception of behavior that contravenes such decency.

In one way or another, Vonnegut has several times made comment on the lack of villains in his fiction. The most memorable instance comes in the first chapter of *Slaughterhouse-Five*, where he quotes his father's saying to him, "You know—you never wrote a story with a villain in it" (8). He explains this as something he learned as an anthropology student. But there are some people, real and fictional, he clearly dislikes. He amplifies the moral distinctions involved in such judgments. In the new introduction to the Twenty-Fifth Anniversary Edition of *Slaughterhouse-Five,* he distinguishes between the Dresden raid and Auschwitz by saying that the former demonstrates "the inhumanity of many of man's inventions to man," while the latter shows "man's inhumanity to man" (xii–xiii). Similarly, in his public interview at the Steppenwolf Theatre in Chicago in September 1996, he said that he did not regard the crews of the bombers over Dresden as immoral, whereas the pilots of the two American fighters who broke away and dived down to strafe his little band of survivors did commit an immoral act.[10] The vengeful Paul Lazarro of *Slaughterhouse-Five,* who calls revenge the sweetest thing in life, embodies the rendering of evil for evil that perpetuates grievance and suffering. Ludicrous figure though he appears, Billy Pilgrim embodies the opposite principle of the person who absorbs evil without passing it on, thus breaking the cycle of pain and retribution. That makes him saintly, and indeed he several times appears as Christ-like. The short stories establish the same opposition, though in less dramatically allegorical extremes. The kindly (though sometimes also mocked) Helmholtz, the caring black soldiers in "D.P.," and Heinz in "Adam" are among those who demonstrate decency. Those who are cynical, acquisitive, self-centered, or judgmental—like Quinn in "The Kid Nobody Could Handle," or Norman Fuller in "Miss Temptation"—demonstrate acts that go counter to common decency. The contention between these ways of behaving reveals the moral affirmation in Vonnegut's writing, that the limits to how much humans can control makes the more imperative their behaving with common decency.

In general the stories illustrate this behavioral standard in homespun, down-to-earth circumstances, although "The Manned Missiles" shows the essential decency of two individuals prevailing against the political rhetoric of their governments. Modesty, honesty, consideration, understanding, treating people with good humor, these are the virtues consistently endorsed in the short fiction. While there may be no more heroes than there are villains, the people affirmed for their behavior—Helmholtz, Charley Freeman of "The Package," Milly Whitman of "A Night for Love," for instance—show just these qualities of decency and consideration. Patience with the behavior of teenagers several times serves as the test, as does treatment of and by children. Add to these the marital relationships that strain or reveal "common decency" and it might appear that part of what the stories advocate resembles what a later generation turned into a political cliché as "family values." Vonnegut extends these same criteria for treating people with respectful decency to broad social issues, making them the underpinnings of the views on social policy he expresses.

Some of Vonnegut's political inclinations, frequently revealed in the later writing, become apparent in the short fiction, though in more subdued hues. Socioeconomic issues crop up repeatedly in the short stories, pointing toward *God Bless You, Mr. Rosewater,* where Vonnegut opens the novel by announcing, "A sum of money is a leading character in this tale about people" and where the politics of economic distribution are central. Sums of money, sudden riches or high incomes have important roles in numerous stories: "The Foster Portfolio," "The Package," "Unpaid Consultant," "Poor Little Rich Town," and "Hal Irwin's Magic Lamp," are conspicuous examples. There are others, like "More Stately Mansions," "Deer in the Works," "Custom-Made Bride," or "A Present for Big Nick," where family income or lack of it becomes a contributing factor in the plot. It seems natural enough that money subjects, like sensible management of family income or dreams of wealth, should be a popular subject for stories tailored to a largely middle-class audience. That would be particularly true during the 1950s and early 1960s when the American middle-class dreams of home, car, and gadget ownership flourished amidst an expectation of perpetual material improvement. But the confidence of many in this optimistic era was qualified by memories of the Great Depression. That memory stayed with Vonnegut, even though he explains that his family never suffered serious hardship, the worst being the psychological impact upon his parents. Consequently his concern for those left out of prosperity remains a constant. In the 1996 Chicago interview he said, "My generation had dreams about what would be after the Depression, then after the war. The dream usually involved socialism or communism, something that would create a more equitable society, that after the war we would make it more just economically. Unfortunately neither socialism nor communism turned out to work very well." "Harrison Bergeron" is an allegory about the difficulties of achieving equality. Stories like "Hal Irwin's Magic Lamp," "The Hyannis Port Story," "This Son of Mine" and "A Night for Love" talk about aspects of economic inequality in society enough to show that the issue was already very much in Vonnegut's mind. His more direct treatments of the subject, and of the political stance that results, come later.

By inversion, people's fears, or what they see as threats, often demonstrate their values. That can be seen in Vonnegut's fiction, too. His anxieties about war in the short fiction reflect those of a period that closely follows the Second World War, overlaps with the Korean action, feels the threat of the cold war, and is heading toward Viet Nam. "All the King's Horses," "The Manned Missiles," and "The Report on the Barnhouse Effect" reflect these anxieties. His own feelings, naturally, had been marked forever by his war experiences, particularly those of the aftermath of conflict. "Adam" and "D.P." emphasize the personal tragedies in the wake of war. All of these stories point toward *Slaughterhouse-Five,* the "anti-war novel" that won its first wide public acclaim in the days of anti-Vietnam War demonstrations, and to many later explicitly pacifist statements. Nor has Vonnegut warned only of destruction by war. The dangers to the survival of the species and the planet posed by overpopulation as envisioned in several short stories have been noted, and continue to concern him. Vonnegut also deplores the threats posed by pollution, exhaustion of natural resources, irresponsible science, and misapplied technology, all mostly fueled by greed and sheer unwillingness to apply common sense. Again, these are topics mostly developed in nonfiction and novels—and later in many Trout plots—but they are apparent in stories as different as "Deer in the Works" and "Tomorrow and Tomorrow and Tomorrow." His frustration at society's lack of willingness to address these threats explodes in passages like that in the Trout story "The Planet Gobblers" in *Palm Sunday* that compares humans to "interplanetary termites" who devour planets with "horrifying destructiveness." And he adds, "It is easy to take good care of a planet" (209). He suggests more than once, in slightly varying language but here as stated in *Fates Worse Than Death*, that humanity could leave a message in huge letters on a Grand Canyon wall: "WE PROBABLY COULD HAVE SAVED OURSELVES, BUT WERE TOO DAMNED LAZY TO TRY VERY HARD" (116).

Such direct outbursts can occur more easily in the novels, especially once Vonnegut has evolved the appropriate narrative voice, and in the nonfiction collections. In his frequent speaking engagements, some of which are recorded in *Palm Sunday* and *Fates Worse than Death,* he is often more outspoken. In these various forms, Vonnegut's concern with social issues greatly influences the tone. In most of the novels, and in essays and speeches, too, his tone combines concern, compassion and humor. The humor, which has been categorized too often simply as "black humor," varies between biting satirical derision, the weary laughter of resignation, the slightly malicious delight of slapstick, and the resort to comedy as the only escape from tears. Humor becomes an important tool for leavening the didacticism, enabling him be blunt on an issue but frequently in a comically irreverent way that lessens the preachiness. The short stories afford less opportunity for pronouncement on issues or for some of the techniques mentioned here, due both to their length and to their location. But, as has been suggested, Vonnegut does indeed inject issues into the short stories, generally in a softer tone and less directly. The shared characteristics, of tone, content, technique and implied values, are extensive and strong enough to argue for seeing Vonnegut's work as all of a piece, though varying predictably according to genre, audience and date of composition.

In sum, then, the short stories proved extremely valuable in the honing of Vonnegut's narrative skills and in his evolution as a writer. Perhaps the fact that through much of this period he was writing up to four, five, or as many as seven stories in one year, rather than pursuing a single novel for more than a year, afforded particularly rich experience in working with a range of voices, plots, types of story and audiences. Being able to draw on this varied experience proves important as he emerges as a novelist. The first four novels, for instance, are remarkably different in form and tone—the dystopian *Player Piano*, the space operatic *The Sirens of Titan*, the darkly confessional *Mother Night*, and the hilariously original *Cat's Cradle*. His ability to actually combine within one novel the kinds of elements found in the range of stories contributes to his eventual evolution as a postmodern novelist. There seems little doubt, as Leslie Fiedler suggests in his essay, that writing popular fiction for the magazines played a crucial role in determining the kind of novelist Vonnegut would become and the success he would enjoy.

Most of the stories wear remarkably well. Some suffer from diction or descriptions of setting or technology that sound dated. Much fiction comes to face that problem, which may be particularly acute in short stories where situations must be created quickly so draw heavily on what is already familiar to a contemporary audience. Yet among these stories, the situations themselves frequently possess a timelessness or universality that lends them endurance. Looking back at them in the magazines in which they were originally published, they often appear strikingly less dated than the advertisements and illustrations that decorate their pages. The DC-6s, cake mixes and hairstyles in the margins are reminders of how much America has changed, while the contents of the stories are usually still relevant and occasionally prophetic. Given that they are written in the first decade or so of a half-century long career, their durability has been more than might have been expected of stories written for consumption by a general audience.

Apart from relevant themes that often relate to the moral choices faced in everyday life, these stories offer plots that involve "human interest" and that create suspense. Fiedler has spoken of popular fiction as reinventing the age-old myths. Vonnegut's novels invoke them; the short stories provide little opportunity to except in the occasional allusion. But they often do act as *exempla* for the kinds of values and behavior extolled in classical myth. They also appeal in endorsing those values for daily living often seen as the traditional American ones, of common sense, optimism, industry, fair play, generosity, and love of children, dogs and underdogs. They are also mainstream Americana in their tall-tale and shaggy-dog humor and their delight in deflating pretension. Their plots are well made and often original. Tempo varies effectively with the situation, and the stories generally move energetically. Their characterizations, while of necessity sometimes scarcely beyond brisk caricatures, usually impart life to the story. In the best, the evolution of a comfortable narrative persona contributes much to the engagement of the reader. All of these characteristics contribute to the quality of the stories, particularly as viewed in terms of the criteria required of their popular fiction genre.

The short stories, then, take their place in the wide range of Kurt Vonnegut's artistic achievement. They do not simply stand beside his novels. The stories have, in effect, become part of those novels, both in their contribution to the skills and experience invested in creating them, and in the continuing place within the longer works for Trout stories, vignettes, and a highly segmented construction. The short fiction remains complementary to the earlier novels much as the short *non*fiction, in essays, speeches and collections, complements the later novels. They are an essential part of Vonnegut's extraordinarily versatile literary creativity, and arguably more central to it than his ventures into drama, poetry, libretto and requiem. But to divide and separate his creative endeavors seems arbitrary and distorting. His engagement with media other than prose has come as natural outgrowth; short stories and novels have led to film, television and stage adaptations. Some of these have been his own doing, and others have involved him to greater and lesser extent. Some have actually occurred without his permission or knowing; yet the seed remains his. He has always drawn and painted, and perhaps inevitably this activity has flowed into his fiction, with drawings in several books—most obviously *Breakfast of Champions*—and artists and art featured in others—notably *Bluebeard*. Later in Vonnegut's career the artwork comes to assume a larger proportion of his artistic production. Perhaps the spare but intense lines of his paintings represent the ultimate compression of message, like the Tralfamadorians' telegraphic novels of *Slaughterhouse-Five*, though Vonnegut claims they are created expressively, without message or moral.

Kurt Vonnegut, journalist, fiction writer, playwright, poet, essayist, lecturer (even stand-up entertainer!), librettist, painter and, yes, public relations writer, has been placing his creations before the public throughout the second half of the twentieth century. The short fiction occupies its own important place under this broad panoply of artistic endeavor. Overshadowed by the novels that eventually replaced them as their author's preferred medium, they retain their importance in their own right and for their place in Vonnegut's artistic evolution. If they may sometimes be seen as unsophisticated, that is often part of their charm, for they are as likely to express the energy and resourcefulness of the young writer who worked into the night hours to produce them. With them he laid the foundations for one of the longest and most prolific literary careers in America in the twentieth century.

NOTES

1.   R. A. Sokolov, Review of *Welcome to the Monkey House*, *Newsweek*, August 19, 1968, 85.

2.   Richard Rhodes, Review of *Welcome to the Monkey House*, *Book World*, August 18, 1968, 4.

3.   James Lundquist, *Kurt Vonnegut* (New York: Frederick Ungar, 1977), 8.

4.   Leslie A. Fiedler, "The Divine Stupidity of Kurt Vonnegut," *Esquire*, September 1970, 196.

5.   In his 1987 interview with William Rodney Allen and Paul Smith, Vonnegut speaks of rules he learned governing the writing of successful short stories. "They were quite sound, and a lot of them were taken from Aristotle's *Poetics*." In William Rodney Allen, ed., *Conversations with Kurt Vonnegut* (Jackson: University Press of Mississippi, 1988), 268.   Hereafter cited as *Conversations*.

6.   *Kurt Vonnegut: A Self-Portrait*, produced and directed by Harold Mantell (Princeton, N.J.: Films for the Humanities, 1976).

7.   In the 1977 *Paris Review* interview, Vonnegut says: "I try to keep deep love out of my stories because, once that particular subject comes up, it is almost impossible to talk about anything else. Readers don't want to hear about anything else. They go gaga about love" (*Conversations*, 185).

8.   An interesting account of such negative views of Vonnegut by Jack Richardson, John Gardner and Roger Sale, and a rebuttal to them, appears in John Irving, "Kurt Vonnegut and His Critics," *New Republic*, September 22, 1979, 41–49.

9.   In the 1973 *Playboy* Interview, Vonnegut says, "As I get older, I get more didactic. I say what I really think. I don't hide ideas like Easter eggs for people to find" (*Conversations*, 108). A similar idea emerges in an interview with Robert Short in 1976 when asked if his fiction will become more didactic: "There'll be more and more for people to complain about in my fiction. People will say it's not fiction any more, it's editorializing." Robert Short, *Something to Believe In* (San Francisco: Harper and Row, 1978), 300.

10. Kurt Vonnegut was interviewed on stage by Dr. Lee Roloff at the Steppenwolf Theatre in Chicago on September 29, 1996. This preceded the opening performance by Steppenwolf of Eric Simonson's stage adaptation of *Slaughterhouse-Five*.

Appendix: Contributions to the *Shortridge Daily Echo* and the *Cornell Sun*, by M. Andre Z. Eckenrode

Shortridge High School, Indianapolis, Indiana
Cornell University, Ithaca, New York
By M. Andre Z. Eckenrode

Kurt Vonnegut, Jr. attended Shortridge High School in Indianapolis from 1936 to 1940. Originally known as Indianapolis High School when launched in 1864, it became the first high school to publish a daily newspaper, the *Shortridge Daily Echo,* in 1898. This premiere daily was one page, the back of which was devoted to advertising, and was put together almost exclusively by the teamwork of three students, with nearly non-existent faculty involvement. The paper lasted for only seven weeks before succumbing to pressure from parents of the few students involved. However, the *Echo* was revived several months later, this time with considerably more student involvement as well as faculty sponsorship. The new *Echo* was two pages, and a separate editorial staff was now established for each day of the school week. By the time Vonnegut began attending Shortridge, the *Echo* had been expanded to four pages.

Vonnegut's name first appeared in the *Echo* during his freshman year, in the Wednesday, January 13, 1937, edition, in a gossip column on the third page going by the name of "Sally Shortridge Sez." Page three of the *Echo* was the nearly exclusive domain of gossip columns throughout the week. Over the next four years Vonnegut would be mentioned many more times, often concerned with which girls he'd been seen with, but sometimes referring to his school activities. While Vonnegut's name was linked with those of several girls in the gossip columns, he was never mentioned in conjunction with Jane Cox, his wife-to-be. Jane Cox garnered only a few gossip mentions herself during Vonnegut's years at Shortridge.

Vonnegut joined the Tuesday staff of the *Echo* as a reporter effective with the April 25, 1939, edition, according to the masthead, and continued to serve in that capacity for the remainder of his junior year. No items attributed to him by name appeared in Tuesday editions, nor any attributable with any degree of certainty. Beginning with the first Tuesday edition at the outset of his senior year, the *Echo* masthead listed Vonnegut as "Second Page Columnist." In this edition there appeared a column entitled "The Inquisitive Reporter Reporting on a Bull Session," and signed "Ferdinand." The author of the "The Inquisitive Reporter . . ." column was clearly following the lead of a series of columns which had appeared in the previous three years' Tuesday editions on page two, titled at various times "Inquisitive Reporter" or "The Inquisitive Reporter." The author maintained the goal of the preceding columns, which was to interview a handful of students on a particular topic each week. (Vonnegut himself had been quoted in the column previously.) The title of the second page Tuesday column varied somewhat in the months following the first one, but the emphasis was shifted to "Bull Session." The signatures were variations of "Ferdinand."

In the Tuesday, January 23, 1940, edition, a news article appeared on the front page accompanied by the headline "Vonnegut, Hitz to Edit Tuesday Edition in Spring," detailing the promotion of Vonnegut and his friend Ben Hitz to co-editors. Phil Huston, listed previously in the masthead as "Second Page Co-Editor," succeeded Vonnegut as "Second Page Columnist." The "Bull Session" column in this edition included a brief farewell from its author. The columns continued to appear on page two of that school year's remaining Tuesday editions, but would usually be signed "Filbert" beginning with the February 6, 1940, edition.

It appears safe to assume that the "Inquisitive Reporter . . ."/ "Bull Session" columns from September 12, 1939, to January 23, 1940, were indeed Vonnegut's, and he is designated as their author in the index that follows this text.

The considerable use of the name "Ferdinand" in the *Echo* during Vonnegut's years at Shortridge provides a source of interest and some confusion. During the fall of his freshman year, two facetious letters appeared under the headline "Freda the Freshman" in Wednesday editions of the paper. These letters were purported to be written by an undereducated, hillbilly female freshman to her mother, and were characterized by poor usage and gross misspellings. Then, in the Monday, February 8, 1937, edition, an introduction was published to "Ferdy the Freshman," a series of letters following identical lines to those of "Freda" but coming from a fictitious male this time, who was said to be from a place called "Punkinseed Junction." These letters appeared in every subsequent Monday edition for the rest of that school year, and resumed in the following school year's Monday editions as "Ferdie the Soldier," then "Ferdie the Ex-Traveler." Several additional letters were published in the fall of Vonnegut's junior year, all in Monday editions, as "Ferdie, Man About Town." None appeared during his senior year.

In the Monday, December 5, 1938, edition, during Vonnegut's junior year, an editorial-review of *The Story of Ferdinand* by Munro Leaf was printed, praising the story's pacifistic overtones. Vonnegut had appended a brief quote from the book onto the end of his November 21, 1939, "Bull Session" column, just before the "Ferdinand" signature. It is evident that his use of "Ferdinand" as pen name for the column, in combination with his choice of column title, was inspired by the tale, which Vonnegut likely identified with due to his own emerging pacifism.

There were several unsigned items of some significance printed in Tuesday editions during Vonnegut's stint as staff member, in each of his three incarnations, which may in fact have been written by him. Two of these make notable use of the word "excelsior," followed by an exclamation point, as Vonnegut did later in the title of his *New York Times Magazine* essay of July 13, 1969, "Excelsior! We're Going to the Moon! Excelsior!"

The unsigned items referred to here are distinguished by a certain style of humor and exaggerated use of vocabulary also evident in Vonnegut's "Bull Session" columns. In the index that follows, these items are designated as *speculated* Vonnegut contributions.

Phoebe Hurty, working for the *Indianapolis Times* and writing Block's department store advertisements for that paper, hired Vonnegut to write Block's ads for the *Echo.* The first appeared in the Thursday edition of October 12, 1939, and others followed throughout the year. His ads were signed with various exaggerations of his name: from the terse "Koort II" to the verbose "Koort Snarfield Vawnyagoot II." A full page Block's ad appeared in the 1939 Christmas edition of the *Echo*, featuring a photograph of Vonnegut, along with Marilyn Clark and another female student, acknowledging their services as the store's representatives at Shortridge. Facing this page was an ad for "Vonnegut's Hardware and Sporting Goods" store. Toward the end of his senior year, the *Echo* announced a high school fashion show, to take place at Block's department store, and listing Vonnegut and a dozen or so other students from area schools, including one Jane Cox, as models.

Vonnegut was quoted briefly in the *Echo* several times, and he was mentioned over sixty times in various news articles regarding *Echo* staff changes, election results, student productions and activities, and the like. He was also mentioned in several Marilyn Clark-penned Block's ads (generally as "Koort"), as well as over seventy times in the gossip columns.

After graduating from Shortridge High School, Vonnegut attended Cornell University in Ithaca, New York, majoring in biology and chemistry. On March 25, 1941, he made his debut on the editorial page of the *Cornell Sun*, an independent commercial newspaper staffed by Cornell students. The following day's editorial page fully detailed "The 1941–42 *Sun* Board," listing name, position, hometown, and expected graduation year of every staff member recruited for the coming year. Vonnegut was included here among the Men's News Board members. A comparable full disclosure of the coming year's staff was published in the *Sun* every March, and "The 1942–43 *Sun* Board" unveiled Vonnegut's promotion to the Assistant Managing Editor post. The December 15, 1942, edition proclaimed yet another promotion for Vonnegut, to the position of Associate Editor. A different individual acted as "News Editor for This Issue" each day, and Vonnegut's name was specified on several occasions during the course of his career at the *Sun.*

Vonnegut's premiere column in the *Sun* appeared as "Innocents Abroad." The title, undoubtedly lifted from Mark Twain's book of the same name, was used quite regularly in the *Sun,* primarily as a jokes column, evidently by whoever felt he had something funny enough to pass along. In most cases, short jokes and witty rhymes were printed, sometimes along with the names of newspapers they were clipped from. Vonnegut contributed eleven of these with bylines, all during the 1941 spring semester.

"Well All Right," another popular editorial page column, also featured semiregular installments by Vonnegut. Twenty-one of these were attributed to him between April 1941 and November 1942; nineteen with bylines, and the remainder with just his initials at the bottom Even in his more serious columns, Vonnegut seemed to write with a gleam in his eye, on the verge of wild laughter at the folly of his subject.

A few of Vonnegut's "Well All Right" columns come across as angry, such as his final entry (" . . . And Then There Was the Publicity Crazy Man That Clipped His Name Out of the Phone Directory for His Scrap Book," November 13, 1942) accusing the university of catering to the war effort at the expense of remaining students for the sake of publicity. This particular installment also accomplished the relatively rare feat of drawing two letters to the editor in response; interestingly, this was his last signed contribution to the *Sun,* though he continued as staff member for several months afterward.

Vonnegut also wrote two columns which appeared under the "Berry Patch" banner, another humor venue, likewise on the editorial page. The remainder of Vonnegut's signed contributions to the *Sun* are revealed in nine installments of a daily sports column, "Speaking of Sports." These appeared between spring 1941 and spring 1942 and were fairly unpersonalized examples of sports reporting, with occasional forays into promotion.

A number of columns printed on the *Sun* editorial page during Vonnegut's career there were credited to fictitious names—such as "Fooh the Wooh" or "The Head"—or to ambiguous initials which did not correspond to any names appearing in the masthead. Several sets of such initials were used repeatedly, but those utilized most numerously and consistently were "VTY." Eighteen columns, mostly "Well All Right" installments, bore these initials as signatures from April 1941 to February 1943.

Frank Curtis Abbott, class of '42 and *Sun* editor-in-chief/editorial director for 1941–42, refers to himself as "VTY," which evidently stood for "Very Truly Yours," in an essay for the 1980 retrospective book *A Century at Cornell.* However, there did appear one column in the *Sun* ("Well All Right/Finding the News in the News," May 22, 1941) which is both preceded by Vonnegut's byline *and* followed by the signature "—VTY." The most plausible explanation for this would seem to be that the signature may have been a typographical error, and for the purposes of the index, the byline is assumed to be correct.

"VTY" columns did continue to appear in the *Sun* for up to eleven months following Mr. Abbott's departure from the newspaper staff, by which time he had also long since graduated from the university. It is hypothesized that his successor, Simon Miller Harris, had elected to carry on employing the signature for himself as well.

Several additional *Sun* items are also considered to have been potentially written by Vonnegut. " 'No Breasts No Torsos'/A Moral Survey of the Nation" purports to offer proof that "The Moral Fabric of our nation is shredded" in four brief newspaper clippings, which tell of the New York City Police Commissioner's decree prohibiting nude night club dancers; of a rapist-murderer who habitually cooks and eats a meal at the scene following his crime; and report on the contemporary legal difficulties of Errol Flynn and Frances Farmer. The other piece is a satire of Mr. Flynn's then-evolving trial for statutory rape. Both published on the editorial page in the January 16, 1943, edition, they bear all the hallmarks of Vonnegut's sense of humor at its most uninhibited.

Vonnegut's name disappeared from the *Sun* masthead without fanfare following the February 16, 1943, edition, almost two years to the day before he would witness the firebombing of Dresden. Although farewells were occasionally bid to staff members departing for the war in progress, no such valediction to Vonnegut could be located in the pages of the *Sun*.

Sources

A Century at Cornell. Daniel Margulis, ed. Ithaca, N.Y.: The *Cornell Sun,* Inc., 1980.

Cornell Sun 1940–1944 (Microfilms kindly lent by Olin Library, Cornell University).

Shortridge Daily Echo 1936–1940 (Microfilms kindly lent by the Indiana Historical Society).

INDEX OF VONNEGUT JUVENILIA

The index is arranged in chronological order. Items are categorized according to Vonnegut's relationship to each as follows:

    Cont (Contributions)

    Spec (Speculated Contributions)

    Quot (Quotes)

For this publication, mentions, notices, and related items have been omitted. It is hoped that these can be included elsewhere in the future; however, the full *Shortridge Daily Echo* list is on file at the Indiana Historical Society. Additional information has been provided where warranted. Bylines and signatures are indicated for those items which included them.

Shortridge Daily Echo

Date	Page	Type	Item
1938			
18 Feb	2	Cont	"This Business of Whistle Purchasing" (signed 'Kurt Vonnegut, English IVx')
26 Apr	2	Quot	"The Inquisitive Reporter" (unsigned)
13 Sep	3	Quot	"A Columnist's Diary" (unsigned)

23 Sep	3	Spec	"Lost" under "Classified Ads" (signed 'Kurt Vonnegut')
4 Nov	4	Cont	Under "Vote for Me for Vod'vil Chairman" (continued from page 1; portion attributed to Vonnegut)
17 Nov	2	Quot	"Boners" (unsigned)
Christmas	20	Quot	"Dear Diary" by Katy Parrish

1939

7 Feb	np	Quot	"In Scenes Near Vodvil Time" (unsigned; quote attributed to both Vonnegut and Ben Hitz)
9 Feb	1	Quot	"Vaudville Vanderings" (unsigned)
21 Feb	2	Quot	"Inquisitive Reporter" (signed 'Sonie' [Jean Bosson])
23 May	1	Spec	"Excelsior!" (unsigned)
12 Sep	2	Cont	"The Inquisitive Reporter Reporting on a Bull Session" (signed 'Ferdinand')
19 Sep	2	Cont	"Bull Session With 5 Girls 5" ('Ferdy')
26 Sep	2	Cont	"Bull Session" ('Ferdy')
3 Oct	2	Cont	"Bull Session" ('Ferdinand')
10 Oct	2	Cont	"Bull Session" ('Ferlferdilfinalfand')
12 Oct	3	Cont	"The Stag at Eve" ('KOORT II')
17 Oct	2	Cont	"Bull Session" ('FERDY')
24 Oct	2	Cont	"Bull Session/Nee Inquisitive Reporter" ('FERDY')
31 Oct	2	Cont	"Bull Session/Nee Inquiring Reporter" ('FOIDINANDO')
1 Nov	3	Cont	"On Being Properly Sloppy" ('KOORT II')
2 Nov	4	Cont	"5 Senior Candidates List Qualifications" (continued from page 1; portion attributed to Vonnegut)
7 Nov	2	Cont	"Bull Session/Nee Inquisitive Reporter" ('Ferdy')
14 Nov	2	Cont	"Bull Session/Nee Inquiring Reporter" ('Ferdy')
15 Nov	3	Cont	"Frozen Assets" ('KOORT II')
21 Nov	2	Cont	"Bull Session/Nee Inquiring Reporter" ('Ferdinand')
28 Nov	2	Cont	"Bull Session/Nee Inquisitive Reporter" ('Sturdy Ferdy')
29 Nov	3	Cont	"Gadget Lore" ('KOORT II')
5 Dec	2	Cont	"Bull Session/Nee Inquiring Reporter/The Care and Feeding of Problem Parents" ('FERDY')
6 Dec	3	Cont	"The Glutz Poll of Popular Opinion" ('KOORT II')
12 Dec	2	Cont	"Bull Session/Nee Inquiring Reporter" ('ERDYFAY')
13 Dec	3	Cont	"The Gab of Gift" ('KOORT II')

19 Dec	1	Spec	"Dear Santy—" ('Heartbroken')
19 Dec	2	Cont	"Bull Session/Nee Inquiring Reporter" ('Ferdy')
20 Dec	3	Cont	"Yuletide Yearnings" ('KOORT II')

1940

9 Jan	2	Cont	"Bull Session/Nee Inquiring Reporter" ('FERDY')
16 Jan	2	Cont	"Bull Session/Nee Inquiring Reporter" ('FERDY')
23 Jan	2	Cont	"Bull Session/Nee Inquiring Reporter"('FERDINAND')
15 Feb	3	Cont	"Spring Song" ('KOORT II')
29 Feb	3	Cont	"Sweet Feet" ('KOORT II')
7 Mar	3	Cont	"Block's Sniffer/Lotions of Love" ('KOORT II')
14 Mar	3	Cont	"Block's Sniffer" ('Koort Snarfield Vonnegut II')
21 Mar	3	Cont	"Block's Sniffer" ('Koort Snarfield Vawnyagoot II')
28 Mar	3	Cont	"Block's Snoozer" ('KOORT II')
11 Apr	1	Cont	"Shortridge Boys Are Successful On Trek" (by Kurt Vonnegut II)
11 Apr	3	Cont	"Block's Sniffer" ('KOORT II')
16 Apr	1	Spec	"Dip and Sway With Denny Dutton; The Ticket Cost is Next to Nuttin'" (unsigned)
17 Apr	3	Quot	"Bluebell—Uglymen Candidates Break Down" (unsigned)
18 Apr	3	Cont	Under "Advice to the Lovelorn" ('Kurt Vonnegut')
18 Apr	3	Cont	"Block's Sneezer" ('KOORT II')
23 Apr	1	Spec	"Rave On" (unsigned)
25 Apr	3	Cont	"Block's Sniffer" ('KOORT II')
2 May	3	Cont	"Block's Sniffer" ('KOORT II')
7 May	1	Spec	"Aes Triplex" (unsigned)
9 May	3	Cont	"Block's Sniffer" ('KOORT II')
16 May	4	Cont	"Block's Sniffer" ('KOORT MCXVIII')
23 May	3	Cont	"Block's Sniffer" ('KOORT MCXVIII')
27 May	5	Cont	"Block's Sniffer" ('KOORT MCXVIII')
29 May	3	Cont	"Block's Sniffer" ('Koort Snarfield Vonnegut II')

Cornell Sun

Date	Page	Type	Item

1941

25 Mar	4	Cont	"Innocents Abroad" (by Kurt Vonnegut)

9 Apr	4	Cont	"Innocents Abroad" (by Kurt Vonnegut)
15 Apr	4	Cont	"Innocents Abroad" (by Kurt Vonnegut)
16 Apr	7	Cont	"Speaking of Sports/Cornell's Rugby Club Tries to Forget Harvard and 38–0" (by Kurt Vonnegut)
21 Apr	4	Cont	"Innocents Abroad" (by Kurt Vonnegut)
22 Apr	4	Cont	"Well All Right/Bayonet Drill at the Rate of Seven in 20 Seconds, or, Oh For a Couple of Nazis" (by Kurt Vonnegut)
23 Apr	4	Cont	"Innocents Abroad" (by Kurt Vonnegut)
30 Apr	4	Cont	"Innocents Abroad" (by Kurt Vonnegut)
1 May	10	Cont	"Speaking of Sports/Mood Indigo on Upper Alumni, or, It Ain't Cricket (by Kurt Vonnegut)
2 May	4	Cont	"Innocents Abroad" (by Kurt Vonnegut)
3 May	4	Cont	"Innocents Abroad" (by Kurt Vonnegut)
9 May	4	Cont	"Innocents Abroad" (by Kurt Vonnegut)
10 May	4	Cont	"Well All Right/In Which We Dare to Enter a Stronghold of Evil" (by Kurt Vonnegut)
14 May	4	Cont	"Innocents Abroad" (by Kurt Vonnegut)
21 May	4	Cont	"Well All Right/Gloomy Wednesday—or Why We Wish We Were an Independent" (by Kurt Vonnegut)
22 May	4	Cont	"Well All Right/Finding the News in the News" (by Kurt Vonnegut)
23 May	4	Cont	"Well All Right/We Impress Life Magazine with Our Efficient Role inNational Defense" (by Kurt Vonnegut)
26 May	4	Cont	"Innocents Abroad" (by Kurt Vonnegut)
22 Sep	4	Cont	"Well All Right/Doomed to Look Like a Freshman All Our Lives" (by Kurt Vonnegut)
26 Sep	4	Cont	"Well All Right/In Which We Get Trimmed and Find the Barber in the Same Boat" (by Kurt Vonnegut)
8 Oct	4	Cont	"Well All Right/Ramblings of One Who Is Weak in the Exchequer, and in the Mind" (by Kurt Vonnegut)
13 Oct	4	Cont	"Well All Right/We Chase a Lone Eagle and End Up on the Wrong Side of the Fence" (by Kurt Vonnegut)
11 Nov	4	Cont	"Well All Right/A Challenge to Superman!!!!" (by Kurt Vonnegut)
4 Dec	12	Cont	"Speaking of Sports/Everything's Okely Dokely with Moalekey" (by Kurt Vonnegut)

1942

11 Feb	4	Cont	"Well All Right/A Worrysome Thing to Leave You to Sing the Blues—in the Night" (by Kurt Vonnegut)
13 Feb	12	Cont	"Speaking of Sports/16 Thousand Witnesses—The Millrose Story" (by Kurt Vonnegut)
19 Feb	4	Cont	"Well All Right/All This and English 2" (by Kurt Vonnegut)
25 Feb	4	Cont	"Well All Right/Unaccustomed As We Are to Public Speaking (by Kurt Vonnegut)
2 Mar	2	Cont	"Speaking of Sports/Madison Square Garden Is No Bed of Roses" (by Kurt Vonnegut)
4 Mar	4	Cont	"Well All Right/In Defense of the Golden West" (by Kurt Vonnegut)
5 Mar	8	Cont	"Speaking of Sports/Cornell's Indoor Track Team Prepares for the First Real Test—The IC4-A's Saturday" (by Kurt Vonnegut)
6 Mar	12	Cont	"Speaking of Sports/ More Dope on the IC4A Gang " (by Kurt Vonnegut)
7 Mar	7	Cont	"Speaking of Sports/Tonight is the Night to Be Bright" (by Kurt Vonnegut)
11 Mar	8	Cont	"Speaking of Sports/And Red Friesell Wasn't Near the Place!" (by Kurt Vonnegut)
24 Mar	4	Cont	"Well All Right/Albino for a Day, or in the Pink" (by Kurt Vonnegut)
24 Apr	4	Cont	"Well All Right/The Drunken Mr.'s Pro and Con" (signed '-KV')
4 May	4	Cont	"Well All Right/The Lost Battalion Undergoes a Severe Shelling" (signed '-K.V.')
26 Sep	4	Cont	"Well All Right/For Whom the Bell Tolls" (by Kurt Vonnegut)
29 Sep	4	Cont	"Well All Right/In Which Mr. Willkie and We Raise Stinks on Opposite Sides of the Fence." (by Kurt Vonnegut)
22 Oct	4	Cont	"Well All Right/How're You Going to Keep 'Em Down on the Farm, After They've Seen Lockheed?" (by Kurt Vonnegut)
24 Oct	4	Cont	"Berry Patch/Mr. Anthony, What I Want to Know" (by Kurt Vonnegut)
2 Nov	4	Cont	"Berry Patch/Adventures with Dynamite in the Land of the 20-20 Duck"(by Kurt Vonnegut)
13 Nov	4	Cont	"Well All Right/ And Then There Was the Publicity Crazy Man That Clipped His Name Out of the Phone Directory for His Scrap Book." (by Kurt Vonnegut)

1943

16 Jan   4   Spec   " 'No Breasts No Torsos'/A Moral Survey of the
                             Nation" (unsigned)
16 Jan   4   Spec   "Kaman Takes the Baton/The
                             Don't-Send-Errol-to-the-Pen Club Is
                             Now in Session" (unsigned)

Bibliography

KURT VONNEGUT: MAJOR WORKS

Player Piano. New York: Charles Scribner's Sons, 1952.

The Sirens of Titan. New York: Dell, 1959.

Canary in a Cat House. Greenwich, CT: Gold Medal/Fawcett, 1961.

Mother Night. Greenwich, CT: Gold Medal/Fawcett, 1962.

Cat's Cradle. New York: Holt, Rinehart and Winston, 1963.

God Bless You, Mr. Rosewater. New York: Holt, Rinehart and Winston, 1965.

Welcome to the Monkey House. New York: Delacorte Press/Seymour Lawrence, 1968.

Slaughterhouse-Five. New York: Delacorte Press/Seymour Lawrence, 1969.

Happy Birthday, Wanda June. New York: Delacorte Press/Seymour Lawrence, 1970.

Breakfast of Champions. New York: Delacorte Press/Seymour Lawrence, 1973.

Wampeters, Foma, and Granfalloons. New York: Delacorte Press/Seymour Lawrence, 1974.

Slapstick. New York: Delacorte Press/Seymour Lawrence, 1976.

Jailbird. New York: Delacorte Press/Seymour Lawrence, 1979.

Sun Moon Star. With Ivan Chermayeff. New York: Harper and Row, 1980.

Palm Sunday. New York: Delacorte, 1981.

Deadeye Dick. New York: Delacorte Press/Seymour Lawrence, 1982.

Galapagos. New York: Delacorte Press/Seymour Lawrence, 1985.

Bluebeard. New York: Delacorte, 1987.

Hocus Pocus. New York: G. P. Putnam Sons, 1990.

Fates Worse than Death. New York: G. P. Putnam Sons, 1991.

Slaughterhouse-Five, Twenty-Fifth Anniversary Edition. New York: Delacorte Press/Seymour Lawrence, 1994.

KURT VONNEGUT: SHORT STORIES
   * Reprinted in *Canary in a Cat House*.
   # Reprinted in *Welcome to the Monkey House*.

"Report on the Barnhouse Effect." *Collier's*, February 11, 1950, pp. 18–19, 63–65.*#

"Thanasphere." *Collier's*, September 2, 1950, pp. 18–19, 60, 62.

"EPICAC." *Collier's*, November 25, 1950, pp. 36–37.#

"All the King's Horses." *Collier's*, February 10, 1951, pp. 14–15, 46–48, 50.*#

"Mnemonics." *Collier's*, April 28, 1951, p. 38.

"The Euphio Question." *Collier's*, May 12, 1951, pp. 22–23, 52–54, 56.*#

"The Foster Portfolio." *Collier's*, September 8, 1951, pp. 18–19, 72–73.*#

"More Stately Mansions." *Collier's*, December 22, 1951, pp. 24–25, 62–63.*#

"Any Reasonable Offer." *Collier's*, January 19, 1952, pp. 32, 46–47.

"The Package." *Collier's*, July 26, 1952, pp. 48–53.

"The No-Talent Kid." *Saturday Evening Post*, October 25, 1952, pp. 28, 109–110, 112, 114.

"Poor Little Rich Town." *Collier's*, October 25, 1952, pp. 90–95.

"Souvenir." *Argosy*, December 1952, pp. 28–29, 76–79.

"Tom Edison's Shaggy Dog." *Collier's*, March 14, 1953, pp. 46, 48–49.*#

"Unready to Wear." *Galaxy Science Fiction*, April 1953, pp. 98–111.*#

"The Cruise of the Jolly Roger." *Cape Cod Compass*, April 1953, pp. 7–14.

"D.P." *Ladies Home Journal*, August 1953, pp. 42–43, 80–81, 84.*#

"The Big Trip Up Yonder." *Galaxy Science Fiction*, January 1954, pp. 100–110.*# ("Tomorrow and Tomorrow and Tomorrow" in *Welcome to the Monkey House*.)

"Custom-Made Bride." *Saturday Evening Post*, March 27, 1954, pp. 30, 81–82, 86–87.

"Adam." *Cosmopolitan*, April 1954, pp. 34–39.

"Ambitious Sophomore." *Saturday Evening Post*, May 1, 1954, pp. 31, 88, 92, 94.

"Bagombo Snuff Box." *Cosmopolitan*, October 1954, pp. 34–39.

"The Powder Blue Dragon." *Cosmopolitan*, November 1954, pp. 46–48, 50–53.

"A Present for Big Nick." *Argosy*, December 1954, pp. 42–45, 72–73.

"Unpaid Consultant." *Cosmopolitan*, March 1955, pp. 52–57.

"Deer in the Works." *Esquire*, April 1955, pp. 78–79, 112, 114, 116, 118.*#

"Next Door." *Cosmopolitan*, April 1955, pp. 80–85.#

"The Kid Nobody Could Handle." *Saturday Evening Post*, September 24, 1955, pp. 37, 136–137.#

"The Boy Who Hated Girls." *Saturday Evening Post*, March 31, 1956, pp. 28–29, 58, 60, 62.

"Miss Temptation." *Saturday Evening Post*, April 21, 1956, pp. 30, 57, 60, 62, 64.#

"This Son of Mine . . ." *Saturday Evening Post*, August 18, 1956, pp. 24, 74, 76–78.

"Hal Irwin's Magic Lamp." *Cosmopolitan*, June 1957, pp. 92–95.*

"A Night for Love." *Saturday Evening Post,* November 23, 1957, pp. 40–41, 73, 76–77, 80–81, 84.

"The Manned Missiles." *Cosmopolitan,* July 1958, pp. 83–88.*#

"Long Walk to Forever." *Ladies Home Journal,* August 1960, pp. 42–43, 108.#

"Find Me a Dream." *Cosmopolitan,* February 1961, pp. 108–111.

"Runaways." *Saturday Evening Post,* April 15, 1961, pp. 26–27, 52, 54, 56.

"Harrison Bergeron." *Magazine of Fantasy and Science Fiction,* October 1961, pp. 5–10. Reprinted in *National Review,* November 16, 1965, pp. 1020–1021, 1041.#

"My Name Is Everyone." *Saturday Evening Post,* December 16, 1961, pp. 20–21, 62, 64, 66–67.# ("Who Am I This Time" in *Welcome to the Monkey House.*)

"HOLE BEAUTIFUL: Prospectus for a Magazine of Shelteredness." *Monocle* (Vol. 5, no. 1), 1962, pp. 45–51.

"2BR02B." *Worlds of If,* January 1962, pp. 59–65.

"The Lie." *Saturday Evening Post,* February 24, 1962, pp. 46–47, 51, 56.#

"Go Back to Your Precious Wife and Son." *Ladies Home Journal,* July 1962, pp. 54–55, 108, 110.#

"Lovers Anonymous." *Redbook,* October 1963, pp. 70–71, 146–148.

"Welcome to the Monkey House." *Playboy,* January 1968, pp. 95, 156, 196, 198, 200–201.#

"The Hyannis Port Story." In *Welcome to the Monkey House,* 1968, although sold to *Saturday Evening Post* in 1963 and not published owing to the assassination of President John F. Kennedy. See text.

"The Big Space Fuck." *Again, Dangerous Visions: Forty-six Original Stories Edited by Harlan Ellison* (Garden City, N.Y.: Doubleday, 1972), pp. 246–250. Included in *Palm Sunday.*

OTHER WORKS CITED

Allen, William Rodney, ed. *Conversations with Kurt Vonnegut.* Jackson: University Press of Mississippi, 1988.

Broer, Lawrence R. *Sanity Plea: Schizophrenia in the Novels of Kurt Vonnegut.* Ann Arbor, MI: UMI Research Press, 1989.

Eliot, T. S. "The Love Song of J. Alfred Prufrock." *T. S. Eliot: The Complete Poems and Plays, 1909–1950.* New York: Harcourt, Brace and World, 1964.

Fiedler, Leslie A. "The Divine Stupidity of Kurt Vonnegut." *Esquire,* September, 1979, pp. 195–197, 199–200, 202–204.

Gardner, John. *On Moral Fiction.* New York: Basic Books, 1978.

Gaus, Laura Sheerin. *Shortridge High School 1864–1981.* Indianapolis: Indiana Historical Society, 1985.

Giannone, Richard. *Vonnegut: A Preface to His Novels.* Port Washington, N.Y.: Kennikat Press, 1977.

Irving, John. "Kurt Vonnegut and His Critics." *New Republic,* September 22, 1979, pp. 41–49.

Joyce, James. *A Portrait of the Artist as a Young Man.* New York: Viking Press, 1965.

Klinkowitz, Jerome, and Donald Lawler, eds. *Vonnegut in America.* New York: Delta Books, 1968.

Klinkowitz, Jerome, and John Somer, eds. *The Vonnegut Statement.* New York: Delacorte Press/Seymour Lawrence, 1973.

Klinkowitz, Jerome. *Kurt Vonnegut.* London & New York: Methuen, 1982.

Leaf, Munro. *The Story of Ferdinand.* New York: Viking Press, 1938.

Leeds, Marc. *The Vonnegut Encyclopedia.* Westport, CT: Greenwood Press, 1995.

Lundquist, James. *Kurt Vonnegut.* New York: Frederick Ungar, 1977.

Mantell, Harold, producer and director. *Kurt Vonnegut: A Self-Portrait.* Princeton, N.J.: Films for the Humanities, 1976.

Merrill, Robert. *Critical Essays on Kurt Vonnegut.* Boston: G.K. Hall, 1990.

Mustazza, Leonard. *Forever Pursuing Genesis.* London & Toronto: Bucknell University Press/Associated University Presses, 1990.

Pieratt, Asa B., Julie Huffman-klinkowitz, and Jerome Klinkowitz. *Kurt Vonnegut: A Comprehensive Bibliography.* Hamden, CT: The Shoestring Press/Archon Books, 1987.

Reed, Peter J. *Kurt Vonnegut, Jr.* New York: Thomas Y. Crowell, 1972.

Reed, Peter J. and Marc Leeds, eds. *The Vonnegut Chronicles.* Westport, CT: Greenwood Press, 1996.

Rhodes, Richard. Review of *Welcome to the Monkey House. Book World,* August 18, 1968, p. 4.

Sale, Roger. Review of *Slapstick. New York Times Book Review,* October 3, 1976, pp. 3, 20–21.

Schatt, Stanley. *Kurt Vonnegut, Jr.* Boston: Twayne Publishers, 1976.

Short, Robert. "Robert Short Interviews Kurt Vonnegut, Chicago—June 8, 1976." *Something to Believe In.* San Francisco: Harper and Row, 1978, pp. 283–308.

Sokolov, R. A. Review of *Welcome to the Monkey House. Newsweek,* August 19, 1968, p. 85.

Vonnegut, Kurt. "Fortitude." *Playboy,* October 1968, pp. 99–100, 102, 106, 217–218.

Vonnegut, Kurt. "Jack the Dripper." *Esquire,* December 1983, pp. 549–553.

Yarmolinsky, Jane Vonnegut. *Angels Without Wings.* Boston: Houghton Mifflin, 1987.

Index

Adams, James, 71, 76
Allen, William Rodney, xi, 109
Anderson, Sherwood, his novel
    Winesburg, Ohio, 144
anti-gerasone, 67, 106
Argosy, 39, 41, 59
Army, U.S., 3, 16, 21–22, 60, 63, 68–
    69, 103, 104
art, artwork, silkscreens, Vonnegut's,
    139, 154
Ashland, Charles, 58
Asleep at the Switch, 132–133

Baepler, Paul, xi
Bane, Joe, 59–61
Bergeron, George, 80–82, 87–88
Bergeron, Harrison, 23, 80–82, 84–85,
    95, 101, 148
Bermuda ern, 128
Billy the Poet, 100, 103, 142–143
Block's, department store, 13–14, 25,
    152, 159, 163,
Boaz, 44
Bokonon, books of, 80, 127, 147
Book World, 137, 155
Borders, Arvin, 77
Bourjaily, Vance, 91, 102
Bratpuhr, Shah of, 125, 141
Brentner, Rice, 78, 80

Broer, Lawrence, 2
Bullard, Harold K., 38–39
Burger, Knox, 3, 28, 71–72, 105–
    106, 139

Cady, Newell, 38
Cahoun, Kitty, 45, 144
Callaghan, Pat, 32, 40, 93
Campbell, Helga, 126
Campbell, Howard, 62, 73, 84, 109,
    126–127, 140–141
Cape Cod 3, 22, 24, 38, 62, 70, 95–
    96, 99
Cape Cod Compass, 62
Capone, Al, 61
chemicals, chemically controlled
    behavior, 32, 66, 85, 106, 129, 132
The Chemistry Professor, 108
Chicago City News Bureau, 3, 22
chronosynclastic infundibula, 66, 108
Cinderella, 48
cold war, 4, 31, 33, 59–60, 78, 81,
    88, 95, 152
Collier's, 3, 27–29, 32–33, 35–36,
    38–39, 41, 59, 71, 75, 91, 105, 149
common decency, 98, 150–151
Constant, Malachi, 4, 145–146, 150
Cornell Sun, xi, 3, 10–12, 15, 33,
    157, 159–161, 163

Cornell University, 2–3, 11, 14, 17–
    18, 20, 22, 25, 49, 104, 157, 159–
    160, 164–165
Cosmopolitan, 28, 50–51, 56, 59,
    68, 75–76
Cox, Jane Marie (also Jane Cox
    Vonnegut; Jane Cox Yarmolinsky),
    18, 27, 71, 76, 92, 157, 159
Crosby, Pop, 37

The Dancing Fool, 131
The Day the World Ended, 126–127,
    147
dehumanizing, dehumanized, 3, 59,
    70, 100, 144–145, 148
Depression, the Great, 27, 49, 57,
    63, 95, 146, 152
dictionary, 95–96, 102–103
didactic, didacticism, 5, 10, 12, 54,
    59, 130–131, 150, 153, 155
Divine, Celeste, 54
Divine, Harry, 54
Donnini, Jim, 43
Donoso, Jose, 91
Dr. Jekyll and Mr. Hyde, 108, 147
dreams, 3–4, 36, 43, 48–50, 53, 57,
    59, 63, 78, 89, 148, 152
Dresden, 3, 6, 24, 27, 63, 69, 73,
    129, 131, 151, 161
Duggan, Leroy, 42
Durant, Nathan, 63–64
Duvalier, "Papa Doc," 128
dystopia, dystopian, 80, 84, 148, 153

Eckenrode, Andre, xi
Ed, writer in *Player Piano*, 46, 125,
    128
Eddie, in "Souvenir," 52–53, 60–61
Edison, Thomas, 38–39, 93, 95
Eisenhower, Dwight David, 98
EPICAC, 6, 28, 32–33, 40, 95, 104,
    114, 145, 147

Falloleen, 45–46, 48, 144, 147
father-son relationships, 2, 4, 27,
    35, 43–44, 48–51, 55–56, 58–59,
    62, 68–69, 71, 78–79, 86–87, 97,
    101–102, 105, 130, 146

Faulkner, William, 37, 108, 114
Fenton, Earl, 37
Fenton, Maude, 37
Fiedler, Leslie A., 138, 153–155
Fields, W.C., 53
Finnerty, Ed, 46, 116, 143
Fitzgerald, F. Scott, 57, 137–138
Foster, Henry, 35, 93, 95, 145, 147
Frankenstein, Dr. Norbert, 105–106
Fraternity, fraternities, 3, 15, 18, 37,
    49, 56–57
Fuller, Norman, 46–47, 101, 151
future, 4, 45, 65, 69, 84–85, 94–95,
    107, 147–148, 161

Galaxy Science Fiction Magazine, 62,
    64, 66–67, 94, 104, 107
Gardner, John, 12, 25, 155
General Electric Company, 3, 9, 14, 19,
    22, 27–28, 32, 70, 72, 96–97, 103
Germany, 19, 68, 73, 93, 96
Get With Child A Mandrake Root, 128
Glampers, Diana Moon, 80–81, 92
Goldwater, Senator Barry, 97, 99

Hacketts, Elmo, 44
Hagstrohm, Edgar, 44, 112–122
Hail to the Chief, 132
Haiti, 128
Haley, Stewart, 42–44
Halyard, Dr. Ewing, 44
handicaps, 6, 81–82
Harger, 55
Harris, "Firehouse," 35
Harris, Simon Miller, 160
"Harrison Bergeron," story, 23, 80–
    82, 84, 85, 95, 101, 148, 152,
Haycox, 44
Heinz, Karl, 151, 168
Hell to Get Along With, 75, 142
Helmholtz, George, 41–45, 49, 78,
    150–151
Higgins, Kiah, 53
Hilton, Gloria, 87
Hinkley, Bearse, 46–47
Hinkley, Herb, 89
Hinkley, Sheila, 89
Homestead, 44, 112–122, 143

"The Honey Fitz," 97
Hoobler, Wayne, 93, 107
Hoover, Dwayne, 81, 100, 118, 132, 145
Huffman-klinkowitz, Julie, xi, 39, 72, 92, 109
humor, self-deprecating, 4–5, 28, 101, 103, 106–108, 159–161
Hurty, Phoebe, 25, 159
Hyannis Port, 88, 90, 95, 97, 99, 109, 145, 152
hyperbole, 20–21, 30, 67, 85, 90, 132, 142

identity, search for, 3–4, 33, 35–36, 49, 66, 69, 80, 83–84, 86, 98, 144–146
Ilium; Ilium Works, 37–38, 48–49, 69–70, 78
Indianapolis, 2, 10, 13, 16, 19, 25, 41, 49, 67, 73, 96, 129, 157
inequality, 23, 75, 129, 133, 152
Investments Counselor, 35, 45, 54, 56, 78
Iowa Writers Workshop, 10, 91, 102, 139
Iron Curtain, 59
irresponsible science, 152
Irving, John, 155
Irwin, Hal, 56–58, 94–95, 148, 151–152
Ithaca, New York, 14, 17–18, 157, 159, 161
Ivankov, Mikhael, 58

John, Jonah, narrator of *Cat's Cradle*, 126–127

Kelly, Colonel Bryan, 33
Kennedy, Edward, 103
Kennedy, Jacqueline, 103
Kennedy, John F., 90, 95, 98–99, 101, 103
Kennedy, Joseph P., 97, 100, 103, 109
Kennedy, Robert F., 97, 103
Kennedy, Sheila, 97
Kilyer, Tom, 86

Klinkowitz, Jerome, xi, 1, 6, 8, 24–25, 39, 72, 109
Konigswasser, Dr. Felix, 64–66
Krummbein, Otto, 45, 49
Kuskin, Karla, 88

Laird, Eddie, 3, 52, 60–61
Lazarro, Paul, 12, 151
Leeds, Marc, xi, 40, 73, 136
Leonard, Paul, 55–56
Lindberg, Karl, 48–49, 86
Lindberg, Rudy, 48–49, 86
Lindbergh, Charles, 19–20, 23
Littauer, Kenneth, 3, 28, 139
Little, Dr. Elbert, 105–106
Louis, Joe, 68
love, of woman; man-woman relationships, 32, 47, 75–80, 83–85, 87–89, 97, 141–145, 147, 150–151
Lundquist, James, 138, 155

Magazine of Fantasy and Science Fiction, 80
Matthews, Hildy, 77
McClellan, George, 36
McClellan, Grace, 36, 84, 144
Melville, Herman, 127
Memories of a Monogamous Casanova, 84, 126
metafiction, 53
Middleton, Andy, 77
Moby Dick, 127
Monzano, Mona Aamons, 46, 128, 144
Mustazza, Leonard, 2
myth, 2, 99, 106, 138, 140, 154

narrator; narrative voice, 5, 30, 32–37, 45, 54, 58, 65, 78, 82–83, 87–90, 96–98, 125–126, 131, 134, 140–141, 144
Nash, Harry, 83, 144–145
Nation, J. Edgar, 100–101
National Review, 80
Nazis, 51, 73, 85, 126, 164
New York Times Magazine, 159
New Yorker, 36, 96

Newsweek, 137, 155
Nim-nim B-36, 134
Now It Can Be Told, 132, 145

O'Hare, Bernie (Bernard), 61–62, 126
observer, 5, 31, 125–126
Orwell, George, 82, 139

pacifism, 17, 134, 150, 152, 158
Pan Galactic Strawboss, 131
Pefko, Francine, 64, 145
Pefko, George, 63–64
Pi Ying, 33
Pieratt, Asa, xi, 39, 72, 92, 109
Pilgrim, Billy, 138, 148
The Planet Gobblers, 134, 152
"playlets," 80, 104, 149
Plummer, Walter, 42
popular fiction, 2, 6, 125–126, 137–
    138, 153–154
Pornographer, pornography, 46,
    126, 128, 131, 135
postmodern, postmodernism, 10, 97,
    127, 139, 147, 153
Potter, David, 69–70
preserving the planet, 85, 108, 152
Proteus, Anita, 35
Proteus, Paul, 4, 44, 70, 112–122, 145–
    146
public relations, public relations
    writer, 1, 3, 9, 14, 21, 27, 69–70,
    72, 88, 96, 105, 125–126, 130,
    154

Quinn, Bert, 43–44, 49, 150

Rachstraw, Loree, xi
recipes, 80, 101, 149
Redbook Magazine, 88
Reed, Peter, 136
Reinbeck, Louis, 47–49, 150
Reinbeck, Natalie, 47–48
Rhodes, Richard, 137, 155
Rivera, Geraldo, 108
Rivers, Jerry, 108
Robinson, Edward G., 62
robots, people as robots, 32, 66, 81,
    131–132, 143–145

Rosewater, Senator Lister, 93, 96,
    98–99, 141, 144, 146, 151
Rumfoord, Beatrice, 150
Rumfoord, Commodore William H. T.,
    97
Rumfoord, Robert Taft, 97–99
Rumfoord, Winston Niles, 99
Russians, 29, 33, 58, 60, 88

Saab dealership, 72, 74
Sale, Roger, 12, 25, 155
Salo, 32, 125, 141, 145, 148
satire, 12, 35, 67, 88, 90, 96, 126,
    148, 161
Saturday Evening Post, 28, 39, 41, 45,
    48–50, 59, 71, 75, 78, 82, 90, 95
Schatt, Stanley, 1, 6, 23, 26, 44, 53–
    54, 73
Schenectady, New York, 3, 14, 27,
    41, 67, 70, 103
Scholes, Robert, 25, 39, 74, 91, 102
science fiction, 1–2, 4–5, 30–32, 62,
    64, 66–67, 80, 83, 87, 91–92, 94–
    96, 104, 128, 130, 135, 137, 146–
    148
Second World War, 11, 13, 21, 25, 50,
    51, 62–64, 68–69, 73, 139, 152
sentiment, sentimentality, 11, 18,
    30, 32, 48, 51, 60, 68, 138, 142,
    147
shaggy dog story, 5, 23, 34, 36, 38–
    39, 90, 93, 95, 147
Shaw, Helene, 83
Shortridge Daily Echo, 2, 10, 16, 24–
    25, 157–159, 161, 163
Shortridge High School, Indianapolis,
    2, 10–11, 14–16, 41, 85, 157–159
The Sister B-36, 134
Snopes, Flem, 107–108
soldiers, 17, 42, 60, 63–64, 68–69,
    76, 103–104, 145, 151
Sousa, John Philip, 43, 50
Southard, Annie, 78
space, 31, 34, 59, 106–108, 131,
    145, 147–148, 150, 153
space flight, 31–32, 58–59, 107
space travel, 4, 58–59, 131, 134,
    145, 148

Space Wanderer, 4, 129, 145
Stevenson, Robert Louis, 108, 139
Suicide; Ethical Suicide Parlors, 6,
  32, 67, 84–85, 99–100, 102, 128,
  135, 142, 145, 148
Suicide, mother's, 3, 146
Sunoco, Dr. Fleon, 135
Susanna, "Miss Temptation," 46, 77,
  95, 101, 143–144
Swift, Dr. Tom, 105

tall tale, 5, 29, 33, 39, 53, 147
technology, 2, 5, 23, 32, 50, 147–
  148, 152–153
Timequake, 133–136
Tralfamadore, Tralfamadorian, 125,
  129
Trout, Kilgore, 20, 39, 73, 80–81,
  84–85, 91, 104, 107, 117, 120, 125,
  128–136, 138, 141, 145–146, 148–
  150, 152, 154
Twain, Mark, 29, 57, 159

Ulm, Arthur Garvey, 128
University of Chicago, 22, 27
utopia, 2, 34, 41, 90, 148

Vietnam War, 64, 152
villains, lack of in his stories, 11,
  62, 79, 87, 150–151
Vonnegut Hardware, 49, 159

Waggoner, Franklin, 48–49, 86
Waggoner, Merle, 48–49, 86
Whitman, Milly, 47, 150–151
Whitman, Nancy, 47
Whitman, Turley, 47
Wilkinson, Max, 28, 139
Wirtanen, Frank, 101, 109, 141
women's roles; women's work, 33,
  35–36, 46, 132, 141–146
women, depiction, characterization,
  35, 44–45, 70, 99, 101–102, 143,
  146
World War II. *See* Second World War
Writer's Digest, 39
Writers, within stories, roles of, 24,
  27, 29, 39, 53, 73, 81, 85, 96,
  125–136, 141

Yarmolinsky, Adam, 76, 92
Yates, Richard, 91, 102

About the Author

PETER J. REED is Professor of English at the University of Minnesota. In 1972 he published the first book-length treatment of Vonnegut, *Writers for the 70s: Kurt Vonnegut*. His biographical sketches of Vonnegut appear in such standard works as the *Concise Dictionary of American Literary Biography*; *Dictionary of Literary Biography*; *Magill's Survey of American Literature*; and *Postmodern Fiction: A Bio-Bibliographical Guide*. He is the editor, with Marc Leeds, of *The Vonnegut Chronicles: Interviews and Essays* (Greenwood, 1996).